# Dragons in the Stacks

To Annah — Thank you! Thank you! Thank you for your belief in this little book, for your efforts toward women in gaming, & for your faith in getting more teens in gaming!

# Dragons in the Stacks

❖ ❖ ❖

*A Teen Librarian's Guide to Tabletop Role-Playing*

**Steven A. Torres-Roman and Cason E. Snow**

Libraries Unlimited Professional Guides for Young Adult Librarians
*C. Allen Nichols and Mary Anne Nichols, Series Editors*

# LIBRARIES UNLIMITED

AN IMPRINT OF ABC-CLIO, LLC
Santa Barbara, California • Denver, Colorado • Oxford, England

**Library of Congress Cataloging-in-Publication Data**

Torres-Roman, Steven A.
  Dragons in the stacks : a teen librarian's guide to tabletop role-playing / Steven A. Torres-Roman and Cason E. Snow.
        pages cm. — (Libraries Unlimited professional guides for young adult librarians series)
  Includes bibliographical references and index.
  ISBN 978-1-61069-261-8 (paperback) — ISBN 978-1-61069-262-5 (ebook)
1. Young adults' libraries—Activity programs.   2. Libraries—Special collections—Games.   3. Libraries and teenagers.   4. Fantasy games.   5. Role playing.   I. Snow, Cason E.   II. Title.
  Z716.33.T67   2014
  027.626--dc23        2014024062

ISBN: 978-1-61069-261-8
EISBN: 978-1-61069-262-5

19 18 17 16 15   1 2 3 4 5

This book is also available on the World Wide Web as an eBook.
Visit www.abc-clio.com for details.

Libraries Unlimited
An Imprint of ABC-CLIO, LLC

ABC-CLIO, LLC
130 Cremona Drive, P.O. Box 1911
Santa Barbara, California 93116-1911

This book is printed on acid-free paper ∞
Manufactured in the United States of America

**Copyright Acknowledgments**
Portions of this book were previously published as part of the following articles:
Snow, Cason. 2008. "Dragons in the Stacks: An Introduction to Role-Playing Games and Their Value to Libraries." *Collection Building* 27.2: 63–70.
Snow, Cason. 2009. "Tabletop Fantasy RPGs: Tips for Introducing Role-Playing Games in Your Library." *School Library Journal* 55.1: 24–31.

*As always, a book is the product of many people above and beyond the authors themselves. To that end, the authors would like to thank the following:*

To Karen, Jennifer, and Lily, for their patience and love.

To the DeKalb Roleplayers Meetup, for sharing our love of the game.

To Angie, Andrew, David, Leif, Matt, Jared, Sam, Vivien, April, Trennel, Rory, Steven, Andrew, Kyle, Julia, Caroline, Tavarras, Sarah, Alex, Owen, and all the teen members of Adventure @ Your Library—you are the future of tabletop role-playing gaming.

To Kaylee and Abigail, hoping that soon you'll be rolling dice rather than chewing on them.

To Sean Patrick Fannon and Jared Nielsen, who kindly gave us permission to adapt their rating system from *The Fantasy Roleplaying Gamer's Bible, Second Edition* for our own use— that book inspired the one you hold in your hand.

To all the people we've ever gamed with, and all the gamers we haven't met yet.

Most of all, to E. Gary Gygax and Dave Arneson, for the spark of creativity that still burns brightly, and to Frank Mentzer, for making it all comprehensible to youth opening that red box for the first time.

# Contents

# Series Foreword

The idea of gaming as an essential library service has come a long way. Once thought of as only recreational and only for boys, we now know that playing games is beneficial and fun for all ages. It requires literacy, socialization, and strategy, just to name a few skills that can help teens in life. Many of you have successfully implemented video gaming programs in your libraries. But what else is there? Don't know the difference between an RPG and a GPS? No worries! Authors Steven A. Torres-Roman and Cason Snow have written this extremely valuable guide to help demystify the world of table-top role playing games. Their advice will help you understand the teen appeal of this type of gaming as well as show you it can be easily implemented in your library. They offer tips on aspects of library service, from selecting to collecting to cataloging to programming. The bibliography provides an excellent resource list for those new to this type of programming and to those who may be seasoned gamers.

We are proud of our association with Libraries Unlimited/ABC-CLIO, which continues to prove itself as the premier publisher of books to help library staff serve teens. This series has succeeded because our authors know the needs of those library employees who work with young adults. Without exception, they have written useful and practical handbooks for library staff.

We hope you find this book, as well as our entire series, to be informative, providing you with valuable ideas as you serve teens and that this work will further inspire you to do great things to make teens welcome in your library. If you have an idea for a title that could be added to our series, or would like to submit a book proposal, please email us at lu-books@lu.com. We'd love to hear from you.

Mary Anne Nichols
C. Allen Nichols
Series Editors

# Introduction

Welcome and well met! Whether you're an old hand at tabletop role-playing games (RPGs) or this is the first you've ever heard of them, we thank you for taking the time to purchase and peruse this book. Presumably, you're a librarian looking for a creative and innovative activity to entertain and involve your patrons, but you might also be an interested gamer looking to start an RPG group and community through your local library. If so, then this is the book for you!

Let's begin by defining what tabletop RPGs are—if you're already well-versed in RPGs, then you might want to skip ahead.

## Tabletop

The types of RPGs we deal with in this book are typically played at a tabletop, where all the players are physically present. Sometimes players will use virtual tabletops, like Roll20 (http://roll20.net), or software applications like Skype and Google Hangouts. Sometimes they'll also use maps as a play space, and miniatures to represent their characters, while other groups imagine and visualize everything in their heads. Either way, tables are handy as a place to put snacks and drinks.

That said, tabletop RPGs do not require players to dress and act completely in character, as if on stage, moving about and enacting, rather than simply describing, what their characters do. That's another form of RPG called Live Action Role-Playing, or LARPing—fun, but not the focus of this book.

This book also does not deal with computer role-playing games (CRPGs). While certainly a lot of fun, and usually visually stunning, they do not require as much creative input from the players, nor do they match the diversity of actions and options available in a tabletop RPG.

So, just to be clear, from now on, when we say RPG, we mean *tabletop* RPG (unless we say otherwise).

# Role

Players in an RPG create characters that inhabit an imaginary world, and players take on the roles of these characters to interact with and imaginatively inhabit that setting. Unlike a role in a play, however, your actions are not scripted ahead of time; players must improvise their characters' dialogue and actions depending on what their characters encounter.

You may take the roles of heroes or scoundrels, warriors or wizards, aliens or superhumans with godlike powers. As part of the roles, your characters should be motivated to participate in the adventures that they undertake. They may be struggling to save a kingdom, or to save their own souls. They may seek to explore the unknown, an inherently dangerous profession, filled with pitfalls and perils aplenty. They may want to protect the innocent by defeating supervillains or slaying monsters. Perhaps your characters are daredevils and thrill-seekers that simply prefer a life of adventure to whatever passes for normal in their world, or maybe they're delving into ancient ruins in the hopes of discovering undreamt of wealth. Whatever the reason, when players take on the roles of characters, they should strive to act the way characters in that setting, and in that genre, should act. (Unless, of course, your particular group prefers a game where the players humorously undermine and subvert genre expectations. You might enjoy playing a schlub who happens to be an accountant, a disappointment to his family, and a vampire: Woody Allen as a creature of the night. Hey, it's your game.)

# Playing

Sometimes the game master (GM) will decide on a particular game, set of rules, setting, and genre to use; at other times, the entire group may decide these details together. In play, the GM describes a setting and situations that the characters experience and must respond to, and takes the role of everything else in the setting beyond the player characters. While some games, even some RPGs, are solo affairs, the great majority of participants play with a group. The group of characters typically has a goal, be it well defined or nebulous, that it can achieve through collaboration and cooperation. This goal, like the types of characters you play, is often determined by the genre of game: you may be a team of secret agents out to foil a terrorist plot, a group of investigators determined to solve a murder, or a band of knights sent to recover a holy relic. The players may accomplish their goal, or they may be defeated—the outcome is never certain, after all, but they always win if they've entertainingly played their characters and contributed to the group's enjoyment.

## Game

RPGs are essentially a structured and fun way to play make-believe. Each game has a set of rules, often called a system or engine, which structures the play experience and provides a means of resolving actions attempted in the game. RPGs usually use dice as randomizers to help determine whether characters succeed or fail.

## Storytelling

Wait, what?! The word "storytelling" isn't part of RPGs!

Well, you're correct, it isn't. However, we would be remiss not to address the issue of story, narrative, and RPGs.

First, the hobby's origins lie with historical miniatures wargaming, with the game *Chainmail* being the direct inspiration for *Dungeons & Dragons* (*D&D*). These games were played on a tabletop using miniature soldiers and scale terrain pieces to show the positioning of the armies, and they used an abstracted rule set to resolve combat and command interactions. RPGs were also clearly and heavily influenced by stories from their very inception. Dave Arneson, one of the founders of RPGs along with E. Gary Gygax, modified his games with influences from *The Lord of the Rings* (Tresca 2011, 61). Indeed, fantasy literature influenced Gygax and Arneson to take the emphasis off larger units of miniatures to emphasize specific characters and their actions, and the first edition of the *Advanced Dungeons & Dragons Dungeon Masters Guide* includes "Appendix N," which lists fantasy and science fiction novels that influenced *D&D*.

Second, RPGs often attempt to emulate the genres, plots, and action found in stories. To this end, many RPGs have rules that attempt to elicit the same feel of the stories they emulate; thus, games using the GUMSHOE system have specific rules to show off the expertise of investigators in crime shows, and *Feng Shui* mirrors action films by allowing players to create characters that are combat machines who can perform remarkable stunts. Many RPGs have rules that influence players, often using in-game rewards, to maintain a particular tone by playing their characters in a manner that aligns with a particular genre. For example, nobody in his or her right mind would walk down a flight of creaking stairs into a dark basement, with nothing but a faulty flashlight, to investigate those wet, tearing sounds. But, because teens do exactly that in slasher films all the time, a particular horror game might reward players for having their characters investigate trouble when sane persons would drive away at top speed while dialing 911 on their cell phones.

Third, whatever emphasis any particular RPG places on genre emulation or manipulating tone by means of rules, it's inevitable that particular storytelling genres influence the gamers playing. Simply put, people are surrounded by stories, whether those stories come from cultural traditions, myths, fairy tales, books, comics, films, or television shows. Most of those stories can be classified into genres, each of which has its own common structures, character archetypes, and tones. Players come to RPGs with this kind of "story information" preloaded and prelearned from simply living in a given society, and it influences both how they play and what they expect. Thus, most players come to RPGs with a sense of genres and narratives, and how they work: they expect knights to be noble, monsters to be evil, and serial killers to be vicious, intelligent, and cunning (and, thanks to characters like Hannibal Lector and Dexter Morgan, rather witty and urbane). Sometimes, a GM will want to violate expectations, for example, by making a particular princess neither weak nor helpless, like Merida in the Disney film *Brave*. Sometimes a monster might be the best friend the characters can have, because only the monster knows the way out of the ancient labyrinth. But regardless of how the action in the game progresses, the fact remains that players come to the table already knowing about and having various expectations of genre, plot, characters, and tone, and GMs and gaming groups will make extensive use of this knowledge when playing.

Finally, simply by having fun and playing the game, players will realize that once they've been adventuring and enjoying their game for a time, the game itself becomes a story after the fact. For example, imagine you watched a football game. There is no "story" imposed upon the game—it's two teams playing a game by certain rules. However, imagine further that later you tell your friend about the game, detailing the triumphs and tragedies, the fumbles and touchdowns that led to one team's victory over another. Whether you intend to or not, the very act of relating the game to a friend often means that you end up describing the game in a narrative form, as if it were a story, a phenomenon called *emergent narrative*.

In other words, even if the RPG rules don't overtly attempt to emulate narrative conventions, if your games are successful and the players are enjoying themselves, then the participants will remember the deadly perils, the noble sacrifices, the victorious triumphs, and even the inglorious defeats, and will retell these stories they've crafted for themselves to their friends. And in doing so, they might attract more players to RPGs.

## The Golden Rule

Every endeavor or hobby has four kinds of people: those who have never heard of it, those who are peripheral to it (they might have friends who play, but don't themselves), those who enjoy it, and those who are fanatical about it. Let's talk about that last group for a moment.

At their best, fans (short for fanatics, you know) can be excited, engaging, and eager to share their hobby with you. At their worst, however, they can be dogmatic and even bullying. The RPG community has a lot of people with a lot of strong opinions about their favorite kinds of games and their preferred styles of play. Forums and blogs abound with people engaging in communication ranging from friendly to hostile. Some people even develop entire philosophies of RPG play and design. In the midst of all of this signal and noise, we want you to remember the golden rule:

> If everyone in your group is having a good time, chances are you're doing it right.

There is no one "true" way to play. There is no single game that is inherently superior to all others. Opinions and preferences abound. If you come upon somebody who insists upon the inherent superiority of [fill in the blank here], you can take a deep breath and evaluate what to do next: engage that person in conversation, decline to comment, offer to buy that person a soft drink, or back away slowly. But you do not have to adhere to anyone else's definition of fun. If all of the players in your gaming group are happy, if they're enjoying themselves, if they're engaged and participating, then that's what matters. They may become fanatics, or they may simply stay involved. Sometimes, they might drift away—that's okay, because life can get busy, and not every hobby is for everyone, but at least they gave it a try! But if your players have a good time, they'll likely talk about the hobby and your group positively, which means more people will hear about the game, and more people might be willing to play.

## Why Libraries?

Libraries occupy a unique position in our society. They are repositories of information, education, and entertainment. They also act as a community center, a safe and neutral space for studying, reading, exploring, and discovering.

Thus, libraries are a perfect spot for youth to congregate.

This position may not be clear to some people, but as more and more teens are willing to self-identify as geeks, libraries can be ground zero for the geek culture in your community. Libraries have a lot to offer, including books, movies, computers with Internet access, music, and, most important for our purposes, programming—much, if not all of it, free, already paid for by patrons' tax dollars.

The best thing about RPGs is that they fit perfectly into library spaces and budgets. If a library has a small conference room or other enclosed meeting space that can fit five to eight people, then you can run an RPG. For anywhere from free to $100 as an initial cost outlay, you can purchase all you need to run programming for *years*—a very important consideration, given shrinking budgets and financial constraints.

## Beginning Your Quest: What This Book Is for and How to Use It

This book is intended as an aid to librarians interested in providing creative and innovative programming at their libraries using RPGs. To this end, we want to give you the tools you need to understand the hobby and explore its origins and boundaries. Basically, this book is the beginner's tour.

Chapter 1 covers a brief history of tabletop RPGs. We provide a quick and dirty grounding in the origins of the hobby that makes note of important names, landmark influential games, turning points in the hobby's direction, and the 800-pound gorillas that everyone's reacting to. You'll learn just enough to be dangerous.

Chapter 2 covers the whys and hows of selection and collection development—where to purchase the games and guidelines for choosing them.

Chapter 3 handles how best to classify and catalog the books and gaming materials you'll acquire.

Chapter 4 covers programming, including the essentials of what every good gaming group needs, and where to go from there. We'll discuss materials, choosing the right game for your group, advertising, planning, and yes, even how to give intelligent and measured responses to objections to the hobby.

Chapter 5 includes a collection of RPG reviews. Each entry within a list is structured in the same way:

- the title of the game

- the author of the game

- the publication information, including publisher and year

- the publisher's website (We list this information because publishers often make support material available at their websites, including errata, free adventures, quick-starts or introductions to the game, forums, etc.)

- genre tags (Many of these games belong to a particular genre or subgenre, while others are a mash-up of genres. If you know the preferences of your players, then you can more easily pick a game that they might enjoy.)

- the type of dice the game uses (or other randomizer, if any)
- an introduction of the game
- a brief overview of the game's system
- the types of character roles that players might assume
- the game's setting, including information about the imaginary kingdom, land, world, galaxy, and/or universe where the game takes place
- a quick numerical evaluation of the game, on a scale of 1–5, based on the following criteria:
  - ○ Complexity: how difficult is this game to learn and play? The lower the number, the quicker and easier it is to grasp and teach to new players.

    1 = You can effectively master the rules in one reading, though over time you may find additional novel and creative ways to use the rules.

    3 = You will need to spend some time learning the finer points of the game, and you may find yourself referencing the rules occasionally during games.

    5 = This rules set is substantially intricate and complex, and may require multiple readings and play experience to grasp completely.
  - ○ Popularity: how popular is this game in the RPG community at large? The higher the number, the more likely you are to find people who already know of and play the game.

    1 = This game is relatively obscure.

    3 = This game enjoys mid-range popularity among tabletop RPG gamers.

    5 = This is one of the most popular tabletop RPGs on the market, so much so that even your non-gaming friends may have heard of it.
  - ○ Support: how much support there is for the game, especially professionally published support. The higher the number, the more material currently exists to supplement the game. Please note that

this score isn't a judgment on the quality of the support material, nor is it a value judgment about the game—some games don't really need any support material, after all.

1 = This game has very little supporting material available.

3 = This game has decent support; the publisher continues to produce material for the game, and there may be considerable fan-produced material as well.

5 = You will have no difficulty finding additional adventures, supplements, and other materials to support your game.

○ Completeness: how complete is the product you're buying? How much more "stuff" (see "Support," above) do you need to buy to make the game a satisfactory playing experience? The higher the number, the more complete the initial product.

1 = This game requires, or at the very least significantly depends on, additional materials beyond the book and dice (or basic set). Those products may be maps, chits, cards, miniatures, counters, or additional books of monsters. The game may simply have a tendency toward power creep, where later published materials offer options to players that are far more powerful than those found in the initial rulebooks.

3 = While this game can be played as-is just fine, players will likely own, and expect to be able to use, the support materials available.

5 = This game is utterly complete as-is. Just add friends and imagination.

○ Versatility: how many different kinds of games, campaigns, or uses can you put this game to? The higher the number, the more versatile the game. Again, this score isn't a value judgment—some games, for example, are designed to be more generic than others, and are able to handle a variety of genres and play styles, while others are intended to do just one genre or play style, and do it well.

1 = This game has a setting and system that are intricately tied to each other, or the game wasn't designed to go beyond a particular genre, subgenre, or setting.

3 = This game, while designed for a particular setting, has rules that can be extrapolated relatively easily beyond the given setting or genre with a bit of effort and creativity.

5 = This game was designed to handle a variety of genres and settings. GMs may need to adjust rules to properly handle the particulars of emulating a specific genre or world.

o Emulation: how well does this game emulate the genre or source material it is patterned after?

1 = This game requires considerable effort on the part of the GM to capture the feel and flavor of a particular genre or setting.

3 = This game does a good job of capturing the style and tone of its source material, or the rules set is easily adaptable and requires only moderate effort to emulate a given genre, sub-genre, or intellectual property.

5 = This game plays just like the stories or source material it is derived from.

- any final comments

- the cost of the game, in both print and PDF format if both are available (Costs are subject to change depending on where you purchase the items. Free PDFs can usually be downloaded from the publisher's website.)

To elaborate further, the guide itself is ultimately a small sampling of the vast array of RPGs available. We based our selections on a variety of criteria, including but not limited to:

- Is the game currently in print, and what is the most recent edition of the game? (These criteria are further complicated by the vast number of once out-of-print games that are now available again as PDFs.)

- Is the game current and popular?

- Is the game primarily geared toward adults due to mature themes and language? (We are, after all, gearing this book toward programming with teens.)

- Is the game iconic or important to the history of the hobby?

- Would we hand this game to a first-time GM?

- Did we represent a variety of genres, systems, and play styles?

Inevitably, we did not include some of what might be or might become your favorite RPGs—mea culpa. Just as inevitably, our selections are somewhat idiosyncratic, and we likely break all of our above guidelines at one point or another.

But that just means you have a lot more to discover and explore! For information on games not found in this book, visit our Web site dragonson thenet.blogspot.com.

P.S.: Before you dive into the rest of the book, we heartily recommend that you read the glossary in the next section. Usually, glossaries are saved until the end of a work, but we're placing it earlier in the book so that you can familiarize yourself with the terms we use throughout this volume.

## Works Referenced

Tresca, Michael J. 2011. *The Evolution of Fantasy Role-Playing Games.* Jefferson, N.C.: McFarland & Co.

# Glossary of RPG Terms

Role-playing games (RPGs), like any other hobby, use a number of specialized terms and jargon. Rather than redefine and re-explain these terms in every game's description, we've decided to include this glossary in order to familiarize readers with these terms and to keep the bibliography entries more concise.

**Abilities.** *See* Attributes

**Advantages and Disadvantages:** Special abilities or difficulties the character might possess. Typically, advantages give the character a bonus at certain tasks in the game or allow the character to bend or break a particular rule, whereas disadvantages penalize the character. For example, a character might have "ambidextrous" as an advantage, or "coward" as a disadvantage.

**Adventure:** The earliest RPGs took place in fantasy worlds like those found in Tolkien's novels, and like Bilbo Baggins, the player characters often left behind hearth and home in search of adventure. Even though RPGs expanded into other genres, the term "adventure" stuck as a description of, essentially, where the player characters go, what they encounter, and what they do—the sum and substance of what occurs in RPG sessions. Adventures may last a single night of play, or may take many sessions to resolve.

**Alignment:** Alignment is a type of personality mechanic. Most commonly used in reference to *Dungeons & Dragons* (*D&D*) and its retroclones (though it also sees use in other games, like Chaosium's *Stormbringer*), alignment reflects both a character's behavior and general philosophical outlook. Alignment in *D&D* is mapped on two axes: the first ranges from Lawful to Neutral to Chaotic, and the second ranges from Good to Neutral to Evil. A Lawful Good character adheres to both the letter and spirit of the law, but also serves the forces of Good. An example of Lawful Evil (adherence to the law and serving an evil purpose) could exemplify a society like the Nazi regime, or indeed Hell, as portrayed by C. S. Lewis in *The Screwtape Letters*, with its hierarchy of evil. *See also* Personality Mechanic

**Archetype:** Character archetypes are common types of characters found in a given game's setting. Often, these archetypes are essentially premade characters, requiring only a little customization before they're ready for use. Some RPGs include archetypes in order to allow gaming groups to begin play as quickly as possible and to emphasize the types of characters for which the game was designed.

**Attributes:** Attributes are those innate qualities that every character has, measuring things like strength, agility, awareness, intelligence, and charisma, ranked on a scale that varies from game to game. *See also* Traits

**Bennies.** *See* Metagame Currency

**Boons.** *See* Advantages and Disadvantages

**Campaign:** A term derived from the miniatures war-gaming roots of RPGs, a campaign is a series of adventures detailing the ongoing exploits of a group of player characters.

**Character:** The role assumed in an RPG. The character is at its root a collection of traits and numbers; it is the player's task to breathe life into the character and give it personality beyond the numbers.

**Check:** When a player rolls the dice to determine the success or failure of an action.

**Chronicler.** *See* Game Master

**Class and Level:** These terms are used to describe the general profession of a character (class) and the character's overall level of competence and power in the setting. Classes range from a set of rigidly defined abilities to more customizable templates where the player can select which abilities a character develops, leading to more variations within a given class.

**Critical Success/Failure:** Many RPGs designate certain results on the dice as critical successes or failures. When a player rolls a critical success or failure, the character's action results in the best or worst possible outcome, respectively.

**Crunch:** Often used in reference to a given rules set. The "crunchier" a system is, the more rules-intensive that system is likely to be, which is to say, more rules are used to achieve a given effect, style, tone, or emulation. *See also* Fluff

**Dice:** You know what these are, right? The six-sided dice you're likely familiar with come in a whole host of board games that you've played. RPGs, however, use dice with many different sides for a variety of purposes, and some games use dice specifically designed for that game. You can purchase sets of dice at your friendly local games store (FLGS), or over the Internet at a variety of online stores. *See also* dX

**Dice Pool System:** Many games have characters roll a number of dice rather than a single die to determine the success of characters' actions. The dice pool is often determined by the sum of different traits. Some games require the player to sum the results of all the dice and compare it to a target number. Other games, like *Shadowrun* or the White Wolf Publishing's *World of Darkness* games, identify a target number, and each die that rolls equal to or greater than that number contributes to a total number of successes. For example, in *Shadowrun*, players roll a number of d6s equal to the sum of the relevant attribute and skill; each die result of a 5 or 6 counts toward the character's success. *See also* dX; System; Traits

**Diceless:** "Diceless" is an adjective used to describe an RPG that uses a method other than rolling dice to resolve actions within the game. Often, diceless games use cards (such as a standard playing deck or a tarot deck) as an alternate randomizer. The *Amber Diceless Role-Playing Game* compares the characters' traits to decide outcomes. One horror RPG, *Dread*, uses a *Jenga*™ stack of blocks to build tension and resolve actions.

**Difficulty Class (DC).** *See* Target Number

**Difficulty Number.** *See* Target Number

**Disadvantages.** *See* Advantages and Disadvantages

**Drama Points.** *See* Metagame Currency

**Dungeon Master (DM).** *See* Game Master

**dX:** A type of die, with the X indicating how many sides the die has. For example, a d6 is the standard six-sided die you see in games like Monopoly and Yahtzee. Some games use a single type of die, while others use a variety of dice. Some of the most common die types used in RPGs are the d4, d6, d8, d10, d12, and d20. While some games use other kinds of randomizers, such as playing cards, and others eschew the use of randomizers altogether, most RPGs use dice to determine the success or failure of a character's actions. Multipliers of dice are typically written out with a number preceding the die type; thus, 2d8 means roll two eight-sided dice. Other modifications to a roll are often in the form of + or − a given amount; 2d8+2 means roll two eight-sided dice, sum the results, and add two to the total.

**dX – dX (dX minus dX):** A system where two dice are rolled, and one is subtracted from the other. Some games always have the lower die subtracted from the higher die; other games simply designate one die as positive and one as negative, in which case a roll can yield negative as well as positive results. Either way, the final result is typically added to a character's trait to yield a final result.

**Edges.** *See* Advantages and Disadvantages

**Engine.** *See* System

**Experience Points (XP):** Many, though not all, RPG systems include a method of enabling players to improve their characters' abilities over the course of their adventures. As the characters adventure and grow in experience, a system of points is often awarded to players, who spend these points to improve their characters' traits.

**Exploding Dice:** In some games, when a player rolls the highest possible number on a die, the player gets to reroll that die and add the new result to the previous roll. Often, so long as the die continues rolling the highest number possible, the player can continue rolling and adding until the die comes up with a number other than the highest possible. For example, in a system that allows for exploding dice, the player may roll a d6 and come up with a 6. The player then rerolls, and comes up with a 4. The total result of that roll is 10. If the player had rolled another 6 on the second roll, then a third roll would be permitted, and perhaps more, until the player rolled something other than a 6.

**Fate Points.** *See* Metagame Currency

**Feats.** *See* Advantages and Disadvantages

**Flaws.** *See* Advantages and Disadvantages

**FLGS:** Friendly Local Games Store

**Fluff:** As *crunch* refers to the rules, *fluff* refers to the narrative elements in a given RPG rulebook or supplement, particularly the setting, and any short stories the authors have included to introduce iconic characters, tone, theme, and mood. *See also* Crunch

**Game Master (GM):** In most RPGs, the GM is the individual responsible for adjudicating the game system. Traditionally, the GM must know the rules and setting well enough to run the role-playing session, determine how other characters in the setting respond to the player characters' actions, describe the setting with sufficient detail for the players to imagine the scenes and interactions, breathe life into the various other personalities inhabiting the game's setting, and award experience points or other rewards to the players for their efforts. Equal parts director, referee, creator, and entertainer, the GM wears many hats. Some recent RPGs have systems that encourage sharing the GM's traditional responsibilities among all players, to mixed degrees of success.

**Game Master Character (GMC).** *See* Nonplayer Character

**Game System.** *See* System

**Generic System.** *See* Multigenre System; System

**Genre:** Pretty much what you'd expect—as with stories, movies, and television shows, genre helps to describe the setting that the RPG hopes to emulate. Common RPG genres include fantasy, science fiction, horror, comic book superhero, pulp adventure, and western. Many RPGs combine (or "mash-up") two or more of these genres in their settings; other games focus on a particular subgenre, like sword and sorcery or space opera (subsets of fantasy and science fiction, respectively).

**GM.** *See* Game Master

**GNS:** GNS stands for Gamist, Narrativist, and Simulationist. In 1999 game designer Ron Edwards wrote a short essay entitled "System Does Matter" (http://www.indie-rpgs.com/_articles/system_does_matter.html), in which he proposes three approaches to game design and argues that RPG designers should focus on one of the approaches to the exclusion of the other two when creating games. While this essay was neither the first work of RPG theory nor the first to use these terms, it did garner sufficient attention to merit its mention. Gamist RPGs are those games that focus on competition, perhaps among the players, between the players and the game, or between the players and the GM. Ultimately, the goal is to win by creatively and tactically using the game's rules to overcome challenges. Narrativist play assumes that the purpose of play is for the players and GMs to construct a story using the RPG. While a "gamist" player would abhor his or her character's death—such an event means that the player has "lost" the game—a "narrativist" player is assumed to accept, and even be enthusiastic over, a character's death if that event makes sense within the genre and the aesthetics of the story being told. Simulationist play focuses primarily on how the RPG creates a setting that is internally consistent and logical, and how the exploration of that setting is shaped by and reinforces this logic and consistency. (Authors' note: In our opinion, the importance, utility, and efficacy of RPG theory as a whole is more dependent on your tolerance level for theorizing and for reading and discussing theory than anything else. There are plenty of pages and pixels spent on the topic. As for us, this entry pretty much exhausts our tolerance for the subject.)

**Hero Points.** *See* Metagame Currency

**Hindrances.** *See* Advantages and Disadvantages

**Home Brew:** A home brew game system is one created by the GM for use with a given gaming group. The term "home brew" may also apply to a setting created by a GM for a particular group that uses an already existing system.

**House Rule:** Used as both a noun and verb ("to houserule")—when a GM and group decide to alter the established rules for a given system so that the game runs more in keeping with their liking. (Not every game system is perfect, and once you buy the game, it's yours to do with what you will and to run the way you and your group will have the most fun.)

**Initiative:** A method of determining which character or group of characters acts first, typically in combat.

**Judge.** *See* Game Master

**Karma Points.** *See* Metagame Currency

**Lifepath Character Creation:** A method of (usually, but not always, random) character creation, where the player will roll or select options from a variety of tables, the results of which determine the character's life leading up to the point at which his or her in-game adventures begin. Usually, this method of character creation will also determine the character's traits as well as background.

**Mash-up:** Typically refers to games that "mash" two or more genres together to create an interesting combination for use in a setting. For example, the *Deadlands* setting is a mash-up of the western, horror, and steampunk genres. More recently, the term has been applied to combining or importing elements from one game system into another to produce a given effect, referred to as a system mash-up.

**Merits.** *See* Advantages and Disadvantages

**Metagame Currency:** Metagame currency is used by some systems to allow the players to alter and directly influence the outcome of a situation. The most typical uses of metagame currency include rerolling a failed die roll or gaining a bonus to a die roll, though some games allow players to spend metagame currency in order to alter certain minor aspects of a situation, such as allowing a player to declare a previous relationship between a player character (PC) and a nonplayer character (NPC), though none had existed until that moment ("The owner of the inn is my uncle!"). The GM may award metagame currency during the course of a game to reward particularly inventive or clever actions by the players.

**Modifier:** A modifier is a circumstantial bonus or penalty that may be applied to a roll or trait check. For example, if a character is trying to climb to a better position, then the GM may apply a bonus modifier to the player's roll if the character was climbing a tree with plenty of branches for support. The same GM might apply a penalty modifier to the player's roll if the character was attempting to climb a wall in the rain (making the surface slicker) while being shot at (rattling the character's nerves).

**Multigenre System:** An RPG system that is designed for use in a variety of settings and genres.

**Narrative Currency.** *See* Metagame Currency

**Narrator.** *See* Game Master

**Nonplayer Character (NPC):** Nonplayer characters are the other characters in the setting controlled by the GM. They exist to aid, oppose, or otherwise interact with the player characters, and to lend some verisimilitude to the setting. If a GM is particularly good at breathing life into NPCs, then the players may become attached to them, and what were once mere side characters, akin to window dressing, take on a life of their own and a role of greater importance in the characters' adventures.

**Old School Renaissance (OSR):** What began as a rejection of the assumption that newer iterations of an existing RPG were necessarily better than previous editions, or that newer styles of play are inherently superior to the style of play evoked by older rules sets, has blossomed into a movement that revels in and revives the fun found in older RPGs and a particular style of play as a whole. For an excellent treatment of the old-school style of play, we refer the reader to *A Quick Primer for Old School Gaming* by Matthew Finch, currently available for free at Lulu (http://www.lulu.com/home/). *See also* chapter 1

**Old School Revolution.** *See* Old School Renaissance

**One-Shot:** A single-session game, as opposed to an ongoing campaign. Most one-shot games strive for the impression of a complete gaming experience, with a discernable beginning, middle, and end. If most RPG campaigns are similar in construction to ongoing serial entertainments like television and comic book series, then a one-shot is like a film, complete in itself (with the potential for sequels).

**Open Game License (OGL):** A particular licensing agreement where the owner/publisher of a game allows others to develop gaming material using the source game's mechanics.

**Opposed Roll:** When two characters want to accomplish a task, and only one of them can succeed, the GM may call for an opposed roll. For example, if two characters lunge for the Unspeakable Artifact of Doom, then they may make opposed Dexterity (or Agility, Reflexes, etc.) rolls to grab it. Sometimes the result is a tie, indicating a stalemate; in the previous example, if the players rolled a tie, then both characters may have hold of the artifact, in which case the GM might call for an opposed Strength roll. Note that some systems make combat a series of opposed rolls between one character's combat trait and another's defensive trait.

**Percentile Dice (d%, d100):** Some systems use percentiles to determine the chance of an occurrence, including the success or failure of characters' actions. These systems use two ten-sided dice, typically of different colors, to determine the outcome. One d10 is chosen as the tens digit, and the other as the ones digit. For example, a roll of 4 on the tens die and a roll of 7 on the ones die generates a result of 47. Since most d10s are numbered 0 to 9, a roll of 00 is often (though not always) read as 100. Some d10s clearly serve as the tens digit, since, instead of 0 through 9, they are numbered 00, 10, 20, etc. Players can buy a die with one hundred sides; the d100 looks like a golf ball, and when rolled takes an inordinate amount of time to come to rest and generate a result. (The authors prefer d10s for percentile rolls.)

**Personality Mechanic:** A personality mechanic is simply a descriptor that highlights an aspect of a character's personality and suggests the character's likely response to a situation, to the character's benefit or detriment. For example, in the original *World of Darkness* games, these were known as Nature and Demeanor; in the *New World of Darkness* games, they are called Virtue and Vice. Other games simply use personality-oriented advantages and disadvantages to perform the same function, or they may use alignments. GMs will often reward a player's adherence to a character's personality mechanic ("playing in-character"). *See also* Alignment

**Player Character (PC):** The role a player assumes in the RPG. Player characters are the primary protagonists, the central roles in the adventure, and the core characters in the action and drama.

**Players:** The people who gather together to play an RPG. While many would argue that the GM is a player too, the majority of RPGs distinguish the GM's position from the players, and grant the GM more authority and responsibility in the session.

**Point-Buy Character Creation:** Instead of using a template or character classes, many games give players an allotment of points that they can spend on traits, advantages, and powers in order to build their characters. Many players like this system, as it allows them to customize their characters and build them from the ground up to fit the imagined personas that the players want to immerse themselves in.

**Power Creep:** The tendency of publishers to produce supplemental material that offers options to players that are comparatively and considerably more powerful than those found in the basic rules. Some players suggest that power creep is a way for publishers to entice players to buy more published material.

**Powers:** Typically used to describe characters' superhuman abilities in superhero RPGs. Powers might also describe the paranormal or supernatural abilities of beings like aliens, vampires, or angels in games that feature those types of characters.

**Random Character Generation:** Many games have players roll dice and compare the random rolls to a table to determine their characters' Attributes and Traits.

**Referee.** *See* Game Master

**Retcon:** A term derived from comics, retcon stands for "retro-continuity" and refers to an after-the-fact alteration of previously established facts in the game world. Sometimes a GM may retcon events in a campaign to allow for new storylines (or, more likely, to smooth over errors).

**Retroclone:** A retroclone takes the rules of a previous, out-of-print game and creates a new game using those rules. The new game is thus compatible with the older game's products, and allows for the publishing of new products compatible with that rules set. Games like *Labyrinth Lord*, *Basic Fantasy*, and *Swords & Wizardry* would be considered retroclones.

**Roll-High/-Low Systems (or, Roll Over/Under):** Just like it sounds. In a roll-high system, the player wants a result as high as possible on the dice, usually trying for a result equal to or greater than a target number to achieve success with a character's action. In a roll-low system, the player is usually trying to roll equal to or lower than a target number to achieve success. Some systems also use degrees of success or failure. In a roll-high system, the rules may provide gradations above the target number to determine just how impressive the character's success might be, and may include gradations below the target number to elaborate on just how badly the character failed. In a roll-low system, the opposite would hold true, with gradations of success below the target number and possible gradations of failure above the target number.

**Sandbox:** An adjective used to refer to both a setting and a style of play. A sandbox setting is one that is already mapped out by the GM and where the GM has prearranged many places of interest, NPCs, and encounters, all of which await the players' discovery. A sandbox style of play is primarily player driven; the players decide where their characters go and what they do, and the GM responds when they come across a location or person of interest. In sandbox play, players need to be especially proactive in engaging with the setting.

**Setting:** Sometimes as small as a city, or as expansive as the multiverse, the setting is the place where the action happens, the "world" that the characters inhabit. Many players and publishers define settings by genre or subgenre.

**Skills:** Skills are traits the character gains that reflect training rather than innate ability. For example, while a character might be naturally agile, such a character would still need to train to acquire skills like acrobatics or juggling. *See also* Attributes; Traits

**SRD.** *See* System Reference Document

**Stats.** *See* Attributes; Traits

**Story Game:** A very loose definition of RPGs whose rules primarily focus on Narrativist (*see* GNS) goals, to create a game experience that is much like a self-contained story. Story games push the boundaries of game design to promote Narrativist play in a variety of ways. Some story games eschew the traditional role of GM and distribute the power to create and continue story events equally among all the players. Many story games promote a more contained, single-session game experience rather than traditional continuing campaign–style adventures. Some RPG theorists argue that story games are something utterly different from traditional RPGs, but it might be more accurate to say that story games are a branch of RPGs that push a particular style of play.

**System:** The set of rules used to play and adjudicate a particular RPG. Some publishers use the same system for a variety of games and settings, while other systems are unique to a particular game or setting. For example, White Wolf Publishing uses its Storytelling system for many of the games it publishes. Sometimes a given system is popular enough that a number of other publishers might use the system under license; the d20 and *Savage Worlds* systems are examples of rules sets that are used in a number of games from companies other than the systems' original publishers.

**System Reference Document (SRD):** System reference documents detail the open content of a given set of rules mechanics derived from a particular source game or system.

**Target Number (TN):** A player compares a roll against a target number to determine the success or failure of a character's action. In a roll-high/-low system, this is the number that must be rolled over or under. In some dice pool systems, there may be two target numbers: the first number indicates whether a die's result is sufficient to be counted as a success, and a second indicates how many successes are necessary to achieve the character's intended goal.

**Template.** *See* Archetype

**Test.** *See* Check

**Traits (also known as Skills, Attributes, Stats, Powers):** Traits help to define a character's capabilities and, sometimes, areas of weakness as well. Traits might be attributes, areas of raw aptitude, like strength, agility, endurance, or intelligence. Traits might also be skills the character has learned, areas of expertise and knowledge acquired through training, or powers and abilities beyond the norm. Some games, rather than split up a character's traits between attributes or skills, define traits even more broadly by citing a profession, like "detective" or "physician," in which case the character possesses all the abilities, contacts, and knowledge appropriate to that profession. Often, traits are assigned a numerical value for relative comparison (Strength: 18, or Stealth: 55%), while some systems assign a die type or multiple dice to a trait (Strength: d8, or Taxi Driver: 4d6).

**Wild Die:** Some systems include a wild die that can reflect even "wilder" intervention of fate and chance in an RPG. Sometimes the players roll it as part of a dice pool; sometimes it is rolled in conjunction with another die, and replaces the other die's result if the wild die's result is better. Wild dice are almost invariably exploding dice, but some roll-high systems also use the wild die as part of a critical failure if the player rolls a 1 on the wild die.

**XP.** *See* Experience Points

## Works Referenced

Edwards, Ron. 2004. *The Forge*. "System Does Matter." http://www.indie-rpgs .com/_articles/system_does_matter.html.

Finch, Matthew J. 2008. *Quick Primer for Old School Gaming*. Mythmere Games. http://www.lulu.com/us/en/shop/matthew-finch/quick-primer-for-old-school -gaming/ebook/product-3159558.html.

# 1

## Let Me Tell You of the Days of High Adventure!; or, A Very Brief (and Admittedly Incomplete) History of Tabletop Role-Playing Games

As you embark upon new adventures, both professional and fantastical, using tabletop role-playing games (RPGs) in your programming, you and your patrons may be interested in the origins of these games. If so, step back in time with us to the mythic hoary days of high adventure . . . or as we like to call them, the 1970s.

### 1974–1989: Days of Wine and Roses

The history of RPGs began in 1974, when Tactical Studies Rules (TSR), the company formed by E. Gary Gygax and Don Kaye, published the original edition of *Dungeons & Dragons*. This rules set was derived from the *Chainmail* tabletop miniatures wargame rules developed by Gygax at the University of Minnesota in 1971. Concurrently, David Arneson developed a proto-LARP based on his experiences at the University of Minnesota while participating in David Wesley's Napoleonic wargame *Braunstein*, where players played various individuals in the fictional town of Braunstein. *Braunstein* focused on individual characters who could establish their own goals in addition to goals generated by the game master (GM). Arneson's game was called *Blackmoor* and introduced the concepts of hit points, class levels, experience points, armor class, and dungeons as adventure settings (Fannon 1999, 124). These concepts were derived from tabletop miniature wargames, which were abstracted to represent large units, and applied to single characters. Gygax and Arneson collaborated and, taking elements from *Chainmail* and *Blackmoor*, created *Dungeons & Dragons* (*D&D*). In 1975, due to the success and growing fan base for *D&D*, Gygax decided to publish a setting for the game written by M.A.R. Barker, *Empire of the Petal Throne*. *Empire of the Petal Throne* introduces the world of Tékumel, which dramatically differed from the generic medieval setting of *D&D*; "socially and culturally, Tékumel is as complex—and as alien to modern thinking— as Byzantium, ancient Egypt, Tenochtitlan, or the India of the Mughals" (Barker 1983, 1).

Seeing the success of *D&D*, other small companies produced fantasy RPGs. In 1977 Fantasy Games Unlimited published *Chivalry and Sorcery*. *Chivalry and Sorcery* was adapted directly from the *D&D* system but focused on medieval society, with a strong emphasis on nobility, and kept magic and monsters in a more mythical role (Livingstone 1983, 110). In contrast, *D&D* featured characters rising up from humble beginnings and eventually attaining great power, had no social rules system in place, and was much more concerned with combat, highly visible spells, and hordes of nonhuman monsters.

In 1978 Chaosium published *Runequest*. This game featured the first use of a system for character skills beyond combat, such as Lore or Speak Language. Other games did not have a skill system at all, or the skills were tied directly to level advancement at fixed rates. *Runequest* was also the first "tie-in" game produced, based on and designed to emulate an existing intellectual property. *Runequest* rules served to emulate the world of Glorantha, a fantasy world using the Roman Empire and Germanic tribes as inspiration rather than medieval Western Europe (Livingstone 1983, 81). (Glorantha was originally depicted in several board games produced by Chaosium.)

In 1977 TSR moved from a small saddle-stitched booklet format to an 8.5 x 11–inch hardcover format to launch its *Advanced Dungeons & Dragons* (*AD&D*) game. This game expanded the rules from the original 1974 release, including random treasure tables and interaction tables (used to determine how nonplayer characters react to player characters). TSR continued to produce books for the *AD&D* line and began to expand the influences on the game to wider mythological and literary fantasy sources. This development was a mixed blessing to the company as it did draw new players, but it also involved TSR in legal battles due to copyright infringement with the inclusion of characters from Michael Moorcock's *Elric* saga and H. P. Lovecraft's Cthulhu mythos in the *Deities and Demigods* (1980) book.

In parallel with the release of *AD&D*, TSR released a boxed set called *Basic Dungeons & Dragons* that included two saddle-stitched books. This set was intended as a bridge game between the original *D&D* and *AD&D*. This basic game only supported play from first through third levels and used a five-category alignment system (an early personality mechanic) as opposed to the three categories in the original and nine in *AD&D*. The *Basic* set underwent a major rewrite in 1981; it was released in conjunction with the *Expert* set, a continuation of the rules from the *Basic* set that covered play from levels four through fourteen. By 1985 three more boxed sets were released: *Companion Rules* (levels 15–25), *Master Rules* (levels 26–36), and *Immortal Rules* (levels beyond 36).

Between 1980 and 1982, Iron Crown Enterprises (ICE) introduced a four-book RPG entitled *Rolemaster*. Unlike all other games to date, *Rolemaster* books acted as supplemental rules for other RPGs, aiming specifically at *AD&D*. With the publication of *Character Law,* ICE included rules that allowed *Rolemaster* to be played as a stand-alone game. While charts for random determination of events were present in RPGs before the release of *Rolemaster*, this game took the use of charts to a new level, incorporating charts for nearly all events.

In 1981 Chaosium released *Call of Cthulhu* (*CoC*), an RPG based on the horror stories of H. P. Lovecraft. Set like Lovecraft's tales in the early part of the twentieth century, the merely human characters sought to foil the sinister machinations of otherworldly abominations; thus, *CoC* emphasized investigation over combat, and the acquisition of clues rather than treasure. The early introduction of a personality mechanic, a Sanity score, simulated the degrading mental state of characters that suffered long-term exposure to the horrors of the Cthulhu mythos.

Chaosium released a game based on the Arthurian stories written by Thomas Mallory, entitled *King Arthur Pendragon*, in 1985. *Pendragon* introduced detailed rules for character personality that, until this point, had simply been a blank space on other games' character sheets, used to record a general demeanor. In *Pendragon,* characters had scores in an array of personality traits and derived in-game mechanical effects from these scores. *Pendragon* also introduced the concept of continuing a game beyond individual characters' deaths. Campaigns in *Pendragon* could span generations and included rules governing the aging of characters and what their descendants could inherit.

The year 1986 saw the publication of Columbia Games's *HârnMaster*. This RPG was a set of rules used to simulate a medieval setting in a fictional world. The Hârn setting, unlike *D&D* or *Chivalry and Sorcery*, was not set during a simulated late medieval period but was established in an earlier period, closer to the eleventh century. *HârnWorld* was published without any rules for *HârnMaster*, so the setting could be run with any rules set that the GM desired. *HârnMaster*'s level of detail and simulation of historical culture (with the almost obligatory addition of magic and nonhuman races) created a devoted fan base, which developed massive amounts of unofficial materials for the game and maintains a very active online presence today.

In 1987 Bard Games introduced *Talislanta*. Many previous fantasy RPGs patterned their settings on medieval Europe, or Norse and Celtic mythology and culture. Stephen Michael Sechi, the creator of *Talislanta*, instead drew heavily from pulp era fantasy fiction, especially Jack Vance's *Dying Earth*, for inspiration. *Talislanta*'s uniqueness fascinated its fans and kept the game alive through a host of publishers.

In 1989 TSR released the second edition of *Advanced Dungeons & Dragons* (*AD&D 2e*). This edition took the numerous volumes of the first edition and condensed them into three core books: the *Player's Handbook*, the *Dungeon Master's Guide*, and the *Monstrous Compendium*. This model of three core books followed by supplements to expand rules would become the standard publishing model for TSR, and later Wizards of the Coast (WotC) and other game companies. The second edition introduced major changes to the rules, altering the game further from its wargame origins. For example, in the first edition the ranges of weapons and spells were measured in varying units (feet indoors and yards outdoors) because different wargames used different scales depending on location. *AD&D 2e* used feet as a standard measurement. Another major change was TSR's adoption of a self-imposed publishing code, similar to the "Comics Code" used by Marvel and DC Comics, arising from pressure placed on TSR by parental and Christian groups who believed that role playing, and *D&D* in particular, led to teen suicide and "Satanism" (see the section "Dealing with Opposition" in chapter 4). This code limited the portrayal of evil characters to the purview of the GM and stressed the teamwork aspects of the game.

In 1986 the British company Games Workshop released *Warhammer Fantasy Roleplay* (*WFRP*). *WFRP* was another tie-in game, spun off from the *Warhammer Fantasy Battles* tabletop miniatures wargame. Games Workshop later chose to refocus its business on the sale of miniatures and to support its tabletop wargames, and licensed *WFRP* to other publishers.

In 1988 Lion Rampant Games published *Ars Magica* (Fannon 1999, 147). This game was set in medieval Europe in the year 1200 and focused on characters called *magi* and their interactions with the people of Europe. The major innovation in this game was the emphasis on the construction of a narrative and strong characterization over combat resolution. The other innovation was the concept of troupe-style play, in which each player created a magus, a companion (skilled non-magi), and a group of grogs (skilled peasants), and used whichever character was most appropriate for a particular scenario.

## 1990–2000: Dark Days

In 1991 a fairly new company, White Wolf, leapt into the market with its first RPG offering: *Vampire: The Masquerade* (*V:tM*). *V:tM* set in motion a new direction in RPGs that took players and GMs away from the adversarial wargame-based design of previous games. In *V:tM* and later RPGs produced by White Wolf, storytelling was the main emphasis of the game, where the GM and players cooperate to tell a story. This idea of cooperative storytelling was a legacy of Lion Rampant's *Ars Magica*.

White Wolf's *World of Darkness* setting, shared by many of the company's games, combined urban fantasy and contemporary horror, and refined and influenced the tone of many games during this period of RPG design. Characters were more commonly conceived of as protagonists and antagonists than as heroes and villains, and morality shifted from "black and white" to "gray and dark."

In 1992 Atlas Games published *Over the Edge*, an innovation in RPG system design. Many games sought to emulate styles of play by expanding and refining their sometimes already complex rules sets. Rather than using long lists of attributes and skills, *Over the Edge* used four free-form descriptors to define a character's abilities. If a character had "police officer" as a trait, then that single descriptor covered everything a police officer should know and do, from comprehension of the law to driving a cruiser to shooting a firearm. *Over the Edge*'s simplicity of design would heavily influence later indie RPG creators.

In 1995 TSR released a revised second edition of *Advanced Dungeons & Dragons*, along with a series of optional rulebooks that expanded and introduced new rules for character design, combat, and magic (Fannon 1999, 155). By this time TSR was beginning to struggle financially due to lagging sales and overextension in the creation of products for its myriad settings. Seattle-based company WotC purchased TSR in 1997, staving off the latter company's bankruptcy. WotC performed a major rewrite of the *AD&D* rules and released the third edition of *Dungeons & Dragons* (*D&D 3e*) in 2000. *D&D 3e* followed the same business model as *AD&D 2e*, having three core books (the *Player's Handbook*, the *Dungeon Master's Guide*, and the *Monster Manual*), and WotC added to the rules of both the first and second editions produced by TSR. *D&D 3e* introduced a strong emphasis on character customization; in addition to the earlier class and race system of previous versions, *D&D 3e* included feats, representing special abilities and advantages. WotC also overhauled the skill system and consolidated the skill list from *AD&D 2e*. *D&D 3e* also had a greater emphasis on and reversion to a wargame-style combat system using a square grid map and miniatures.

Insofar as the RPG industry was concerned, perhaps the most important change in the third edition of *D&D* was the introduction of the Open Game License (OGL). This license allowed creators besides WotC to use the mechanics designated "open game content," including a large portion of the third edition core books, in order to create their own games and sell them. The actual document used in the OGL is available online as the System Reference Document (SRD). The OGL opened a floodgate for companies who were now able to release settings without needing to create systems for them. Additionally, these companies could brand their products with the d20 logo and indirectly tie their games to *D&D*. WotC released a revision of the third edition of *Dungeons & Dragons* (*D&D 3.5*), in 2003; it repaired major design problems with the third edition.

## 2000–2007: The Indie Revolution

The first decade of the twenty-first century saw the revival of many older games as publishers renewed interest in, and released new editions of, classic RPGs. These revived games included: *Runequest* by Mongoose Publishing; *Warhammer Fantasy Roleplay*'s second edition by Black Industries and Green Ronin; *Chivalry and Sorcery*'s fourth edition by Britannia Games Design; and *King Arthur Pendragon*'s fifth edition by ArtHaus, which is owned by White Wolf.

While the established companies rereleased their games in new editions, the year 2000 saw Ron Edwards publish a PDF of his independently produced RPG *Sorcerer*, roughly marking the beginning of the "indie" game movement. *Sorcerer* evolved from discussions on a website, Hephaestus' Forge, created by Edwards and Ed Healy in the 1990s. Hephaestus' Forge began to promote independent ownership and publication of games, as opposed to corporate ownership. The website went inactive for years and was renamed and relaunched by Edwards and Clinton R. Nixon as simply The Forge (Rhoer 2007). (The Forge shut down in 2012; the Story Games website [http://www.story-games.com] is now one of the leading forums for discussing indie RPGs.) In 2001 Ron Edwards published *Sorcerer* in print format and showed independent game designers the way to publish their own games (Rhoer 2007).

The year 2001 also saw the publication of *Exalted* by White Wolf. *Exalted* uses a modified version of the Storyteller system that White Wolf had used since the company's first offering, *Vampire: The Masquerade*, in 1991. The setting for *Exalted* distinguished it from other RPGs—the creators chose to use as few traditional fantasy influences (i.e., "Tolkienesque" elements) as possible. They drew their influences from Classical Greek and Roman, Mesopotamian, and Asian mythologies, as well as from pulp fantasy stories. *Exalted* also featured elements of modern media that quickly emerged into mainstream awareness, namely *anime, manga*, and *wuxia* films, as well as popular video games like the *Final Fantasy* series.

The year 2003 saw the release of *FATE*. This game sought to create a rules set for the emulation of narrative rather than a simulation of "reality." *FATE* is a generic rules set that mainstreams several indie RPG elements: the use of metagame currency (fate points) by both players and GMs to push or pull the story in a certain direction, a high level of character competence, and a de-emphasis on long lists of character powers and equipment.

In 2007 Greg Stolze published *Reign*, a game that "expands the frontiers of fantasy gaming by elevating the action to an international stage. Monarchs, mercenaries and merchant princes gamble armies and fortunes to win nations in a rich and vibrant fantasy setting. *Reign*'s simple but complete rules model the triumphs and disasters of societies as small as a village or as large as a realm-spanning religion" (Stolze 2007).

Other innovations came from Clinton R. Nixon with his games *Donjon* and *The Shadow of Yesterday*. *Donjon* permits players to take temporary control of the narration depending on their degree of success. *The Shadow of Yesterday* incorporates the use of keys, or goals that the player has established, that pay off in experience points when resolved. These games, coupled with work by Edwards, paved the way for "story games" that often consist of highly focused and tightly scripted rules and scenarios. Many of the games even provide a limited character selection and play out much like a murder mystery party game.

## 2006–Present: What Is Old Is New Again

In 2008 WotC released the fourth edition of *D&D*. However, eight years earlier, an older generation of gamers had already refused to update their games to the third edition. They didn't see the need to change systems when they had decades invested in earlier editions that were largely cross-compatible. The fourth edition of *D&D* only served to polarize this group further.

With the gaming world replete with newer generations of gamers, a movement began to reintroduce the older editions of *D&D*. These editions were long out of print, often very expensive to acquire, and sometimes suffered from poor or archaic organization. The idea underpinning the movement is that the actual system used in an RPG is a mathematical formula, and algorithms are not copyrightable. Thus, if an author stripped out all of the copyrighted elements of the game, then it could be republished with little changed in the way of gameplay. Such a republished game would allow newer players to discover the older games, would be compatible with the older game books and supplements, and would allow publishers to publish new content compatible with those older games.

Independent publishers used modern technology and thirty-plus years of changes in publication trends and layout innovations, and the resulting revived games and movement collectively became known as the Old School Renaissance (OSR). The first of these games was *OSRIC*, a simulacrum of *AD&D*, published in 2006. *OSRIC* was followed by *Labyrinth Lord*, which emulated *Basic Dungeons & Dragons*, in 2007. *Swords & Wizardry*, an original *D&D* simulacrum, came out in 2008 and rounded off the initial push of the OSR. These games were initially released for free as PDFs and are now available in print format through print-on-demand services. After a period of time the OSR developed two distinct schools of thought and design. The first is of the simulacra, designed to adhere as closely as possible to earlier, long out-of-print editions of *D&D*. The second style is of the retro clones, where these games attempt to maintain the feel of old school games but incorporate newer elements in game design and their own innovations. An excellent example of the retro-clone is Goodman Games's *Dungeon Crawl Classics*.

Meanwhile, in 2009 Paizo published the *Pathfinder Roleplaying Game*, a revision of the *D&D 3.5* SRD that sought to streamline some of the more cumbersome aspects of the source game. Paizo embarked on an extensive open playtesting of its *Pathfinder* rules, a risky endeavor that won over many fans and, thanks to player feedback, helped to shape and refine the game. While retaining the overall mechanics and reward of system mastery found in its parent game, *Pathfinder* proved to outcompete *D&D* for market share.

Some new games use special proprietary dice or cards with unique icons on them to represent in-game elements or resolution systems, a production decision that harks back to the wargame roots of RPGs. Two good examples of this trend are Fantasy Flight Games's *Warhammer Fantasy Roleplay*, 3rd edition, and *Star Wars: Edge of the Empire Roleplaying Game*. The use of special dice, cards, and tokens can be traced back to the use of special dice and chits in tabletop wargames. The fact that these unique items can be copyrighted is a significant factor, in that they make the production of simulacra more difficult and protect the publishers' and creators' intellectual properties.

## A Publishing Revolution

In the early years of RPGs many of the companies were small endeavors and rarely staffed full-time employees. In the 1990s some of the companies grew to a considerable size, and given rising production costs, these companies held a significant advantage when it came to publishing materials. While smaller publishers could use desktop publishing software to create products of a similar high visual quality, the cost of printing still held them back. A major advance in the democratization of RPG publishing came on three fronts.

The first major advance was the popularization of print-on-demand (PoD). Prior to PoD services, small publishers were limited to offering digital copies of their products; PoD allowed a small publisher to provide hard-copy products to customers with little initial outlay of money, unlike traditional publishing venues. Crowdfunding sites, like Kickstarter or Indiegogo, provided the second major advance. A successful crowdfunding endeavor raised capital for a project; a failed crowdfunding endeavor indicated that the project was not financially viable. The third major advance was the implementation of the Open Game License (OGL) concept. Pioneered with *D&D 3e*, the OGL allowed companies other than WotC to use the system when designing a game. Other companies followed suit, and soon there were several systems with open content, triggering a huge output of materials for these games and creating more commercially successful games on the market.

## The Future

The OSR helped to ensure that entirely new generations of gamers can experience and appreciate classic RPGs. Meanwhile, WotC busily republishes deluxe versions of earlier editions of *D&D,* including original *D&D, AD&D, AD&D 2e,* and *D&D 3.5e,* and there is an entire website devoted to purchasing PDF versions of *D&D* products, called Dungeons & Dragons Classics (http://www.dndclassics.com). The year 2014 will see the fifth edition of Gygax and Arneson's brainchild, *D&D,* as well as a seventh edition of the venerable *CoC* RPG.

At the same time, innovations abound, many conceived of by indie creators and financed through crowdfunding sites. There is an RPG for every patron, and as the sheer number of RPGs attests, there is always room for innovation, for a new look and take on an old genre, theme, or interest. There has never been a better time for creative people to experience the world of tabletop RPGs . . . and even design some of their own.

Won't you join us?

P.S.: For those readers interested in a fuller account of the history of RPGs, we refer you to the upcoming four-volume series by Shannon Appelcline, *Designers & Dragons,* to be published by Evil Hat Productions. (Hint: Patrons will check out these volumes from your library's shelves!)

# Works Referenced

Barker, M.A.R. 1983. *Swords & Glory*. Gamescience.

Fannon, Sean Patrick, Aaron Acevedo, and Brett Link. 1999. *The Fantasy Roleplaying Gamer's Bible*, 2nd ed. [USA]: Obsidian Studios.

Livingstone, Ian. 1983. *Dicing with Dragons: An Introduction to Role-Playing Games*, rev. American ed. New York: New American Library.

Rhoer, Clyde L. 2007, May 15. "Interview with Ron Edwards." *Theory from the Closet*. Audio podcast. http://theoryfromthecloset.com/2007/05/14/show008-interview-with-ron-edwards/

Stolze, Greg. 2007. *Reign: A Game of Lords and Leaders*. Self published.

# 2

# Selection and Collection Development

As a librarian, you have a limited budget and limited space for your collections. You want to purchase high-interest items so that the patrons will borrow them, resulting in a high circulation rate. You want a high circulation rate to justify maintaining and increasing the collection, which will please your patrons even more, and lead to more borrowing—a perfect cycle.

This chapter will help you to build that high-interest collection; if you couple an excellent role-playing game (RPG) collection with solid advertising and quality programming, then you have all the ingredients of a recipe for success!

## Make Sure You're Covered

The first issue that selectors need to address includes the policies for collection development, materials selection, and dealing with challenges to library material.

More specifically, make sure that the library where you work *has* policies for collection development, materials selection, and dealing with challenges to material. If you have them, then follow them carefully. If you don't have them, then it's time to get them. Stop reading this book and have a conversation with the director of your library, or whoever writes and decides upon policies at your place of employment. (For example, if you work at a school library, then you may need to discuss developing policies with the school board.) The American Library Association website (http://www.ala.org) has guidelines for developing these policies, and you might want to research the policies adopted by other libraries in your area.

## The (Nearly) Zero-Point RPG Collection; or, "Yes, Virginia, There Is a Santa Claus!"

As a selector, you need to consider how much money you can devote to a new collection, and how much space you have to house that collection.

The beginning point for many librarians should be what we call the (Nearly) Zero-Point RPG Collection. Consider—what if you could reduce the cost of your RPG materials, and the shelf space required for those materials, to zero. Sounds impossible, doesn't it?

The good news is that many publishers offer RPGs online that you can try out for free. Yes, you read that correctly: free. Some publishers simply offer their games for free at their websites, or offer free "quick-start," stripped-down playable versions of the game. Publishers may also choose to adopt an Open Game License (OGL) and offer an online System Reference Document (SRD) that has much of the mechanics and information necessary to play the game. Other publishers may publish their games under a Creative Commons license. Whichever flavor of free is available, that's good news for an already overburdened budget.

Even if they don't give the rules away, many publishers have free adventures and scenarios available at their sites that you can use after you purchase the game. These adventures are very useful because while a game might sound fantastic and read well, it may offer so many different options and styles of play that the game master (GM) and players are left scratching their heads as to which to choose. Adventures offer a direction and structure to players and GMs new to a game.

Many free RPGs use the ordinary six-sided dice you're familiar with, so at the very least you can raid other games to acquire and use them; you can also purchase them rather cheaply at a local dollar store. For those RPGs that use other polyhedral dice, there are a number of free dice-rolling apps available for smart devices—just search for "dice" in iTunes or Android and see what comes up! If you want physical dice at the table, and many players do, then you can get a variety pack called a "Pound-O-Dice" (produced by Chessex games) for around $20 to $25 from a local games store or an online retailer. Another option is to purchase polyhedral dice from an educational supply store, brick-and-mortar or online; this tactic may be easier to justify to a director or board. With dice and one of the free RPGs available online, you can run programs . . . pretty much forever, really.

You see? Zero cost, or very low cost if you have to purchase dice.

Even better, since pretty much all the free RPGs are PDF files, the only space they take up is on your hard drive or server—no library shelf space required. You can also have each of the players download copies, so everyone can own and read the rules, and many of these free games will allow you to make a print copy of the rules as well.

Thus: (Nearly) Zero Cost + Zero Space = The (Nearly) Zero-Point RPG Collection.

## Moving from Virtual to Physical: In-Print RPGs, from Popular to Generic

However, just as every library will want a variety of books on its shelves to appeal to a variety of reading interests, you will want a variety of games in your collection to satisfy the genre preferences and gaming styles that will become evident in your groups. Also, as you generate interest in RPGs at your library, your patrons will want physical products that they can borrow.

RPGs can be rather expensive products. Many games are published as 8.5 x 11–inch hardcover books that often range around $50 or $60 in price. Fortunately, most such games will have all the rules necessary to play the game between two covers, including a beginning adventure or scenario, and all you'll need to provide are dice, paper, pencils, and interested players. However, not all games are complete in a single volume. For example, almost all editions of *Dungeons & Dragons* (*D&D*) beyond the original boxed set require the purchase of multiple books in order to run the game, including a *Player's Handbook*, a *Dungeon Master's Guide*, and a *Monster Manual*. Other publishers have followed *D&D*'s example, either splitting the rules for players and GMs into two separate rulebooks, or having a bestiary or tome of monsters and antagonists separate from the main rulebook. Some publishers have all the rules in one book and offer detailed settings as entirely separate books. Some do all of the above, and more. Selectors need to be aware that when they purchase a particular game, that game may not be complete in and of itself, and may require additional products in order to run properly.

Selectors should also note that, beyond dice, some games simply have a lot of "stuff" that goes with the games, such as cards, miniatures, and tokens, that might be useful, or even necessary, to running the games. This growing trend in the mainstream market may be replicated in indie games with the popularity of Kickstarter stretch goals. While some of this stuff can be substituted with cheaper nonproprietary versions, like using poker chips for tokens, these paraphernalia may add considerably to the cost of a game, and selectors should take them into account when making collection development decisions. Should the library purchase this extra material and make it available for lending? Or should the library simply lend out the game rulebooks and let the patrons and borrowers supply any additional bits and pieces? (We strongly recommend the latter, with a few rare exceptions.)

You'll certainly want to spend your valuable collection dollars on games that are popular and likely to circulate. According to ICv2 (http://www.icv2.com), an excellent source of gaming industry news, as of this writing the most popular RPG on the market (as determined by available sales figures) is *Pathfinder*, a fantasy RPG published by Paizo. *Pathfinder* has even beaten out *D&D* sales since the second quarter of 2011.

In fact, the bestselling RPGs have been remarkably consistent over the past few years. Both *Pathfinder* and *D&D* typically command the top spots, although recently (but not surprisingly, despite its use of proprietary specialty dice) another big seller has been the new *Star Wars* RPG line published by Fantasy Flight Games. The *Dragon Age* RPG boxed sets, published by Green Ronin, and the *Warhammer 40,000* line of RPGs published by Fantasy Flight Games (including *Dark Heresy*, *Rogue Trader*, *Deathwatch*, *Black Crusade*, and *Only War*) have commonly been in the top five, and both are connected to other game lines (a video game franchise and a miniatures wargame franchise, respectively) that certainly help to raise their profiles among gamers familiar with those properties. A recent best-seller is the *Iron Kingdoms Full Metal Fantasy Roleplaying Game* by Privateer Press, also connected to a popular miniatures wargame franchise.

As the *Star Wars* RPG sales demonstrate, it never hurts to acquire games connected to hot intellectual properties (IPs). Given the overlap in geek culture, Cubicle 7's *Doctor Who: Adventures in Time and Space* RPG and Margaret Weis Productions' *Firefly* RPG will certainly circulate. And, of course, by the time this book reaches print, the newest edition of *D&D* will be a must-buy for your RPG collection.

Note, however, that the above RPGs, whether popular in themselves or connected to a popular IP, are not inexpensive. In print, *Pathfinder* currently retails at $49.99, and each of the *D&D* volumes will be comparably priced. *Star Wars: Edge of the Empire* currently retails at $59.99 (and that's before you buy the special dice). Each of the *Warhammer 40,000* RPG core rulebooks costs $59.95, and the new *Firefly* RPG is set to debut at $49.99. Even with distributor discounts, these books are a bit pricey, and those are just the core rulebooks—additional supplements carry their own price tags.

(Of course, just because a game is popular doesn't mean it's an excellent purchase for your collection, which is why we strongly recommend spending considerable time reading reviews and researching games before adding them to the shelves—see "Information and Reviews" later in this chapter.)

In addition to popularity, a librarian looking at RPGs should consider utility. Selectors who want the most bang for their gaming buck should seriously consider generic RPGs, those games that can emulate a whole variety of genres using a single rules set. For example, the *Savage Worlds Deluxe: Explorer's Edition* is a full-color, digest-sized softcover RPG that costs only $9.99. Now, of course, Pinnacle Entertainment Group, the publishers of *Savage Worlds*, has a whole slew of products that they'd like to sell you that use the *Savage Worlds* system (in fact, a large number of third-party publishers would like to sell you their licensed *Savage Worlds* items as well), but the core book alone is sufficient to fuel a large number of games in a large number of genres. *Fate Core*, published by Evil Hat, is another very popular RPG choice; it is available for free at http://www.faterpg.com, has its own SRD at http://fate-srd.com, is incredibly easy to teach and learn, and is already the engine for a number of publishers' games, from fantasy to transhumanist science fiction to the popular *Dresden Files* franchise, based on the series by Jim Butcher.

Several more excellent generic RPGs include Chaosium's *Basic Roleplaying*, S. John Ross's *Risus*, and Precis Intermedia's *GenreDiversion 3E*, and all of them share the same benefit: these game systems are perfectly able to emulate just about any kind of game you'd care to run in your preferred genre. The primary advantage of a generic rules set is that the group has only one set of rules to learn and has no need to learn new rules for each new game or setting; you can use the rules set to run a series of fantasy games, then use the same rules set when the group switches genres to science fiction or horror or post-apocalypse. Creative use of a generic rules set also means that prospective GMs can use that same rules set to run games based on favorite television shows, movies, novels, and comics, whether or not those IPs already have games attached to them. The potential disadvantage of a generic rules set is that the prospective GM may need to do all the "world creation" from scratch, or spend a bit of time and thought adapting the generic rules set to a given IP. Fortunately, many generic RPGs offer advice on just this sort of adaptation. RPGs tend to attract imaginative, creative types, and some of the best games we've ever run had a strong "do it yourself" component.

In any event, the bibliography section of this book should offer enough suggestions to help you construct your first in-print collection, so take your time, read through the entries, and take note of prices. With that information at your fingertips, you should be able to select and assemble a winning beginning collection.

## Dollars and Cubits: What to Buy and Where to Put It

Considering the cost and placement of a new RPG collection isn't always easy: budgets are tight, space is tight, and each library has its own challenges. However, we recommend a starting budget of $200 for a beginning in-print RPG collection for a small library, serving a population of up to 5,000 people. A medium-sized library, serving a population between 5,000 and 150,000, should consider a beginning budget of approximately $1,000. Larger libraries, with greater funds and space and serving larger populations, might consider a beginning budget of $5,000 or more.

When rolling out a new collection, it's often best to give the collection its own prominent spot. Many public libraries that use the Dewey Decimal Classification system, for example, assign a call number of 741.5 to their graphic novels but separate out their graphic novel collections from the rest of the 700s. Separating out the RPG collection makes it more visible to the patrons and more likely to attract their attention.

The physical shelving space should be tall enough for the 8.5 x 11 books to rest comfortably—since most hardcover novels are smaller, you will likely have to adjust the shelves in a given shelving unit. If you can, make enough space for the covers to be facing out so that patrons will see the often-beautiful cover art that many RPG books sport.

If you have a target audience in mind, then clearly you will want to consider placing your new RPG collection in an area where that audience will notice it. This book assumes, for example, collection and programming for young adults (typically teens, though many gamers started playing RPGs in their tweens, or even younger), so you might consider putting a new RPG collection near the young adult or teen collections. Don't be afraid to decorate the area and make it flashy—after all, you want patrons to notice the collection.

## Audience

And speaking of audience, in addition to placement of the collection, consideration of your target patrons will also affect your decisions about what you buy and advertise. While many RPGs want wide audiences and thus attempt to have content and art that isn't offensive (or, at the very least, isn't any more offensive than what is on public network television), other games are intended for more mature audiences. Fortunately, most of those games that market to mature audiences advertise appropriately. That said, some games intended for a teen audience will have swearing and curse words in the text—as does much teen fiction. Due diligence, which includes reading reviews and publisher's websites, will yield sufficient information about the products and enable librarians to make decisions about age-appropriateness.

As you consider your audience, think about the patrons who you think would be interested in the program. Beyond issues of age-appropriateness, for example, you should consider a game's learning curve: some games are simply easier to learn than others; some players might be discouraged by particularly intricate games, while others would enjoy the challenge of learning and mastering those same games. (We've assigned a Complexity rating to each of these games for that very reason.)

Consider, too, what is currently popular among your patrons. Fantasy tends to be the most popular genre for RPGs, but as we mentioned earlier, you might want to consider various popular series and IPs. For example, if many of your teens are still carrying a torch for Stephenie Meyer's *Twilight* series, then the game *Monsterhearts* might be just what they're looking for. You might also anticipate a surge of interest in Fantasy Flight's *Star Wars* line of RPGs should current owner Disney release a new film in the near future. In fact, just as considerable crossover exists among many fantasy, science fiction, graphic novel, video game, manga, and anime fans, many of these fans might be willing to give RPGs a try.

Ultimately, as the collection grows and becomes more popular, you might find further crossover between the interests of adults and youth. Just as many adults enjoy reading superhero comics and manga, adults might start checking out the RPGs as well. Coming full circle, adults' interest in RPGs could lead to requests for more mature games, which might affect where you shelve the games. Some libraries might handle this situation as they've handled the graphic novel situation, by having separate graphic novel collections for adults and youth. Some libraries might consider adding "mature readers" stickers to RPGs, while others may simply refuse to purchase certain RPGs based on their content. You know your library and community best—use your best judgment.

## Information and Reviews

Publishers' websites are the first source of information about a game. Often, a publisher's website will describe the game in detail, including which items are necessary for play and which items are incidental. Many publishers' websites also have additional useful material, including PDFs of character sheets that players can print out, and official errata to correct errors in the printed versions of the game. And while publishers' websites are understandably biased in favor of the games they sell, they will often post links to reviews of their games.

Most librarians base their book purchasing decisions on collection development policies, personal expertise and knowledge, and reviews from various trade publications like *Library Journal, School Library Journal, Publishers Weekly, Booklist,* and *Kirkus.* Unlike books, RPGs currently don't have publications or sites dedicated to professional reviews of materials with the same influence or breadth. Nonetheless, there are many blogs and websites that review games; sometimes professionals in the industry write the reviews, but most of the reviewers are fans, and librarians should give these latter reviews the same weight as reviews posted to Goodreads or Amazon.

Some prominent sites for RPG reviews include: RPG.net (http://www.rpg.net), The RPG Site (http://www.therpgsite.com), and RPG Geek (http://rpggeek.com). *Wired*'s GeekDad column (http://www.wired.com/geekdad/) occasionally has RPG reviews. Kurt Wiegel posts reviews as short video clips on Game Geeks RPG (http://gamegeeksrpg.com), and Wil Wheaton's Tabletop (https://wilwheaton.net/category/tabletop/) occasionally reviews RPGs in between his many board game reviews.

Beyond publisher and review sites, selectors should also visit RPG awards sites. The Game Manufacturers Association (GAMA) announces the venerable Origins awards (http://www.gama.org/OriginsAwards/tabid/2720/Default.aspx) at the annual Origins Game Fair, including the categories of "Best Roleplaying Game" and "Best Roleplaying Supplement." Gen Con, the primary U.S. gaming convention, hosts the Diana Jones Award for Excellence in Gaming (http://www.dianajonesaward.org) and the ENnie Awards (http://www.ennie-awards.com/blog/), sponsored by EN World. The Indie RPG Awards (http://www.rpg-awards.com) represent some of the best non-traditional RPGs.

## Where to Acquire RPGs

So you've done your homework and you know which RPGs you want to purchase for your collection. Now you need to know where to go to buy the items. A library has several options for acquiring RPGs, and at the top of the list is to purchase them from the friendly local game store (FLGS). The gaming community often considers this choice to be the best option because the purchasing library supports the local economy, and because these local stores keep the industry afloat.

A local games store comes with several benefits. The manager and staff can give advice as to which RPGs are popular in the area, and which might best fit the library's collection. If you find a game at the FLGS, then you have the option to examine the game in person before purchasing it for the collection. The FLGS may run demonstrations of games, and you can experience playing the game yourself. Local games stores also provide a physical location for both the librarian and players to socialize and network with the larger gaming community.

Locating a local gaming store can be challenging as many of them are run on small profit margins and can close or move locations unexpectedly. Good resources for locating stores would include simple Internet searches as well as the local phone directory under headings like Gaming, Games, and Game Supplies Retail. If there are no dedicated gaming stores in the area, then try comic book shops, which often double as gaming stores. A purchaser should consider Comic Shop Locator (http://www.comicshoplocator.com/Home/1/1/57/575).

The second best option is to purchase the books directly from the publishers. Many publishers offer a bundle including the electronic version of the book for free or at a substantial discount upon purchase of the physical copy. In fact, Bits and Mortar (http://www.bits-and-mortar.com) is a cooperative venture of many RPG publishers that offers free electronic versions of RPGs upon proof of purchase of a physical copy from any brick-and-mortar game or book store. (Another benefit to going to the publisher is that the website often has a forum available for people to discuss the game and ask questions.)

A third option is large online booksellers. These websites do well in stocking books from the larger gaming companies, namely Wizards of the Coast and Paizo, but can be fairly unreliable in acquiring games from smaller companies.

A fourth option is to use online retailers, for example, RPGNow (http://www.rpgnow.com), DriveThruRPG (http://rpg.drivethrustuff.com), and Indie Press Revolution (http://www.indiepressrevolution.com/xcart/). These sites may offer physical copies through print-on-demand, or bundles of the physical book and an electronic version, although most of their selection usually consists of electronic versions of the books.

## Selection beyond the Shelves: Including the Free RPGs in Your Collection

Remember that zero-point RPG collection we talked about? Even though they aren't on the shelves, selectors can make sure their patrons know about those delightful free RPGs, just as if they were part of the collection. One way to inform the patrons about these games is to use them in library programming. However, another important way to represent them as "part of the collection" is to prominently include them in the advertising.

When advertising the new collection, you will likely use posters and brochures to highlight it. Have separate posters and brochures for the free RPGs that include the URLs where patrons can find those RPGs. Enterprising librarians might create QR codes, using free apps or sites like Unitag's QR Code Generator (https://www.unitaglive.com/qrcode), that link directly to the websites. Adding these QR codes to the posters enables patrons to go straight to the sites using their smart devices.

Librarians can also create an RPG "metabook" to represent the game on the shelf. This metabook would be a piece of cardstock with the cover of the game printed on it in addition to a QR code. Librarians can laminate and shelve these metabooks face-out with the other games, use them in a display, or collect them in a binder.

## Core Collection 1: Games to Fill Your Shelves

Likely, you've gotten some good ideas as to which games to include in your core collection from the games we've mentioned in this chapter, and you'll certainly see some of those listed here.

And now for the part you've all been waiting for: the RPGs we think should be in your core collection.

### Dungeons & Dragons (Wizards of the Coast)

As this book goes to print, Wizards of the Coast is about to release the core rulebooks for the next edition of *D&D* (a.k.a. *D&D Next* or *D&D 5e*). Libraries may want to try out the *D&D Starter Set*, which contains rules, dice, and an adventure for novices, but will certainly want the three core rulebooks (the *Player's Handbook*, the *Monster Manual*, and the *Dungeon Master's Guide*) for their collections. As the latest incarnation of the world's first and best-known RPG, *D&D* will certainly be a best-seller and a must-have game.

### Pathfinder Roleplaying Game: Core Rulebook (Paizo Publishing)

Was there any doubt? It's been the best-selling RPG on the market for years, has extensive support, and boasts a lot of players in its already existing fan base. Yes, it's a bit rules intensive, but *Pathfinder* uses those rules to offer many options for individualizing characters, and some players will enjoy the challenge of mastering the system.

### Fate Core System (Evil Hat Productions)

This revolutionary game changed how a lot of people conceive of RPG systems and gameplay. Also, like we've said earlier, it's easy to learn, easy to teach, and easy to play. If you have a little extra room, definitely pick up *Fate Accelerated* as well. (It's a great "starter" game and is available in print for only $5!) Also, the proprietary dice are easily substituted with a d6-d6 mechanic.

## Savage Worlds Deluxe: Explorer's Edition (Pinnacle Entertainment Group)

The buzzwords for *Savage Worlds* are "Fast! Furious! Fun!" and this game delivers on its promise. This generic RPG has a wide range of applicability to emulating and adapting a variety of genres, and has extensive support. Plus, the core rulebook is only $9.99.

## Traveller Core Rulebook (Mongoose Publishing)

Mongoose Publishing has done a fantastic job of resurrecting this grandparent of science fiction RPGs, and it covers a wide gamut of sub-genres and play styles.

## Stars without Number (Sine Nomine Publishing)

*Stars without Number* is a science fiction game that uses the system compatible with older versions of the world's most popular fantasy RPG and adapts it to a remarkably complete science fiction RPG. *Stars without Number* comes in two versions: one free, the second at a cost, but with additional material.

## Icons (Adamant Entertainment)

We know that this is a controversial pick, as there are many well-loved and better-known superhero RPGs on the market like *Champions* and *Mutants and Masterminds*. We chose *Icons* for its simplicity of rules and surprising breadth of adaptability—whether you're emulating a well-known superhero comic or animated series, *Icons* does the job.

## Vampire: The Masquerade 20th Anniversary Edition or Blood and Smoke: The Strix Chronicle (White Wolf / Onyx Path Publishing)

Take your pick: either the original game of personal darkness and the children of the night in a "best parts" twentieth anniversary edition, or its most recent incarnation. Be warned: both of these books are a bit pricey, but they will find their audiences.

### Star Wars: Edge of the Empire Roleplaying Game Core Rulebook (Fantasy Flight Games)

Despite the special proprietary dice you'll need to run or play this game, its popularity demands a place on the shelf. (Perhaps you can package a set of dice with the core rulebook as a kit?)

### Shadowrun: Fifth Edition Core Rulebook

Take a blender. Fill it with all of the classic fantasy tropes of elves, orks, dwarves, trolls, and magic. Add noir and cyberpunk and really big guns. Purée. This insanely popular game is a bit rules intensive, but fans will gladly master all the fiddly bits in order to wipe out their rivals.

### The Call of Cthulhu (Chaosium) (Currently in edition 6, but likely in edition 7 when this book sees print.)

*Call of Cthulhu* is the original game of mystery, horror, and the unknown, based on the prose works of pulp horror and science fiction writer H. P. Lovecraft. While many other games let fans play out power fantasies, in *Call of Cthulhu* characters are normal people caught up in extraordinary events who risk life, limb, and sanity in order to hold back the darkness for just one more day.

### Legend of the Five Rings: 4th Edition Roleplaying Game (Alderac Entertainment Group) or Qin: The Warring States (7th Circle)

Both games are excellent examples of fantasy role-playing with Asian cultural and martial tropes. *Legend of the Five Rings* aims for the samurai and folklore of Japan, while *Qin: The Warring States* models itself on the *wuxia* martial arts genre from Chinese films like *Crouching Tiger, Hidden Dragon* and *Hero*.

## Core Collection 2: Free PDFs for Your Virtual Shelf

### D&D Basic Rules (Wizards of the Coast)

In an effort to draw in new and lapsed players, and to give everyone a chance to try the latest edition of *D&D*, Wizards of the Coast has a free *Basic Rules* PDF document that details character creation and the fundamental rules players need, as well as complete character creation and advancement rules for the four core fantasy character races (human, elf, dwarf, and half-ling) and character classes (cleric, fighter, rogue, and wizard). GMs will need more information to run the game, but this document pairs well with the *D&D Starter Set*. Wizards of the Coast also promises to update the *Basic Rules* (currently classified as version 0.1) over time to incorporate any errata and changes in the game over time.

## *Risus* (Cumberland Games & Diversions)

*Risus* is a game we recommend to every new GM. Its minimalist approach to rules is surprisingly versatile and freeing. It's easy to learn, easy to teach, and fun to play.

## *Savage Worlds: The Wild Hunt* (Pinnacle Entertainment Group)

This PDF includes the *Savage Worlds Test Drive* rules—a stripped-down version of the complete rules with everything you need to determine if this game is right for your group. It also includes a free adventure and paper miniatures you can print out. If your group likes *Savage Worlds*, then the Pinnacle Entertainment Group website also has a host of free one-session adventures, called *One Sheets*, in a variety of genres—enough free material to keep a gaming group going for quite a while.

## Retroclone-a-Palooza

No, that's not the title of the game. Glance back at the glossary for the term *retroclone*, and then continue reading.

Most retroclones are compatible with earlier editions of the world's most famous fantasy RPG and come in a variety of flavors. We recommend starting with either the *Swords & Wizardry Core Rules*, by Mythmere Games, or *Labyrinth Lord* by Goblinoid Games. If your players want a bit of post-apocalypse science-fantasy gaming, complete with robots, mutants, and weird technology, try *Mutant Future* by Goblinoid Games. Yes, the free rules are sans-art, but hey, they're free. If you want art, use Google image search and supply your own.

## SRD-a-Palooza

And speaking of "the world's most famous fantasy RPG," Wizards of the Coast has SRDs for *D&D* edition 3.5 (http://www.wizards.com/default .asp?x=d20/article/srd35) and edition 4 (http://www.wizards.com/default

.asp?x=d20/welcome), as well as its *D20 Modern* game (http://www.wizards.com/default.asp?x=d20/article/msrd).

Current best-seller *Pathfinder* also has an official SRD available for players, the *Pathfinder Roleplaying Game Reference Document* (http://paizo.com/prd/).

## *Fate Core System* and/or *Fate Accelerated* (Evil Hat Productions)

Even if you didn't purchase the books for your print collection (and you probably should), you can get PDF versions of these fantastic games for free at the *Fate RPG* website (http://www.faterpg.com), or use the HTML versions at the *Fate Roleplaying Game SRD* site (http://www.fate-srd.com); the latter site also includes the *Fate System Toolkit*, a treasure trove of ideas for modifying *Fate* for the setting you create or genre you want to emulate.

## *Marvel Super Heroes: The Heroic Role-Playing Game* (TSR)

By our count, the Marvel Comics IP has gone through four different RPGs, with Margaret Weis Productions being the last company to try its luck. All the previous versions are currently out of print, or in the process of going out of print, but this particular older edition is available for free online. TSR (former owners of *D&D*) originally published *Marvel Super Heroes: The Heroic Role-Playing Game* in 1984, and it was revolutionary in its ability to emulate comic book superhero role-playing.

## *D6 System* (West End Games)

This particular game has had quite a publishing history. Variations of the system were originally used to run RPGs based on the *Ghostbusters*, *Star Wars*, and *Indiana Jones* franchises. West End Games reworked the rules into a series of books for various genres, including *D6 Adventure*, *D6 Fantasy*, and *D6 Space*. You can find all of these, as well as the SRD and additional supplements for these games, at Open D6 (http://opend6.wikidot.com) and DriveThruRPG (http://rpg.drivethrustuff.com/index.php).

## Prose Descriptive Qualities System: PDQ and *PDQ#* (Atomic Sock Monkey Press)

Like *Risus* above, the *Prose Descriptive Qualities System* is remarkably simple and versatile, and can fuel years of RPG campaigns for zero dollars. The *PDQ#* (*PDQ Sharp*) version was developed for optimal swash-buckling action!

## Stars without Number (Sine Nomine Publishing)

We have rarely been so impressed with a science fiction game, and since there's a free version, we're going to mention it twice. Even if you don't purchase it in print, definitely get a copy of the free version—it may convince you to buy the game later.

# 3

# Cataloging

Now that you know where to go for information on role-playing games (RPGs) and where to buy them, this chapter considers that intermediate stage between selection and purchasing, and making the materials available to patrons. How should RPGs be classified? Where is their place in the library's collection? What are the challenges involved in maintaining the collection? This chapter will examine the stages that happen behind the scenes.

## Electronic Documents in the Collection

While many libraries offer e-books through a distributor like Overdrive, the distributor handles access to the documents, storage, and electronic security. Since there are currently no RPG e-book distributors, the library needs to have a policy in place to address issues of accessing electronic versions of purchased RPG books. In a recent communication with DriveThruRPG, one of the leading PDF and print-on-demand (PoD) retailers, a company representative stated that it currently has no policy to cover library use but would be willing to develop one if the demand increased (Scott Holden 2013, pers. comm.). In order to minimize copyright infringement or other piracy issues, libraries should make unsecured PDFs accessible only to library staff. While some might argue that the library could load copies of the files onto tablets for patrons' use in the library, this action enters into a legal gray area that we are not qualified to comment on. The best bet here is to talk to the publisher and work out a mutually acceptable arrangement. An alternative would be for the library to keep the electronic documents as noncirculating copies available only for the programming librarian's use.

Speaking of use, many of the RPGs available in PDF are formatted for a print display, usually as a double column on an 8.5 x 11–inch page. This format hampers navigation and readability on a standard computer monitor and can be an even greater problem when using tablets or other handheld devices, depending on screen size. Some RPGs include multiple layouts ranging from full color, double-column versions to bare bones, grayscale (or no art) versions. However, some publishers have begun releasing their RPGs in electronic formats other than PDF, including epub and mobi versions. Publishers may also have System Reference Documents (SRDs) for their games that freely include much of their games' systems. Players, patrons, and librarians can easily access these SRDs on any Internet capable device.

## Cataloging

From a cataloging standpoint RPGs are not that difficult to work with. The first question a cataloger would ask is what format should be used to designate the game in hand. The vast majority of games are treated as monographs, with some possibly cataloged as monographic sets; the *Dungeons & Dragons* (*D&D*) core rules (*Players Handbook, Dungeon Masters Guide,* and *Monster Manual*) come to mind as an example of a potential monographic set, as in previous editions they had consecutive volume numbers. Other accessories fall into fairly straightforward categories as well: maps go without saying; dice, if you are so inclined to catalog them, would be realia, or possibly a game; boxed sets, if they include dice and other bits, would be kits; miniatures would be realia as well; cards would get shoehorned into flashcards as they, typically, provide ready reference for various in-game abilities or items.

Once the catalogers decide upon format, they need to choose which cataloging rule set they will use. The vast majority of libraries will use either AACR2r or Resource Description and Access (RDA). Both have their advantages. Librarians have used AACR2r for decades, and a wide array of records for many of the most popular RPGs are already in the OCLC database. These records can provide a good jumping-off point for original cataloging in either rule set. RDA will be able to, in the future, more easily show the interrelationships between games, which for most RPGs is fairly straightforward, as each edition replaces the previous edition. For RPGs like *D&D* and all of its iterations, variations, and spin-offs, catalogers can make these relationships more apparent using semantic relationships in RDA.

## AACR2r

This cataloging scheme needs little introduction as it has been used for many years. There are a large number of good records available for a librarian to use outright or as templates to derive new ones.

## RDA

Recently implemented, RDA is a new content standard for cataloging that provides instructions and guidelines on formulating data for resource description and discovery. This content standard is based on the concepts contained in the Functional Requirements for Bibliographic Resources (FRBR). These requirements are defined by the four user functions: Find, Identify, Select, and Obtain. The four tasks are summarized here:

- To *find* entities that correspond to the user's stated search criteria (i.e., to locate either a single entity or a set of entities in a file or database as the result of a search using an attribute or relationship of the entity);

- to *identify* an entity (i.e., to confirm that the entity described corresponds to the entity sought, or to distinguish between two or more entities with similar characteristics);

- to *select* an entity that is appropriate to the user's needs (i.e., to choose an entity that meets the user's requirements with respect to content, physical format, etc., or to reject an entity as being inappropriate to the user's needs);

- to acquire or *obtain* access to the entity described (i.e., to acquire an entity through purchase or loan, or to access an entity electronically through an online connection to a remote computer). (IFLA 1998, 82)

These tasks are important to keep in mind, especially when it comes to RPGs, as we will see in the examples below.

We base the following examples on our interpretation of FRBR and RDA, and arguments can be made for alternate interpretations. Both standards are much less prescriptive than AACR2r is, and both leave many decisions to the cataloger's discretion. Both of these analyses are concerned only with the core rules for a game. Additional books, including rules supplements, adventures, and setting books, should be cataloged as separate works with the appropriate linking information in the record.

At its core the RDA model is centered on WEMI: Work, Expression, Manifestation, and Item. This hierarchy of bibliographic entities attempts to "comprise the products of intellectual or artistic endeavor that are named or described in bibliographic records" (IFLA 1998, 13). The *work* is the thought that forms from the intellectual endeavor. For example, the thoughts of Gygax and Arneson to take miniature wargame rules and modify them for a skirmish-level game with extended campaign play would be the *work* level for *D&D*. The *expression* level is the physical realization of a *work*. The *expression* level for *D&D* was when Gygax and Arneson sat down and wrote out the English language text for the game. The *manifestation* level is an embodiment of an *expression*. The entire print run of the original little brown books, in their boxed set, would be a *manifestation* of *D&D*. The *item* level is a particular instance of a particular *manifestation*. My copy of the original boxed set, signed by Gygax, would be an *item* of this *manifestation*.

The first example for analysis is *Basic Roleplaying* (*BRP*), by Chaosium. This game is derived from another work, *Runequest*. The work-level entity would be when Steve Perrin decided to write a percentile-based generic role-playing system derived from *Runequest*. The expression is the English language text of the rules. Additional expressions would be the various foreign language editions of the game. A manifestation of the work would be the print run of the first edition printed in 1980 of *BRP*. There are additional manifestations of *BRP* as new editions, published in 1981, 2002, 2008, and 2010. These newer editions are considered new manifestations, as they are backward compatible. Each book printed then becomes an individual item. An additional set of works could be added under *BRP* as there are a number of RPGs that use *BRP* as their system, such as *Stormbringer* or *Call of Cthulhu*. In a FRBRized catalog, all the editions of *BRP* would display under a single work record.

The second example is more complex. *D&D* has a long and complex intellectual and publication history. What sets *D&D* apart and makes it a prime example for a more complex WEMI example is the introduction of a work set or super work. This is not supported by FRBR and the WEMI model as currently written but has been established as an entity for more than a decade (Hickey et al. 2002). Here a work set is defined as a group of works that all derive from the same intellectual base. *D&D* fits that definition, in that the original concept of the game has been maintained throughout all the different editions, even though there have been significant changes to the system over the years. Each new, major revision that is incompatible with the previous editions constitutes a separate work. In this case there are six separate works for *D&D*. The first work is *Original Dungeons & Dragons* (*OD&D*) sometimes called 0E or the LBB (little brown books) edition. This work actually required a second work, the miniature wargame *Chainmail*, to function as a game. This rules set was very sparse as it was written with the idea that the players would have a firm grounding in tabletop miniature wargames.

A second work is that of *D&D* including the *Basic Set*, continued in the *Expert, Companion, Master*, and *Immortals* sets and their compilation into the *Rules Cyclopedia*. The third work gathers together two editions of the game, including the first and second editions of *Advanced Dungeons & Dragons*. The fourth work is editions 3 and 3.5 of *D&D*. The fifth work is the fourth edition, and the sixth work is the soon-to-be-published *D&D Next* (or fifth edition).

Now we will discuss each work and its dependent expressions, what most gamers refer to as editions. The first work, *OD&D*, will have one expression and multiple related works. Another work, *Chainmail*, is required to play this game and must be noted in the record with the appropriate linking data. The related works are either rule supplements, such as *Eldritch Wizardry* or *Gods, Demi-Gods & Heroes*, or setting books, such as *Greyhawk* or *Blackmoor*. The second work of *D&D* has several expressions. These are the boxed sets in the BECMI series, including the *Basic Set*, *Expert Set*, *Companion Rules*, *Master Rules*, and *Immortal Rules*. The *Basic Set* actually is three separate expressions as three different editors wrote substantially different versions of the rules for the set; these are the Holmes, Moldvay, and Mentzer sets distinguished by the editors. These sets build one upon the other, further expanding the rules. An additional expression is part of this work, the *Rules Cyclopedia*, which consolidates the BECMI rules into one book. The expressions for the third work are the *Players Handbook*, *Dungeon Masters Guide*, and *Monster Manual* for each edition for a total of six expressions. These three books form the core rules, and without one the game becomes difficult to play or comprehend, if missing the *Dungeon Masters Guide*, to impossible, if missing the *Players Handbook*. The fourth and fifth works follow the same as the previous work: they both have three expressions. The sixth work cannot be defined as at the time of publication the books to be released have not been determined.

Practically speaking, how does this interact with a MARC21 record? This discussion will not cover all of the differences and interactions between MARC and RDA. That has been discussed elsewhere in more detail. The key difference will be in the use of the 33x fields. As previously discussed most RPGs will be cataloged as books and follow those rules. Therefore, when cataloging a game book in MARC21 using RDA, the cataloger would use the following 33x fields:

336 bb text $b txt $2 rdacontent

337 bb unmediated $b n $2 rdamedia

338 bb volume $b nc $2 rdacarrier

Things get interesting when cataloging nonbook material; for example, poster maps would use:

336 bb cartographic image $b cri $2 rdacontent

337 bb unmediated $b n $2 rdamedia

338 bb sheet $ nb $2 rdacarrier

Many games use miniatures for the characters and monsters. A miniature would use:

336 bb tactile three-dimensional form $b tcf $2 rdacontent

337 bb unmediated $b n $2 rdamedia

338 bb object $ nr $2 rdacarrier

## Classification and Location

Placing RPGs in a collection has two facets. First, where in the classification scheme do these games belong? Second, where in the library should these books be physically located? No matter where the physical books live, they should be classified using the system the library uses.

## Classification

The first facet is fairly simply dealt with as the Library of Congress Subject Headings (LCSH) and Dewey Decimal Classification (DDC) have established classification numbers for RPGs. While not the most intuitive, LCSH places all RPGs in the "Fantasy Games" subject heading with general works about RPGs classed at GV1469.6 and specific rule sets at GV1469.62, Cuttered by title. There are a good number of Cutter numbers already established as well. On the Dewey side, all RPGs are located in 793 "Indoor Games and Amusements," subdivision .93 "Adventure Games." Note that if mass combat is the primary focus, as with *Battlesystem*, a *D&D* supplement published as an add-on mass combat game, such an item would be classified in 793.9 "Other Indoor Diversions, Including War Games."

With regard to subject analysis, some of it will be universal, and some will depend on the game being cataloged and on established local practices. As stated above, LCSH places all RPGs in the "Fantasy Games" subject heading. This heading is linked to the broader terms of "Games," which encompasses all facets (ethnological, social, educational) of all types of games (physical, board, and role-playing). The other broader term is "Role Playing," which hews closer to psychology. So all games, fantasy or not, will fall under "Fantasy Games." This can be subdivided using either "Handbooks, manuals, etc." or "Rules," depending on local policy.

A whole host of narrower terms has been established for "Fantasy Games" consisting of the title of the game followed by the qualifier "(Game)," for example, "GURPS (Game)." Some of the terms can seem ambiguous at first glance; for example, "Werewolf (Game)" could be *Werewolf: The Apocaplypse*, *Werewolf: The Forsaken*, or possibly *Werewolves of Miller's Hollow*. Fortunately, in the authority record, the 670 field provides clarity—it is for *Werewolf: The Apocalypse*. If a library had both *Werewolf: The Apocalypse* and *Werewolf: The Forsaken*, then there would be difficulty locating the second in the catalog by subject as no specific heading is presently established. Unfortunately, at this time there is no subfield to denote an RPG.

## Location

The second facet is a bit less clear-cut: the physical location of these games. Should these games be in the main collection or broken out into a separate collection? Should they be publicly accessible or behind the reference desk or somewhere in closed stacks? Some librarians do not like the idea of breaking out collections based on genre; they would argue that the library becomes a Balkanized series of collections within collections, and that too many locations leads to patron confusion. RPGs lend themselves already to being grouped together on the shelf by the nature of the call numbers assigned. But if a library wishes to emphasize RPGs on a programmatic level, then, using graphic novels as a guiding principle, the library should place RPGs in a separate collection. If a library is keeping games in a separate location, then a placeholder directing patrons to the actual location can be made and placed in the general stacks. For example, we have seen pieces of wood cut to the size of a book, with a call number label affixed to the narrow edge and a map on the face of the woodblock showing the location of the collection.

Accessibility to RPGs is a double-edged sword for libraries. Some librarians would keep RPGs behind the reference desk or in some other closed stacks area, and limit use to in-building only. This method keeps the games useable by staff and patrons, and helps to minimize the risk of damage to the physical copies. These materials are frequent targets for theft or vandalism, resulting in frequent replacement. Also no RPGs are printed with library bindings, and many of the PoD books have glued, not sewn, spines. As with graphic novels, RPG books will likely see heavier use and will have a shorter shelf life than other books in the collection.

That said, many librarians are adamant that books should be read, and games should be played. In an academic library (and we wonder if there are any academic libraries with extensive RPG collections for preservation and research), limited access makes sense, but in public libraries, where the collection is meant for public use, limited access seems to defeat the purpose. While libraries may need to replace RPGs often, if patron interest and circulation are high enough, then they're worth replacing.

## Preservation

RPGs face many of the same preservation issues as other print and electronic resources. No RPGs are published in a library edition, and while available in either hardcover or perfect-bound softcover, they have a wide variability in printing and binding quality. This variability can present preservation challenges for heavily used games. What to do when the book is damaged beyond repair is up to the individual library, which should follow its own current collection development policies.

Theft is the most prevalent threat to physical copies of RPGs. This chiefly comes from two segments of society. First are the people who steal books from libraries to simply possess them. RPGs can be fairly expensive, especially for their target audience, and the temptation to keep the book is quite high. The second group is "concerned" patrons who are still mired in the Satanic panic (see chapter 4), thinking that RPGs are a gateway to occultism and other antisocial behaviors, and take it into their own hands to remove these items from the collection. In the same category as theft is vandalism, which can range from people tearing out illustrations they like or blacking out "offensive" illustrations, to books being burned in the building. Sufficient damage will cause librarians to withdraw the item in an untimely manner, with the same result as if it were stolen.

While the placement and preservation of RPGs in a library's collection pose many challenges, these challenges are not new; librarians have faced these challenges many times with a variety of materials in the past and can certainly overcome these challenges in the present.

# Works Referenced

Hickey, Thomas B., Edward T. O'Neill, and Jenny Toves. 2002. "Experiments with the IFLA Functional Requirements for Bibliographic Records (FRBR)." *D-Lib Magazine* 8, no. 9:1–13. Doi: 10.1045/september2002-hickey.

IFLA Study Group on the Functional Requirements for Bibliographic Records. 1998. *Functional Requirements for Bibliographic Records: Final Report.* München: K. G. Saur.

# 4

## Programming

If you've read the earlier chapters, then you have a basic grasp of the vocabulary and history of tabletop role-playing games (RPGs), you know where to purchase them, and you know how to add them to your collection.

But what do you *do* with them? We're glad you asked. But before we get into the *how* of RPG programming, we think it's important to talk a bit more about the *why*.

### Why Play RPGs?

When people play RPGs, they're stretching a lot of mental muscles and making a whole host of connections that may not be obvious until you examine the activity a bit more closely. As you read through this section and start playing RPGs with your patrons, consider how many of these activities match directly to learning standards that your schools and/or state boards of education use as their guidelines. (Hint: Teachers in states that have adopted the new Common Core State Standards will discover that RPGs reinforce a considerable number of standards in both Mathematics and English Language Arts and Literacy.)

### Mathematics

Most RPGs use dice as randomizers to determine whether or not a significant action succeeds or fails. This means that every time players decide something that could significantly affect their characters, they have to roll the dice and do math; addition, subtraction, and number value comparisons ("Did I roll more or less than the target number?") are all commonplace activities in RPGs. Given that most players will want to maximize the likelihood of their characters' success, they will become interested in probability and the chances of their characters succeeding at a given action.

Also, many, perhaps most, RPGs have a point-value system of creating characters. These games assign players a set number of points to construct their characters, and different traits, abilities, and powers have different costs. Thus, character creation can involve addition and subtraction, multiplication, and division. (In one game we're aware of, the players sometimes have to figure cube roots during character creation, but that's a rare case.)

And the very statistics that delimit characters' attributes and traits are values that players must interpret into fictional "realities"—for example, just how much can a character with a Strength value of 8 lift? Thus, knowledge of the system leads to descriptive modeling of game situations—for example, the likelihood that my character, with a Strength value of 8, will be able to move that big rock.

Because players usually have a limited pool of points available to construct their characters, players must also use resource management skills and prioritize which aspects of their characters need the most emphasis. Resource management can also be a factor in-game: if the group of characters only has a week's worth of supplies when entering a vast dungeon, then they'd better factor in how long it will take to find their way out and resupply. Gold and jewels are nice rewards, but they won't keep an adventurer from starving.

## Spatial Skills

In many RPGs, all of the action occurs in the players' imaginations. However, many other RPGs make optional or required use of maps, miniatures, and other materials at the game table. In these RPGs, tactics become a factor in successful game play, and such play reinforces spatial skills. Players need to look at the map and comprehend what their characters perceive; they need to be able to convert map space (often divided into one-inch squares or hex spaces) to "game" space (each square may represent five feet), and, for example, consider if their enemies are in their characters' line of sight. (Of course, players who are more visually oriented learners might benefit from having maps and miniatures as visual references, even if the map space isn't the play space.)

## Socialization

Tabletop RPGs are a social activity. At their most basic, RPGs require players to take turns, each allowing the others to describe their characters' actions, contribute ideas, and roll the dice.

Beyond the basics, RPGs are typically cooperative endeavors among the players and their characters. In a given adventure, the players' characters have goals to accomplish and must often rely on one another to attain those goals, not to mention survive their undertakings. Thus, players must be aware of how their characters' actions affect the other characters, and successful groups usually demonstrate teamwork as the players use their characters' strengths to progress the group's goals, assist one another, and compensate for their teammates' weaknesses. As Sarah Lynne Bowman (2010) mentions in *The Functions of Role-Playing Games*:

> Gaming offers the opportunity for a diverse group of people to interact in new and exciting ways. Because most games emphasize cooperation, both players and characters have to learn to work through personal differences in order to achieve common goals. [. . .] These moments of shared adversity can build bonds between people, offering them the chance to look beyond surface forms of identification such as age, race, sex, and occupation. (60–61)

You will likely discover that the players' teamwork will lead to interesting strategy and tactics within the game. Players might, for example, plan ambushes against monsters that are too powerful to fight head-to-head, or use their characters' skills, spells, and abilities in novel and creative ways in order to overcome obstacles.

Just as RPGs can enhance teamwork, they can also develop leadership skills. Gamers are typically a fairly fractious lot, and trying to get a group to decide on an action in-game can seem like herding cats. The ability to deal with a diverse group of people comes to the fore when interacting with a group of players. A good leader has the skills to address issues that will come up during play. Players can also develop their leadership skills by practicing during play sessions, refining their techniques both in-game and out.

While the group may come to acknowledge one of the players as the characters' party leader, just as often, particularly with more traditional RPGs, the game master (GM) must assume the mantle of group leader. The GM typically reads all the rules, adjudicates the rules, considers players' proposed ideas and courses of action, sets the conditions for success, describes the consequences of failure, and must be fair with all the other players, all while trying to entertain the players at the same time. Impartial, thoughtful GMs who care about their players' enjoyment of the game and cooperate with them will often have a full table; petty despots who see the game as something they can win by beating the players may soon have no players at all.

An additional potential social benefit of RPGs is the development of empathy. RPGs, by their very nature, require players to inhabit another point of view, even if that point of view belongs to an imaginary character, and the ability to consider another's perspective is key to developing empathy. Marsh states that empathy is achieved through "identity alteration," where players play characters that differ from themselves. Playing a character can develop three types of empathy:

> Compassionate empathy can be demonstrated by player-characters responding kindly to other characters. Cognitive empathy can manifest itself through players knowing how other characters are feeling by observation of spectatorship, or through interacting with other characters. Emotional empathy is similar to cognitive empathy, but in addition to knowing how other characters are feeling, the players feel these emotions as their own. (Marsh 2006, 203)

## Genre and Narrative

While RPGs are not in themselves stories, strictly speaking, they have a lot in common with stories and narratives. In fact, RPGs have a recursive relationship with stories and popular culture in general. As we established in the introduction, speculative fiction played an important role in the birth and development of RPGs, and genres like fantasy, science fiction, horror, espionage, and superheroes still define most of these games.

Of course, some RPGs are direct adaptations of specific intellectual properties and franchises (e.g., the *Buffy the Vampire Slayer Roleplaying Game* or *Star Wars: Edge of the Empire*). Players expect the games to play in the same manner as the narratives from the source material. If main characters in the franchise are lucky, competent, and survive many adventures, then the players expect their characters to be just as lucky and competent during game play. Even if a particular RPG derives its content and tone from a more general genre or subgenre rather than a specific franchise, then players familiar with those genres and subgenres carry their expectations from the narratives to the game. Games that fail to evoke the spirit of their source material will likely disappoint players and GMs alike.

But just as stories and popular culture influence RPGs, RPGs influence popular culture and stories. Wizards of the Coast (and earlier, TSR) has a thriving book publishing industry beyond RPGs and produces several lines of novels and fiction featuring characters and settings from the *Dungeons & Dragons* (*D&D*) game. Pinnacle Entertainment Group has several works of fiction and comic books based on its RPGs, particularly the weird Western RPG *Deadlands*. And most of the current electronic and video gaming industry wouldn't exist without *D&D* (Mackay 2001, 24–25).

Players bring their expectations of general narrative structure and tone to RPGs, whether through the expectation of a clearly delineated beginning, middle, and end in a one-shot adventure; the influence of novels and films; or the ongoing plots and subplots and recurring characters in a longer campaign, as found in other forms of serial entertainment like comics and television shows. RPGs use and reinforce this comprehension of genre and narrative structure.

## Literacy

Just as RPGs derive some of their aspects from novels, many RPG writers list their literary and media influences in their books. The first edition *Advanced Dungeons & Dragons Dungeon Masters Guide*, for example, contains "Appendix N," listing many authors and novels that inspired and influenced the game. Many other RPG rulebooks have bibliographies in the back that players can, and often do, use as reading lists.

In the same manner, many RPGs, like *Aces & Eights* or *Victoriana*, use historical and alternate-historical periods for their settings, and many RPGs encourage players interested in these settings to read more about the historical eras in question. Games like *D&D* (with its long history of borrowing from various mythologies in supplements like *Deities & Demigods*), *Scion* (in which the player characters are demigods), and *Changeling: The Lost* also encourage reading myths, legends, fairy tales, and folklore from all over the globe.

## Creativity

RPGs give players and GMs alike ample opportunity to exercise their creativity. While many players often begin by playing characters very much like themselves, or their idealized selves, they must still demonstrate the ability to inhabit another perspective as soon as the game begins. Because RPGs are improvisational by nature, players must learn to think quickly and come up with novel on-the-spot solutions to obstacles and challenges, whether finding a way into the wizard's tower or negotiating a peace treaty between kingdoms.

But even the best-laid plans of the most creative players often go awry, and defeat is always a possibility. Fortunately, RPGs are a safe, virtual space where players can experience negative consequences under the most benign circumstances: even if the worst occurs, the characters die, and a sadistic alien empire conquers the universe, the players can always roll up their sleeves, come back to the table, and play the next generation of plucky rebels.

As the campaign progresses, players often contribute to the game in other ways. Some participants might take careful notes during the games and post session summaries to a blog, exercising their storytelling skills. These players might also go a step further and relate the session's events through their characters' perspectives, giving the campaign its own fan fiction. Other players might contribute artwork to add visuals to the campaign, drawing the group's characters or settings that their characters encounter in the game. Some players have even prepared cuisine appropriate to the historical and cultural setting of the game. Smart GMs will encourage and reward these endeavors.

## Agency

In a tabletop RPG, the players and GM interact with one another to steer the game in one direction or another. Some games even have a meta-game currency that allows varying degrees of narrative control on both sides of the screen. Agency, the ability to affect the game through making choices and decisions, greatly increases the characters', and by extension the players', involvement in the story.

> [T]he *nature* of that social contact is one that involves a high degree of agency. . . . Being able to negotiate face-to-face allows players actual narrative agency, not just the chance for interaction. [. . .] While the DM [dungeon master] can limit the player's actions, in reality, the players have a great deal of agency in creating the story of the TRPG. (Cover 2010, 48–49)

Developing and exercising this sense of agency in-game can give young players the confidence they need to exercise greater agency outside of the game.

## Growing Popularity and Community Building

Granted, popularity isn't something that is evaluated by educational standards, but just in case you were concerned that you might not get teens to attend the programs, according to the website ICv2, a news leader in the gaming and comics industry, hobby game sales continue to grow (http://

www.icv2.com/articles/news/27526.html). While admittedly, the collectible card game market showed the highest increases, sales increased across all gaming categories. In addition, a healthy increase in Gen Con attendance in 2013 is another useful indicator, as Gen Con is one of the biggest gaming conventions and has a strong RPG component.

Remember, too, that RPGs have been part of the popular culture for more than thirty years now, and geek culture as a whole has become part of mainstream popular culture—just take a look at shows like *The Big Bang Theory* and *Community*. Libraries that have RPGs in the collection, that host and sponsor RPG programming, send a message to interested teens and will create social networks and circles of camaraderie built on common interests.

## Running Youth Programming Using RPGs

### The Basics: Safety First

Just as with any teen program, the gaming table has to be a safe space for the teens. They need to know that what they say, what they do, what they think, and what they believe matters. The librarian running the program has to provide an environment where respect is a prerequisite to participation.

Public and school librarians may need to take additional steps to ensure the safety of their youth patrons. Programmers could require participants to have their parents sign permission slips prior to participation; these permission slips could also ask parents to note any information on allergies (particularly food allergies, as many games have snacks nearby), relevant medical issues, and parental contact information in case of emergency. (See the sample form at the end of this chapter.)

Libraries often take pictures of their programs in order to advertise and promote the programs, and as a reporting tool for evaluations. Librarians should get parental permission before posting pictures of participating youth on websites or in advertising and newsletters.

### Advertising

New programs often require a lot of advertising to attract participants. As mentioned in chapter 2, librarians should decorate their RPG collection so patrons will notice it; this space is, of course, a good area to place colorful posters, fliers, and handouts that advertise the RPG program.

Creative librarians can find a myriad of ways to advertise a program. Most libraries, for example, have their own websites, and many also have some form of print or electronic newsletter. Most libraries also make use of social media and have a Facebook account, a Twitter account, and a variety of other spots to post notices about an RPG program. Does your library have any agreements or contracts with local newspapers? How about local radio or television stations? Do you have a local game shop or comics shop? Those are also excellent places to advertise.

When we perform exit interviews and evaluations of programs, we often find that most patrons learn about library programs while in the library. Beyond posters and fliers, make sure you feel comfortable approaching the members of your target audience when they come to the library. Practice your delivery so that you feel comfortable interacting with local teens and telling them about the library's programs. And be sure to enlist the help of your library's friendly circulation staff. Ask them to mention the programs to teens and youth, especially the teens who show an interest in crossover activities and check out comics, anime, manga, and fantasy and science fiction books and movies.

And, of course, once you get your first group of gamers together, encourage them to mention the group to their friends. Successful programs can be their own best advertising, second only to teens and word of mouth!

## Preparation

If gaming is popular in your area, then you may need to limit the number of players in your first game. The group size we've found that works best is a GM and anywhere from four to six players. Of course, with a program just finding its feet, you may not need a sign-up list when you start.

You will, of course, need to read the rules of the game you intend to run well beforehand. If the game has a beginning adventure included in the rulebook, then we strongly recommend running that adventure; if it is a good adventure, then it will likely be engaging and entertaining, and will highlight the more common rules and the major aspects of the rules set. For example, the adventure that comes with the *Star Wars: Edge of the Empire Beginner Game* box set has the players involved with negotiations, combat, flying starships, dogfights, and all the other exciting activities one expects from the *Star Wars* media. Reading and running adventures will give you a sense of structuring an adventure, developing scenes, and transitioning from scene to scene.

Players may not even know what an RPG is, so be ready to give an overview of the activity. Be sure to communicate clearly to the players the genre of the game, the tone of the game, who the player characters are, and what they'll be expected to do in the adventure. In fact, you should be able to phrase the adventure in terms of "your characters are [X] that [do Y]"— for example, "your characters are knights that must protect a village from monsters."

In addition to the rules and adventure, you'll need a space to play that is big enough to accommodate the group, quiet enough that players won't need to shout over one another to be heard, and separated sufficiently from other areas so that the game doesn't disturb anyone else. (There are few noises louder than a gaming group's exaltation over a critical success.) There should be sufficient chairs and a table large enough for maps, miniatures, elbow room, snacks, and rolling dice. And, yes, you'll need to bring dice, snacks, pencils, scratch paper, and character sheets.

For your first game, you may want to provide pre-generated characters for your players to choose from. If you're using a published adventure, then it may already have pre-generated characters included, but if not, then you'll want to create at least one for every player, and maybe one or two more just to have a sufficient variety of choices. These characters should be capable of dealing with the challenges in the adventure, have all the gear they need listed on the character sheets (so players aren't tempted to go into an hour-long shopping spree before the adventure begins), and have their own areas of specialization, to make each character unique.

If possible, we recommend that your first game be a simple, short one-shot adventure, with a clear beginning, middle, and end—just enough to give the players a taste of the activity. If all goes well, then they can continue play in later games with the pre-generated characters, or you can help them generate their own characters at the next meeting!

Of course, if all goes well, then you'll need to set a regular time for the gaming group to meet. If you have a Teen Advisory Board or similar group at your library, then you might ask the members about a good time to play. Some libraries find that after-school programs garner the best attendance, while others don't want to compete with already existing activities like sports and clubs, and so meet in the evening or on weekends. Either way, consider a weekly or biweekly meeting of approximately two hours if your program meets on a weekday or weeknight, or a biweekly meeting of two to four hours if you meet on the weekends. This allows ample time for gamers to blow off a little steam at the beginning, get their heads in the game, play for a significant amount of time, and fill out a postgame evaluation. (See sample evaluation form at end of chapter.)

## Designing Adventures

Eventually, you will likely design your own adventures for your gaming group. Before you do, once again, we recommend running one or two published adventures beforehand. We also recommend obtaining a number of free adventures offered by a variety of publishers at their websites and reading them—you might even be able to adapt them for your game!

Reading and running published adventures will help you to learn about the structure of a successful adventure, and how to progress from scene to scene.

And when you feel confident enough to write your own adventures, we heartily recommend the following guidelines:

1. Make It Clear

   Once again, be able to boil down your adventure premise to a single sentence, "Your characters are [X] that [do Y]." Granted, that's pretty broad, so here are a few more examples: "your characters are explorers and adventurers looking for ancient artifacts"; "your characters are heroic rebels battling against an evil empire"; "your characters are a bunch of teens exploring the old house down the street, the one that the other kids say is haunted." Remember to boil your adventure down to a single sentence, so your players know what's expected of them.

2. Start with Action

   Think about all the television shows and films that you enjoy. Nearly every beginning scene starts with the characters *doing something*. When you start your adventure, bypass the shopping trips and other potential distractions. If the opening scene is one of tension, put the characters in the moment. If the characters are kids exploring the neighborhood's haunted house, then the adventure should begin on the porch of the haunted house long after dark, as the kids are opening the creaking door after sneaking out of their rooms with their backpacks. The adventure should not begin with the characters in their own rooms, gathering what they think they'll need. In the situation with the rebels, start in the middle of a firefight. In the example with the explorers, start at the entrance to the ancient tomb.

3. Imagery Is Key

   Remember that *you* are the senses of the player characters. They only sense what you describe. Feel free to ham it up without going overboard. In key scenes, spend a little extra time setting the scene, so they know it's a bit more special than previous scenes/encounters. In the opening scene with the haunted house, describe the partially broken windows, the cobwebs that stick to their clothes and faces (and the largish spiders in those webs), the cold drafts, and the painting with eyes that seem to follow you as you walk about the room. Emphasize how dark it is, and how little the flashlights actually illuminate. (Remember, if they're pointing the flashlights ahead, nobody's shedding light behind them.) Use words like 'scurrying' and 'skittering' to describe sounds. Tell them about the musty scents and the thickness of the dust. Don't do this for every room, but definitely ham it up at the beginning, and during key scenes. If you need to, draw a quick map so players can orient themselves.

4.  Reward Good Play
    If the players come up with a good idea, then reward them for it. If they think of something genuinely clever, then give them a bonus. If they say something so funny it cracks up everyone at the table, then reward them with experience, metagame currency, or whatever else the game you're running uses as an incentive.

5.  Don't Be Afraid to Warn Your Players, but Let the Characters Face the Consequences of Their Players' Decisions
    It really is okay to ask, "Are you *sure* that you want to go into the basement *alone*, where the wet chewing noises are, without a properly functioning flashlight?" However, if the player says, "Yes, I do," then let the dice fall where they may.

6.  Multiple Paths to Success, and Progress after Failure
    The key to the entire adventure shouldn't depend on stumbling across the secret diary hidden in the mattress of the master bedroom on the second floor. If it does, then your players are likely toast and will justifiably feel frustrated after the game. As you develop your adventures, in every scene, consider both how the players will progress if they succeed, and how they will progress if they fail. Consider multiple possible paths to successfully completing the adventure, and allow for player cleverness to think of a few more.

7.  Steal Shamelessly
    You're not likely going to publish any of your adventures, so feel free to steal ideas and plots from any and every source—movies, television, comics, animation, Internet news articles—when creating scenarios for your players, then modify them so that they fit into your game. Did you recently watch a particularly brilliant episode of your favorite television show? What was the plot? Who was the antagonist? What was at stake? What drove the conflicts between the characters? Answer these questions, and then figure out how you can plug those aspects into the game you're running, altering enough details so that the source isn't obvious—you don't want other fans of the show knowing how your game will turn out, after all—and so that the elements fit the genre, style,

and tone of the game you're running. As you create scenarios, you'll realize that most plots are readily transferrable from one medium and genre to another, and only require a bit of fine-tuning and some statistics for your antagonists to make them useable.

And if you really want to surprise your players, then steal from sources that they *don't* tend to read or watch, and see their heads explode. They'll think you're a genius.

## Continuing the Program

As you progress, you may want to run a variety of different one-shots set in different genres, or you may want to continue running the same characters through subsequent adventures. Whether you choose one-shot adventures, mini-campaigns of six to eight sessions, or longer term campaigns that go on for months (and possibly years) as your regular format, remember: As long as everyone is having fun, then you're doing it right.

Over time, you will also get a sense of which aspects of the game your players consider fun, what they want out of the game, and what brings them back to the table. Robin Laws identifies a number of player "types" in his book *Robin's Laws of Good Game Mastering*; other manuals for GMs have their own classifications. Some players will want to know their characters' motivation and will take time to structure a complex persona and history for their characters. Other players will simply want their characters to look cool performing their characters' specialties; the party tanks will want to be the baddest monster stompers around, and the group's ninja will want to be the ninjiest ninja that ever ninjaed. Other players will enjoy the challenge of mastering a given set of rules, learning every intricacy, and discovering every exploitable loophole. Some players want their games to feel like narratives, and they see the activity as group storytelling. Other players are simply playing just to hang out with their friends—and that's a good thing, because socialization is an important aspect of tabletop RPGs.

When you learn what it is your players want, then try to give them more of it, if possible, and make sure that every adventure has something for each character to do, at least one scene where each character can shine. If you have players who love to stomp monsters, then give them monsters to stomp. If some players like to be sneaky, then give them something to infiltrate. If some players love to dig deep into their motivations, then give them recurring nemeses and tantalizing hints as to how their histories fit into the fabric of the campaign. And those players who love studying the intricacies of rules systems—get them on your side! When you need to reference the rules, ask players to do it when possible, and they may feel appreciated for their expertise.

## Evaluation

Remember to have players fill out an evaluation with every program. Ask them questions that will collect data that are relevant to how your director or supervisor might evaluate your program. You can keep the evaluations anonymous, but you might want to ask for basic demographic data, like gender and ethnicity/race. You could ask the evaluators if this is their first time at the program, how they heard about it, and how they liked the program. Even more importantly, you can ask questions like, "Does playing this game lead you to want to read more books in that genre?" or even "Has playing this game positively affected your reading habits?" (Of course, it helps if GM librarians have handy read-alike lists available for participants!) You might inquire if the game has affected their sense of teamwork, or even if they've made any friends through the program. Of course, instead of a formal evaluation, you could simply ask the participants to write a letter or email about the program and any positive impact it has had on them and their lives. You could reasonably ask for this kind of evaluation semiannually or annually.

Ultimately, what you want to learn is if the game, the program, or the interaction with a librarian-mentor has a positive, long-term impact on the players. If you can demonstrate that your program makes a long-term positive impact on the players' lives, reading habits, and friendships, then you will have a program that more teens will want to attend and that other librarians will want to emulate.

## Plan for Growth

One of the limiting factors of RPGs is the number of players that can easily play at once in the same game. While early groups of role-playing gamers could reach numbers as high as fifteen or twenty, we think that you'll find a group of five or six teens more than enough to entertain. Larger groups tend to descend into chaos, since players experience too long a time between their turns, become frustrated, get distracted, and distract others from the program. RPGs, in this sense, tend to be a quality-over-quantity type of program.

So what happens if you find that there are more players interested in your group than you can handle? One solution is, of course, to run more than one group; for example, you could run weekly games, but have two groups, and each group meets every other week.

We know. We can hear the laughter from here. "I barely have time to run one program a week/every other week/every month," you might say. "How can I run multiple programs for these gamers?!"

Well, if your library has a meeting space that the community can use, then we have a potential solution for you: nurture the players, see which ones could be potential GMs, and have them run some games.

One of your friendly and helpful authors has been a teen librarian for more than a decade. Over the ten years I've run games for local teens, I've challenged them to run games for one another, giving each one a shot at the GM's chair. Some of them discovered that they were very capable, very creative GMs, and they ran games for their friends at their homes, or (if they demonstrated sufficient maturity) even in the library. Libraries often allow other community groups to run programs in their conference or study rooms, so why can't teens do so, if they're kept to the same standards as other groups?

Again, you'll need to consider this possibility in terms of your library's policies and procedures, and of course you'll need to know that you can trust the teens, but part of mentorship is giving the teens moments where they can demonstrate success. Sometimes they might disappoint you, but we think you'll be surprised at how many will rise to the occasion and value the trust given them.

## On the Other Hand . . . Dealing with Difficult Players

We're not naïve. Nobody's perfect, and while many teens respond well to an adult's positive interest and respect, there will still be occasional, difficult times. What happens when some youth refuse to play well with others?

Unlike some other activities, in most geographic regions, the number of tabletop RPG groups is comparatively limited. These groups are typically closed groups of friends who rarely add players, and usually only by invitation, although some popular tabletop RPGs have a fairly interconnected network that can, theoretically at least, exchange players on a regular basis, given a sufficiently large region. Either way, groups quickly identify disruptive players, and word spreads even more quickly.

Players can be disruptive for a number of reasons, but the two main issues are often either lack of social maturity or boredom. For younger players, involvement in RPGs can help develop some sense of social maturity: "If some players experience difficulties in day-to-day interactions, we would suggest that involvement in any social group would be, on some level, beneficial to developing important interpersonal skills and promoting extraversion" (Bowman 2010, 54).

If a player appears bored, then the GM should take the time to discuss the matter with the player in private. Perhaps the player is dissatisfied with the character, or wants or expected more of something in the game, whether fights with monsters or puzzle solving or some other aspect of the genre. See what the player wants, and try to reach some sort of accord to meet that desire.

Sometimes, conflict may arise in play. If the friction is entirely between the characters, and not the players themselves, then it can be entertaining to play out and observe, just like watching two characters in your favorite television show snipe and snark at one another. As long as the interaction is entertaining for the group, then let the players have fun. However, sometimes intercharacter conflicts escalate to interplayer conflicts. In fact, conflicts may arise between players over occurrences in-game, or can be brought in from outside interactions. If the conflict arises over rules, then the GM should make a judgment call and move on. If the conflict is more serious, then it may be necessary to halt the game and deal with the conflict in a respectful, rational manner.

Sometimes, a participant's behavior is sufficiently disruptive that the GM needs to take the player aside, preferably outside of game time, and discuss the situation. However, if a player persists in being disruptive of the game and disrespectful to the other players, then it is not only reasonable but also necessary to ask that player to leave the group permanently. The only thing worse than no game is a game where nobody is having fun, and if you don't remove the difficult player, then you're guaranteed to lose the other players.

## For More GM Advice . . .

While this book is intended as a starting point, it is by no means large enough to present an exhaustive treatise on running games. Be assured that there is no substitute for experience; the best thing you can do is prepare adequately, get the program organized, roll up your sleeves, and start running games. It's how most of us learned, after all.

However, once you've started running games and gotten your feet wet, you will discover areas that you excel at and others that you need to work on a bit more. Fortunately, there are a large number of books that can help you become an even better GM.

Robin Laws is a veteran of the RPG industry, and *Robin's Laws of Good Game Mastering* is an excellent primer for new GMs. Laws's advice on preparing games, considering the audience you're running for, and structuring adventures is extremely helpful to novice GMs. Librarians can purchase this item as a PDF at the Steve Jackson Games website: http://www .sjgames.com/robinslaws/.

*Gnome Stew: The Game Mastering Blog* is another excellent resource for new and experienced GMs, and has a variety of reviews and articles that are both entertaining and informative. Phil Vecchione, a regular contributor to *Gnome Stew*, published *Never Unprepared: The Complete Game Master's Guide to Session Prep* through *Gnome Stew*'s imprint, Engine Publishing. In *Never Unprepared*, Vecchione instructs GMs on how to create their own process for minimizing their workload in preparing adventures for game sessions. Vecchione's second book, cowritten with another regular *Gnome Stew contributor*, Walt Ciechanowski, is *Odyssey: The Complete Game Master's Guide to Campaign Management*. This book is for those programs where the GM is managing a long-term campaign. If you want to keep your players interested and on their toes, if you want to see them coming back to the table amazed at how you keep everything fresh, intriguing, and entertaining, then you need to plan for the long game—that's what *Odyssey* is for.

## Reaching Out

If you have a local game or comics shop, then pay careful attention to gaming events occurring at the shop, especially Free RPG Day (http://www. freerpgday.com). See if you can partner with your friendly local game stores (FLGs) for events like these by advertising for one another. Perhaps you can even run a game on Free RPG Day that will get people talking about your program and spread the word even faster.

And, remember, the publishers want to reach out to you and your players with company-sponsored programs that will engage your players in large-scale campaigns where they can affect the outcome! Catalyst Game Labs has its *Shadowrun: Missions* program (http://www.shadowruntabletop.com/ missions/), Paizo has a brochure on getting the *Pathfinder* RPG into your library (http://paizo.com/pathfinder/libraries), and librarians who are willing to work with their FLGS can get involved with Wizards of the Coasts' *D&D Adventurers League* (http://dndadventurersleague.org)!

## Dealing with Opposition

For some of you, this is the section you've been anticipating, wondering when we'd get around to dealing with the negative perceptions of RPGs. Well, here we are.

Some of you remember the virulent opposition to RPGs in the mid-1980s. In *Gaming as Culture: Essays on Reality, Identity, and Experience in Fantasy Games*, J. Patrick Williams, Sean Q. Hendricks, and W. Keith Winkler reference Stanley Cohen's book *Folk Devils and Moral Panics*, where Cohen describes a moral panic as:

A condition, episode, person or group of persons [which] emerges to become defined as a threat to societal value and interests; its nature is presented in a stylized and stereotypical fashion by the mass media; the moral barricades are manned by editors, bishops, politicians, and other right-thinking people; socially accredited experts pronounce their diagnoses and solutions; ways of coping are evolved or (more often) resorted to; the condition then disappears, submerges or deteriorates and becomes less visible. (Cohen 2002, 1; quoted in Williams et al. 2006, 8).

As Williams et al. continue to relate, *D&D* "was defined as a threat to societal values and interests [. . .] manifested primarily in fears of occult worship [. . .] and negative psychological conditions including suicide, all of which the mass media presented in a stylized and stereotypical fashion" (2006, 8). They go on to discuss how "In [. . .] popular culture sources, staff writers, apparently unfamiliar with fantasy games, reported the concerns of adults—parents, politicians, police, and religious leaders—over fantasy games as a source of child corruption" (2006, 8).

The "Satanic Panic," as it came to be called, resulted in "media hysteria directed at role-playing games in general, and *Dungeons & Dragons* in particular" (Appelcline 2011, 21). At the forefront of this hysteria was Patricia Pulling and her group, B.A.D.D. (Bothered About Dungeons & Dragons); Pulling's son committed suicide on 9 June 1982, and she blamed his death on *D&D* (Appelcline 2011, 21). Another suicide, that of James Dallas Egbert III, further fueled the flames of hysteria. Egbert was a depressed, suicidal young man who dabbled in drugs and had a difficult relationship with his parents; he felt like "everything about [his] life had to be a secret," including the fact that he was gay (Dear 1984, 270). When he went missing during his time at Michigan State University, he had entered the steam tunnels beneath the university. Investigators assumed that Egbert was acting out due to a combination of drugs and *D&D*, lost in the fantasy he had created (Dear 1984, 142). This incident became popularized by Rona Jaffe's fictionalized account of it in her novel *Mazes and Monsters* (later also becoming a film starring a young Tom Hanks). The facts of the case only came out after Egbert's final and successful suicide attempt in 1980; with Egbert's death, the lead investigator in Egbert's case, William Dear, felt he could finally relate the entire account in his book *The Dungeon Master: The Disappearance of James Dallas Egbert III*.

The panic lasted about as long as *D&D* remained incredibly popular; as RPGs went from widespread fad to simply another hobby, the fearmongers sought new prey elsewhere. However, the damage had been done:

reductionist and sensationalized psychological theories about RPGs caused people to doubt the sanity and motives of players, and the media frenzy had frightened well-meaning parents, churches, and schools, and had done no one any good whatsoever.

Fortunately, defenders of the hobby did come forward. Mike Stackpole, author and game designer, published "The Pulling Report" in 1990. In this document, Stackpole utterly demolishes every false claim and calumny that Patricia Pulling and B.A.D.D. ever made about RPGs. "The Pulling Report" is available for free online at http://www.rpgstudies.net/stackpole/pulling_report.html.

Later psychological studies became more refined, as researchers stopped assuming that RPGs were a symptom or cause of pathology. In fact, time after time, researchers "studied role-players in contrast to non-gamers and found no significant differences on measures of antisocial behavior, affect by emotions, depression, suicidal ideation, psychoticism, or neuroticism" (Williams et al. 2006, 9).

However, the shadow of the Satanic Panic looms large still. Even in the twenty-first century, library directors might be leery of public reaction to RPG programs. Some programs have decided to relabel themselves as "storytelling game" programs, but that is ultimately a poor fix to the situation. So librarians who are interested in running RPG programs will need to become advocates of RPGs as well as teen advocates.

The first step you should take was mentioned way back in chapter 2, in the section "Make Sure You're Covered." Be sure that your library has official policies for collection development, materials selection, and especially, challenges to library material.

The second step we recommend is to read Stackpole's "Pulling Report," as it rationally addresses and debunks many of the hysterical myths that have arisen around RPGs. Librarians might also want to peruse other materials available at the website Studies about Fantasy Role-Playing Games (http://www.rpgstudies.net).

The third step is to take a deep breath and thank W. J. Walton for his website, The Escapist (http://www.theescapist.com/index.htm). We could write hundreds more pages on the subject of gaming advocacy and clearing up the myths and misconceptions surrounding RPGs, but frankly, Walton has done a better job than we ever could in arranging and compiling the information. We recommend going to his award-winning website *right now*, reading his "Basic RPG FAQ" (http://www.theescapist.com/basic_gaming_faq.htm), and downloading the PDFs entitled "Facts and Fictions about Role-Playing Games" (http://www.theescapist.com/facts-and-fictions-about-RPGs.pdf) and "The Role-Playing Game Fact Checker" (http://www.theescapist.com/RPGfactchecker.pdf). The Escapist is an excellent source of information and a welcome island of sanity in the RPG universe, and we are very thankful for it.

## Works Referenced

Appelcline, Shannon. 2011. *Designers & Dragons: [A History of the Roleplaying Game Industry]*. Swindon, England: Mongoose Publishing.

Bowman, Sarah Lynne. 2010. *The Functions of Role-Playing Games: How Participants Create Community, Solve Problems, and Explore Identity*. Jefferson, N.C.: McFarland & Co.

Cohen, Stanley. 2002. *Folk Devils and Moral Panics*, 3rd ed. London: Routledge.

Cover, Jennifer Grouling. 2010. *The Creation of Narrative in Tabletop Role-Playing Games*. Jefferson, N.C.: McFarland & Co.

Dear, William. 1984. *The Dungeon Master: The Disappearance of James Dallas Egbert III*. Boston: Houghton Mifflin.

Mackay, Daniel. 2001. *The Fantasy Role-Playing Game: A New Performing Art*. Jefferson, N.C.: McFarland & Co.

Marsh, Tim. 2006. "Vicarious Experience: Staying There Connected with and through Our Own and Other Characters." In *Gaming as Culture: Essays on Reality, Identity, and Experience in Fantasy Games,* edited by J. Patrick Williams, Sean Q. Hendricks, and W. Keith Winkler, 196–214. Jefferson, N.C.: McFarland & Co.

Williams, J. Patrick, Sean Q. Hendricks, and W. Keith Winkler. 2006. *Gaming as Culture: Essays on Reality, Identity, and Experience in Fantasy Games*. Jefferson, N.C.: McFarland & Co.

# Sample Permissions Form for a School Library
## *Tabletop Role-Playing Game Program Consent Form*

Student's Name: _____

Grade: _____

Address: _____

Parent's / Guardian's Name: _____

Home Phone: _____

Cell Phone: _____

Work Phone: _____

Email: _____

## Emergency Contact

Name: _____

Relationship to Student: _____

Phone: _____

## Medical Information

Does the student have any health problems, necessary medication, allergies, or other medical issues that the staff should know of?

_____

_____

_____

_____

_____

_____

_____

*Dragons in the Stacks* by Steven A. Torres-Roman and Cason E. Snow.
Santa Barbara, CA: Imprint Name. Copyright © 2014.

# Sample Program Evaluation Form

What is your gender? _____

What is your age? _____

Which ethnic background do you most identify with?

African-American          Asian                    Caucasian

Hispanic/Latino           Native American          Multiracial

Other: _____

How did you hear about the tabletop RPG program?


Is this your first time attending?


Did you enjoy the program? If so, what aspects did you enjoy the most? If not, is there anything that would make the experience better for you?


Does playing this game lead you to want to read more books in this genre?


Did you use library resources or check out material as a result of this program?


Has this game positively affected your reading habits?


Have you made any friendships over the course of participating in this program?


*Dragons in the Stacks* by Steven A. Torres-Roman and Cason E. Snow.
Santa Barbara, CA: Imprint Name. Copyright © 2014.

# 5

# A Guide to the Games

Our tastes in role-playing games (RPGs) are wide and varied, and our preferences contain multitudes. However, we only have so much space left to share our love of RPGs with you, and in this section we want to present you with a whole host of games that are just as varied as your and your patrons' interests.

To that end, this chapter features a multitude of RPGs that we think will pique your interest and provide hours of fun and fantastic programming. When selecting these games, we had numerous criteria in mind. We asked ourselves: Is the game current and popular? Is there a hardcopy edition available, even by print-on-demand, as well as an electronic version? Does it have ties to a popular book or intellectual property (IP) that people will recognize? Just how complex are these rules, anyway? For whom is the game age-appropriate? Did we represent a goodly number of genres?

And occasionally we broke the above rules because we considered a game too good to be excluded.

Of course, we couldn't possibly include every game we'd have liked to write about, much less every game on the market. And we've invariably left out somebody's favorite game, for which we apologize in advance. Still, we think you'll agree that this is a pretty solid list to start with, and we have no doubt that your own exploration, experimentation, and edification will yield further favorites!

---

The evaluation format of this guide is adapted from Sean Patrick Fannon's *The Fantasy Roleplaying Gamer's Bible, Second Edition*. Ponte Verda Beach, Fla.: Obsidian Studios, 1999. Used with permission of Jared Nielsen and Sean Patrick Fannon.

## *All for One: Regime Diabolique*

Paul "Wiggy" Wade Williams
Triple Ace Games, 2010
http://www.tripleacegames.com
Genre Tags: Alternate History, Fantasy, Historical
Dice: d6 (Actually, the system can use any even-sided dice, or special
Ubiquity system dice, but six-sided dice are the most commonly
available type, and the book mentions them specifically.)

### Introduction

*All for One: Regime Diabolique* is a high-adventure historical fantasy game of Musketeers defending the nation and slowly becoming aware of the supernatural horror that threatens their land.

### System and Characters

*All for One* uses a point-buy system to build characters—players assign points to primary attributes (Body, Charisma, Dexterity, Intelligence, Strength, and Willpower), factor secondary characteristics, choose a background and motivation for their characters, spend points on skills, and choose talents (see "Advantages and Disadvantages" in the glossary).

All characters are Musketeers in service to the crown, but characters have particular talents and specialties depending on their backgrounds to prevent them from being carbon copies of one another. Players resolve tests by building a dice pool with a number of dice equal to either a relevant skill or attribute rating. Players then add or subtract dice, depending on modifiers to the roll. Players roll the dice, count up the number of dice showing an even result, and compare that sum against a target number or opposed roll.

Player characters also have access to a metagame currency resource called style points. Players gain style points through actions in-game or through contributing to the campaign, and can use them to gain bonus dice, boost their talents, and resist injury, and can even spend them on behalf of other characters.

Appropriate to a game of high action and tempting fate, *All for One* has a fantastic mechanic called chance dice. Effectively, when a character really needs to make an action count, the player can ask the game master (GM) for chance dice. For every two chance dice the player receives, up to ten, the GM increases the target number of the action that the character is attempting by one. Players using chance dice take the risk that they can garner enough successes to offset the higher target number, and they may fail dismally or succeed spectacularly.

As befitting a game of sword-wielding, swashbuckling action, the players may also have access to particular fencing schools, and the book has particularly flavorful options for interested players. As befitting a game of supernatural horror, some characters may also have an aptitude for the magickal arts (all in the service of the crown, of course!), and the core rulebook has plenty of mysterious mysticism for player characters and antagonists to bring to bear. Be warned, however: France in 1636 considers all forms of sorcery to be the Devil's work, and careless player characters with magickal powers could find themselves on the wrong side of a peasant mob!

*All for One* has various rules for gear, advanced rules for combat, and a section on allies and antagonists for characters to encounter, carouse with, duel, or destroy.

## Setting

The year is 1636. Louis XIII rules the nation, but Cardinal Richelieu may actually be the most powerful man in France. A terrible evil gnaws at the heart of the kingdom, and all that stands between chaos and the king are his Musketeers!

Obviously, *All for One* takes as its setting a mash-up between the France of Alexandre Dumas's novels and Gothic horror. Fortunately for GMs, the core rulebook spends some time breaking down the swashbuckling genre into its narrative elements and tropes, and gives GMs options on dialing up or down the levels of action and supernatural activity to fit their gaming groups. (We think all the dials should go up to 11!) The GM section also has a list of adventure seeds to spark the GM's creativity.

Now, we've heard some groups go on and on about how all Musketeers were men. Considering, however, that Dumas added a veneer of high action and romance, and that the game adds even more fantastical elements, we don't think that it's such a stretch to have female Musketeers—do you?

## Evaluation

Complexity: 2

Popularity: 2

Support: 5; take a look at the publisher's website for freebies, and then see what else might be available to purchase.

Completeness: 3

Versatility: 3; *All for One* uses the Ubiquity game system, the core system for pulp games like the *Hollow Earth Expedition* RPG and the *Leagues of Adventure* Victorian steampunk RPG.

Emulation: 4

## Comments

As you can tell, we were pretty impressed with this game and its ability to handle the mash-up of Musketeers and supernatural monsters. Introduce players to Alexandre Dumas's work if they haven't tried it yet, as well as to *The Phoenix Guards* by Steven Brust. And whatever you do, make sure the players watch the anime *Le Chevalier D'Eon.* At the very least, the GM should watch this excellent animated series, as it is a treasure trove of ideas for *All for One.*

Cost: $34.99 hardcover; $24.99 PDF

## *Artesia: Adventures in the Known World*

Mark Smylie
Archaia Studios Press, 2005
http://www.archaia.com
Genre Tags: Comics, Fantasy
Dice: Primarily d10; d4, d6, d8, d12, d20 also used

### Introduction

*Artesia: Adventures in the Known World* is based on the author's series of graphic novels centered on the eponymous heroine.

### System and Characters

The system used in *Artesia* is based on the Fuzion system created by R. Talsorian games. Fuzion is a very simple system that uses a d10 and adds attribute and skill modifiers to beat a target number. This basic resolution mechanic is a unified mechanic and applies to all rolls in the game.

Character creation follows a lifepath system. The customized lifepath system is setting specific and has several additional elements that are important to the world. The lifepaths are divided by culture and social level within the culture. Other tables include astrological signs, omens, and lineages, which all have some game effect on the character. These tables are incredibly useful in shaping characters that will fit into and have ties with the richly developed setting.

The experience point system is fairly unique to this game. *Artesia* uses two groups of experience points: training and arcana. Training points are just that—points acquired by doing nothing but training at whatever characteristic or skill a character wishes to improve. This method is fairly slow, in game time, and can only be used to improve mundane skills. Arcana points are earned by the character's actions. There are twenty-two arcana representing various stages of life. Each arcanum rules a different set of attributes, gifts (supernatural abilities that are inherent to the character), skills, and bindings (primarily mental and social burdens that can be mitigated over time). Characters are awarded a number of points in specific arcana based on their actions taken, and these points can then be used to improve the characteristics ruled by those arcana. Another point to keep in mind is that these arcana reflect the cosmological laws of the Known World and not the cultural laws, so for actions to be rewarded they must further some cause or goal noteworthy enough to garner divine attention.

## Setting

The setting is based visually on our world's fifteenth century. *Artesia* portrays several cultures drawn from real world models. The RPG greatly expands the world established in the graphic novels and allows players to tell their own stories set in this rich world. They also have the option of including the events of the graphic novels.

One major feature that makes this game stand out from many other fantasy RPGs is the amount of thought that went into religion and its effects on society. Unlike most fantasy games where there is only one pantheon and all cultures follow the same gods, in *Artesia* there are two major pantheons of gods that are venerated. One pantheon is a patriarchal group with the sun god at the head; the other is a matriarchal group centered on an Earth Mother and draws heavily from a Classical Greek model.

The magic in *Artesia* is also different from most other fantasy games. In this world anyone can learn and use the various forms of magic. The types of magic range from quickly cast Incantations to longer Rituals, Divinations, and Enchantments to Runes and Sigils to make magic items. Much of the magic is divine in nature, where the characters call upon the favor of the gods they follow. Here again the author's research into Classical religion shows, as sacrifice and spiritual pollution both play important roles in the workings of magic.

## Evaluation

Complexity: 2; the Fuzion system is fairly easy to learn, but the experience system is very complex.

Popularity: 1

Support: 1; no supplements were ever published.

Completeness: 5

Versatility: 3; typical campaigns range from war to investigation to intrigue, but all take place within the setting of the graphic novels.

Emulation: 5; this game has a customized rule set and setting designed and written by the author of the graphic novels on which the game is based.

## Comments

Currently, the print copy of *Artesia* is out of print, though at the time of this publication a new edition is in the works, and secondhand copies can be purchased at or below retail price.

Cost: $39.95 hardcover; $19.99 PDF

## *Basic Roleplaying: The Chaosium Roleplaying System, Second Edition*

Jason Durall et al.
Chaosium Inc., 2011
http://catalog.chaosium.com
Genre Tags: Multigenre
Dice: d4, d6, d8, d10, d12, d20, d%/d100

## Introduction

*Basic Roleplaying* (*BRP*), also known as "The Big Gold Book," is a time-tested system nearly four decades old that has handled games in nearly every popular genre, and is still a strong and simple game of choice for many RPG players.

## System and Characters

Characters in *BRP* have seven attributes called Characteristics: Strength, Constitution, Size, Intelligence, Power (your character's willpower and aptitude for magic or other superhuman or supernatural powers), Dexterity, and Appearance, with an optional eighth characteristic, Education. These characteristics range from 3 to 18, with Intelligence, Size, and Education ranging from 8 to 18. Players generate these Characteristics randomly, although the rulebook does have an optional system for assigning points instead. Players then multiply these characteristics by five to determine percentages for Characteristic rolls, which can range from 15 percent to 90 percent. Players then decide on a profession and gain points to spend on their skills, which can range from 0 to 100. Depending on the genre and setting, players may get additional points to spend on powers, including magical or sorcerous abilities, mutations, psychic abilities, or superpowers.

*BRP* is a percentile-based, roll-low system. Players will attempt to roll under their Characteristic's percentile roll, or their skill value, in order to succeed. In the case of an opposed roll, such as in combat, opposing characters make their checks, and the results are compared to one another on a table to determine success. In the case of particularly difficult tests, players will need to roll equal to or under one-half of their skill rank or Characteristic percentile.

*BRP* has a host of special rules for various settings and genres. One of the best aspects of this RPG is that so many of its rules are modular—you can use them, not use them, or alter them to your gaming group's desires, and it won't affect the playability of the rest of the game.

## Setting

Because *BRP* is a multigenre game, it doesn't have a single system ascribed to it, but it can handle, and has handled, a variety of game settings. *Runequest*, a fantasy game now published by the Design Mechanism (http://www.thedesignmechanism.com), uses a variant of *BRP*, as does Chaosium's own *Call of Cthulhu*. Variants of *BRP* have also served as game engines for *Superworld*, various RPGs based on the works of author Michael Moorcock (including his *Elric*, *Corum*, and *Hawkmoon* properties), and the *Elfquest* RPG based on the comics by Wendy Pini, among others. Chaosium also sells a large number of published settings and adventures specifically for use with *BRP*, ranging from fantasy to science fiction, post-apocalypse to pulp adventure, giant mecha to historical and horror campaigns, and many more!

## Evaluation

   Complexity: 2/3; the basic system is simplicity itself, with additional modular rules adding various levels of complexity.

   Popularity: 4; over the years, many gamers have used the *BRP* system in one form or another.

   Support: 4; Chaosium and third-party publishers have plenty of material for *BRP*.

   Completeness: 5; *BRP* is about as complete as anyone could ask for.

   Versatility: 5; over the decades, the *BRP* system has handled just about every genre.

   Emulation: 3; GMs may need to tinker with *BRP* to make it fit a particular vision for a genre or setting, but the game is a perfect toolkit for that kind of tinkering.

## Comments

What easier way to tell a player that they have a 60 percent chance of success than saying exactly that? The system's ease of use, tried-and-true mechanics, and modular components for varying types of play make it an excellent system to use with novice players. Plus, the free quick-start PDF, available at Chaosium's website, has all the essential rules for players as well as several free adventures!

Cost: $44.95 hardcover; $21.97 PDF

## Black Crusade

Sam Stewart
Fantasy Flight Games, 2011
http://www.fantasyflightgames.com
Genre Tags: Science Fiction, Space Opera
Dice: d%/d100

### Introduction

*Black Crusade* is a darkly themed space opera where the characters serve unknowable entities of the Warp in trying to overcome the Imperium of Man. This game is a dark reflection of the other RPGs in the *Warhammer 40,000* universe published by Fantasy Flight Games.

### System and Characters

Players create characters in *Black Crusade* using a hybrid of random generation and a point-buy system. Unlike many other games, *Black Crusade* represents basic combat training as attributes rather than skills. The role of each character is further defined by the selection of an archetype. There are eight archetypes available, four human and four Chaos Space Marines (superhuman soldiers in powered armor). Each archetype fulfills a specific role and has a set of skills useful to that role. All of the characters in *Black Crusade* begin with more experience, which is figured in at character creation, than do equivalent starting characters in the other *Warhammer 40,000* games. Psychic powers are initially restricted to certain archetypes, but all characters may develop them over time. Unlike the other games in this series, psychic abilities are not tightly controlled or frowned upon in *Black Crusade*, as they are a sign of power and blessing by the powers of Chaos.

At its core *Black Crusade* uses a percentile system for determining success. This basic resolution mechanic is used in nearly all tasks, both mundane and psychic. There are some rules in this game that are noteworthy and show the game's direct lineage as a tabletop miniatures wargame. As servants of Chaos, characters in *Black Crusade* will earn Corruption and Infamy. These serve as the measure of favor that a character has from the

Ruinous Powers and their peers, respectively. In a game where the characters are all fairly self-interested and could very easily have conflicting goals, the rules for cooperation are included in the form of compacts. Compacts provide a framework for the characters to pursue their goals and are goal oriented, providing the group a clear goal.

## Setting

The characters in *Black Crusade* are divided into two groups: humans and Chaos Marines. Humans are people who have decided, for myriad reasons, to break with the Imperium ruled by the Emperor and to venerate Chaos. The Chaos Marines initially began as loyal Space Marines, who 10,000 years ago decided to rebel against the Emperor and the Great Crusade. They followed the traitorous Warmaster Horus and fell to venerating the powers of Chaos. Some of the fallen legions chose a specific power of Chaos to swear allegiance to; for example, the Death Guard follows Nurgle, Lord of Corruption, while others, such as the Night Lords, follow Chaos Undivided.

The setting of *Black Crusade* is the Screaming Vortex, which is a large and obscured region of space largely unknown to the Imperium of Man. Groups can play out entire games without the need to worry about Imperial interference. This region is saturated with psychic energy, and the strong influence of the Ruinous Powers gives the region a surreal and menacing feel. Here the characters' opponents will be other Chaos powers, either mortal or supernatural. Information is also included about the regions of Imperial space detailed in the other games of the *Warhammer 40,000* line, providing GMs suggestions on running a Chaos-themed game in the various sectors.

## Evaluation

Complexity: 4; based on a miniatures wargame rule set, *Black Crusade* includes multiple subsystems.

Popularity: 4; *Warhammer 40,000* RPGs have proven very popular, according to available sales data.

Support: 3

Completeness: 4; complete rules in the core book; other books add options for play.

Versatility: 3

Emulation: 5; a faithful translation of a miniatures wargame to an RPG.

## Comments

There are three common modes of play in *Black Crusade*. First is that of militants, where the characters actively take the fight to the temporal powers of the Imperium. Second is that of corrupters of men, where the characters attempt to subvert the powers of the Imperium and turn them to the service of Chaos. Thirdly are the seekers of forbidden knowledge, as the Imperium has kept many subject areas hidden from the populace due to the dangerous nature of such knowledge, and here the servants of Chaos have broken free of this ignorance and seek to "enlighten" the masses and over-throw the benighted Imperium. The major themes of this game are glory, hedonism, power, and vengeance. All of these themes speak to the very indi-vidual nature of each character in this game, rather than to a group unified by a common cause; these characters are all highly motivated individuals working together temporarily for mutual convenience and profit.

Games Workshop's *Warhammer 40,000* franchise has a very strong fic-tion line that may already be on library shelves. Teens interested in the books or miniatures wargame will gleefully try out this RPG. We also included this RPG because, without fail, there are always players who want to try their hand at being the bad guys, and *Black Crusade* does an excellent job of scratching that itch.

Cost: $59.95 in print; $30 in PDF

## *The Burning Wheel Fantasy Roleplaying System, Gold Edition*

Luke Crane et al.
Crushing-Malloy, Inc., 2011
http://www.burningwheel.org
Genre Tags: Fantasy
Dice: d6

### Introduction
*Burning Wheel* is a fantasy game that places a strong emphasis on what characters believe and how they respond to a situation.

### System and Characters
Players create characters in *Burning Wheel* through a combination of lifepaths and point buy. The lifepaths cover the past of the characters before they became involved in the story. Each lifepath gives the character access to certain skills, talents, and points to be used later in character creation. *Burning Wheel* characters have six primary stats—Will, Perception, Agil-ity, Speed, Power, and Forte (toughness)—and the number of points avail-able to spend on these stats depends on the starting age of the character and

bonuses from lifepath selections. Players also purchase skills using a pool of points.

The most intriguing parts of *Burning Wheel* are the BITs—Beliefs, Instincts, and Traits—that help define a character beyond simple mechanical definitions. Beliefs are things that your character firmly believes in, or are short-term goals they can accomplish in the game. Beliefs are meant to be challenged in the game and give an indication as to what type of situations a player would like to see during play. Instincts are actions that a character can take that bypass the normal sequence of events. Players select Traits, like Brutal or Determined, based on the most prominent aspects of a character. Players should play their Traits to the hilt, even (and especially) if those Traits cause trouble for the players. When players depict their BITs in a game session, they earn the metagame currency, called Artha, that players can spend to alter dice rolls and situations in-game.

The system in *Burning Wheel* is a simple dice pool mechanic based on d6s. Players determine success by counting the number of dice rolling over the target number, or obstacle. Different power levels have different target numbers that players must beat. *Burning Wheel* divides conflict into three discrete types: the Duel of Wits (social), Range and Cover (ranged), and Fight! (melee). Each player scripts, or predetermines, his or her next three actions during a conflict. This system gives the game a certain level of tactical thinking that does not require the use of maps and miniatures. Also if this system does not suit the group, then the rulebook includes quicker methods of resolution as well.

## Setting

The setting of *Burning Wheel* is intentionally left undeveloped to allow a group maximum flexibility. The life paths available in the book do steer the setting strongly toward a Tolkien-inspired Western medieval default. With some work, groups can shift the setting to other cultural milieus, and *Burning Wheel* has been adapted to different genres, including science fiction.

## Evaluation

Complexity: 3/4; the basic rules (Hub and Spokes) is straightforward, but the scripted conflict mechanics add a level of complexity.

Popularity: 2; fairly popular with the indie gaming population

Support: 1; nothing has been published for *Burning Wheel Gold*, but the previous edition's supplements are still useful.

Completeness: 4

Versatility: 3; character-driven game and random character generation can create a wide array of stories, but all fall in a medieval fantasy world.

Emulation: 4

## Comments

*Burning Wheel, Gold Edition* currently has no supplements, but the ones available for the older revised edition are nearly completely forward compatible. This game should be used for a very character-driven story.

Cost: $25.00 hardcover; a free "Hub and Spokes" quick-start document is available at the *Burning Wheel* website.

## *Cartoon Action Hour: Season 3*

Cynthia Celeste Miller et al.
Spectrum Games, 2013
http://www.spectrum-games.com
Genre Tags: Cartoons, Multigenre, Younger Gamers
Dice: d12

### Introduction

Do you remember pouring yourself a big bowl of sugary cereal and sitting down for a long run of Saturday morning cartoons? *Cartoon Action Hour: Season 3* (*CAH*) emulates the wacky and fantastic fun of 1980s-era cartoons and integrates all their features—from black-and-white morality to toy merchandizing—into the game!

### System and Characters

Once the GM has set the parameters for the Series (see "Setting" later in this entry), he or she decides on guidelines for the player characters (PCs) that determine the power level of the PCs: human, superhuman, or cosmic. Players get a Star Power rating equal to their status as protagonists (minions have lower Star Power, and archvillains may have higher Star Power) and Oomph, a type of metagame currency that players use to enhance their actions. Players then decide on three qualities for their characters: one signature quality that defines the character, and two others that flesh out the character's personality or background. Players make up traits for their characters and assign points to those traits based on the character's power level. Traits are typically things that the characters can do or powers and equipment they have.

Once players have decided on traits, they get to choose Special Rules for their traits that might enhance their utility (like giving their power armor the ability to transform into a vehicle), and upgrades for their characters for further boosts (like getting traits that can exceed the series maximum by a small amount). One of the neater upgrades is the ability to contribute points toward a Playset. Do you remember the action figures that 1980s cartoons advertised? Many of those series of action figures had giant playsets (sold separately, of course) that depicted important bases and locales. In the same manner, PCs might have a special base—their Playset—that they can create and enhance, and that gives them access to its powers when they are at that location. As a further homage to the cartoon-toy connection, the PC sheet provided in the book looks like the packaging for an action figure, complete with a Proofs of Purchase spot that tracks points for character improvement.

*CAH* uses a roll-high system against a target number or opposed roll. Players roll 1d12, add their relevant trait rating to an action, and try to beat the GM's 1d12 roll plus target number, or opposing character's trait. Rolls of 1 are automatic failures, or Flubs, and rolls of 12 gain the boon of adding double the character's Star Power to the roll. Various other factors can add to a player's roll, including appropriate character Qualities that come into play and spending points of Oomph. If a player fails a crucial check—a test that could endanger the character—then the character gets Setback Tokens. Remember that 1980s cartoon characters—both heroes and villains—didn't die, so neither do *CAH* characters. However, if a character accumulates more Setback Tokens than it has Star Power, then it is defeated and knocked out of the action for the rest of the scene due to circumstances that the GM narrates in-game.

Game time is important in *CAH*. When a group completes a Season (approximately six Episodes, or sessions, of games), characters can spend Proofs of Purchase to improve their characters and Playsets. The rulebook has additional special rules for Transforming and Merging (powers that were common in cartoons like *Transformers* and *Voltron*), and a host of optional rules that add flavor to the game. Our favorite optional rule was "The Movie," where the next one to three sessions represent taking the series to the big screen. In "The Movie," major changes can happen—characters can even die!

Finally, at the end of every episode, characters play out an After-Show Message, the "Now you know" moral segment of the show. Players can get as wacky as they like and earn Proofs of Purchase for an entertaining performance!

*CAH* contains additional guidelines directed at helping GMs *and* players get into the style of 1980s cartoons, and creating entertaining episodes for games.

## Setting

In this game, the GM (and perhaps the whole gaming group) decides on the features of the setting. The game campaign—the Series—gets a title and a tagline, like "Transformers: Robots in Disguise!" GMs then decide on a genre, any "twists" that make the setting unique, like "all player characters pilot giant robots," and a tech level for the campaign, like "galactic civilizations" or "medieval fantasy." Most series also have an overall goal that the characters work toward—even something as basic as "Keeping the world safe from alien invaders"—and some kind of nemesis or villainous organization that the characters oppose.

GMs then set the Dials on their series to better define their style and tone. Dial types include Seriousness (how comedic—or not—is the series?), Realism, Violence, and Continuity (are the adventures entirely episodic and stand-alone, or are we building an epic storyline?).

### Evaluation

Complexity: 1
Popularity: 2
Support: 2
Completeness: 3
Versatility: 5
Emulation: 5

### Comments

*CAH* takes its unbridled love of 1980s cartoons and fully embraces it, and the game is fun and flavorful enough that players will love it too! This RPG touches on all the tropes of its source material, no matter how cheesy, and seamlessly incorporates them into the game. The rulebook is even entertaining to read, with a long list of 1980s cartoons that players can watch for entertainment and inspiration, and three in-book "co-hosts"—*CAH* cartoon character icons—to help guide readers through the rules.

And lest anyone wonder about the feasibility of running a game for today's youth that consists of 1980s cartoon material, we would remind doubters of how many of these cartoons—including *He-Man and the Masters of the Universe* and *Thundercats*—have made comebacks as animated series in the 2000s, and that *Transformers* is quite the successful franchise even after thirty years! Even better, *CAH* is a nice, safe introduction to RPGs for younger players as well.

Cost: $14.99 PDF

# *Cat: A Little Game about Little Heroes, Revised Edition*

John Wick
John Wick, 2004
http://www.johnwickpresents.com
Genre Tags: Animals, Fantasy
Dice: d6

## Introduction

Every one thousand years, cats and dogs compete to see which will act as guardians of the world. Recently the cats won. In the *Cat* RPG, the players take on the role of cats protecting humanity from danger both mundane and in their dreams.

## System and Characters

Character creation in *Cat* is very short and straightforward. Players create cat roles that have six attributes, called traits, and nine lives. These traits determine how many dice are rolled during a test. Each character also begins play with several reputations, which are used like skills in other games.

The system in *Cat* uses a die pool of d6s based on the trait being tested, with success measured by how many even numbers are rolled. Players may roll additional dice at the GM's discretion based on the player's engagement with the scene or if a particular reputation is applicable. Damage, called scars, removes dice from your dice pool. Success in excess of the target number can be used to directly alter the scene or saved as automatic successes on later rolls. *Cat* magic uses the same system as the rest of the game. These tricks have various levels of difficulty and produce singular effects.

There is a lengthy chapter on storytelling with advice for this style of game. *Cat* gives players more authorial control than do many conventional RPGs, and these can be challenging to run. The game also provides adventure hooks to assist GMs in getting the game going.

## Setting

Most of the action in *Cat* takes place in the real world. The main goal in this game is for cats to rid their human companion's home of boggins, incorporeal manifestations of negative thoughts and emotions. Though cats spend most of their time in the physical world, they may enter the Kingdom of Dreams and adventure in a surreal landscape made up of their human companion's dreams.

## Evaluation

Complexity: 2
Popularity: 1
Support: 1
Completeness: 5
Versatility: 2
Emulation: 3

## Comments

Cat lovers will enjoy this opportunity to play as their furry friends. Librarians could use this game to emulate a more magical version of the *Warriors* series of novels by Erin Hunter.

Cost: $5 PDF

## *Cold City, v. 1.1*

Malcolm Craig
Contested Ground Studios, 2010
http://www.contestedground.co.uk
Genre Tags: Alternate History, Conspiracy, Historical, Horror, Investigation, Spy
Dice: d10

## Introduction

*Cold City* takes place in Cold War Berlin. Members of the Reserve Police Agency (RPA) hunt down the remnants of Nazi twisted technology, occult science and the nightmarish horrors it spawned, all while pursuing secret agendas and working under a constant state of paranoia, wondering if they can truly trust their colleagues.

## System and Characters

Characters are agents of the RPA. Agents are selected from one of the various nations with a presence in Berlin—the United States, U.S.S.R, France, Britain, and Germany—and are expected to cooperate for the greater good of discovering, covering up the existence of, and eradicating (or covertly obtaining) Nazi twisted technology. RPA agents must also pursue the secret agendas of their home country, further their personal agendas, and be on the alert for double-crosses and betrayals by their fellow agents. Who said being a spy was easy?

Players decide on their characters' names, nationalities, and backgrounds, including how their characters were drawn into the RPA.

Characters have three Attributes: Action (any physical action), Influence (a measure of charisma, willpower, and personal presence), and Reason (intellectual ability, perception, deduction, etc.). All Attributes range from 1 (poor) to 5 (almost superhuman).

Characters also begin play with five Traits, broad areas of skill, quirks, and talents. Players can be as creative as they like with their Traits, allowing for a wide variety of options. When the character is created, at least two of these Traits must be negative.

Finally, characters have two Hidden Agendas (a national agenda dictated by the character's superiors/country of origin, and a personal secret agenda the character is trying to further) and a Trust score. Trust is a numerical score that ranges from 0 (I don't trust you at all) to 5 (I would place my life in your hands); each player assigns a number of trust points to each of the other members of his or her team.

When conflicts arise, the player and GM must determine the Stakes, and the player builds a dice pool to roll. To determine Stakes, the player and opposition state clearly what they want to get out of the conflict. This determination can be as simple as, for example, "I want to interrogate the spy for information about his mission" and "The spy tries to resist giving up any information." Then, the player and GM determine the Attribute that makes most sense in the context of the situation, and the player gets a number of d10s equal to that attribute. Additional dice can be gained if Hidden Agendas, Traits, and Trust come into play.

Both parties then roll their dice pools and try to roll numbers that are higher than the highest number rolled by the opposition, a result that translates into Consequence points. These points are then applied, by means of a chart, to either positive consequences for the player who won the die roll, negative consequences for the losing opposition, or both. Players then creatively narrate outcomes in cooperation with the GM. If a die representing a negative trait has the highest number in the conflict, then something unfavorable occurs tied to that Trait—sometimes victory has a bitter taste.

## Setting

*Cold City* takes place in post–World War II Berlin circa 1950, a still-recovering city divided by the supposedly allied governments of the United States, Britain, France, and the U.S.S.R., as well as the reestablished German government. The book gives an overview of major Cold War events through 1950, including the U.S.S.R. gaining nuclear weapons, the rise of the People's Republic of China, and the beginning of the Korean War. In addition, the British and French have their own countries to rebuild, and they want to withdraw from Germany. And to top it all off, as Operation Paperclip proved, all the nations involved are eager to siphon off whatever scientific breakthroughs the Nazis may have achieved. With the various nations eager to acquire and proliferate twisted technology, the countdown to Armageddon may have already begun.

The Nazi twisted technology includes a variety of possibilities, including portals to other dimensions, where monstrous horrors wait to possess unwitting innocents, the walking dead, and super soldier experiments gone wrong. Given the plethora of fiction and conspiracy theory surrounding Nazis and the occult, the possibilities are endless.

The book also familiarizes readers with the city of Berlin and provides street and sector maps, detailing which countries control which areas, and a list of important sites, both within and outside Germany, that can serve as potential twisted tech hotspots. Lists of relevant overt and covert scientific, military, and espionage agencies, and their relation to one another, provide plenty of potential origins and antagonists. Most important of all, however, is the author's description of the mood in post–World War II Berlin, the paranoia and uncertainty, the lingering despair, the necessities of the black market, and the creepy nature of the labyrinthine Berlin underground. A reference to inspirational novels, films, websites, and more rounds out the book, and gives both GMs and players further inventive ideas for adventures.

### Evaluation

Complexity: 2; collect dice, roll, look for the highest numbers.

Popularity: 1; it's a little-known game that deserves more play.

Support: 1; the original book did have a companion, but it was combined into version 1.1.

Completeness: 4; almost everything you need in one small digest-sized book.

Versatility: 2; it does what it does very well, but it's a very specific game written for a specific setting.

Emulation: 5; a perfect example of how a system can be used to evoke a genre effectively.

### Comments

*Cold City* has a very simple game system that manages to be remarkably versatile. The setting is evocative and creepy, and will keep players on their toes. And who doesn't like to stand against the surviving machinations of Nazis?

If your players like spy stories or *Hellboy* comics, then this is the game for them. Additionally, you could use this game as an introduction to comics like *Hellboy*, media like the *X-Files*, and even more contemplative espionage fiction like the works of John le Carré. You could even use Traits to give the players' characters minor weird abilities of their own!

If your players like this game, then be sure to introduce them to its sequel, *Hot War*, where the world powers finally use the twisted technology they found against one another. *Hot War* is by the same author and publisher as *Cold City*.

Cost: $24.99 softcover; $10 PDF

## Conspiracy X 2.0 (a.k.a. Conspiracy X, Second Edition)

David F. Chapman et al.
Eden Studios, 2006
http://www.edenstudios.net
Genre Tags: Conspiracy, Horror, Investigation, Spy
Dice: primarily d10, though the game also uses d4, d6, d8, and d12

### Introduction

*Conspiracy X* posits a world where aliens, supernatural horrors, and psychic powers exist, and shadowy organizations vie for information and control over the truth.

### System and Characters

*Conspiracy X* (*CX*) characters are agents of Aegis, the United States' first defense against the extraterrestrial and unknown. As such, you research and investigate the paranormal while concealing the truth from the public.

*CX* is a point-buy, roll-high game that uses the Unisystem game engine, Eden Studios' in-house system. Players spend points on their characters' Attributes (Strength, Dexterity, Constitution, Intelligence, Perception, and Will), Profession (Aegis recruits agents from a variety of backgrounds), Qualities (defining aspects of the character that can range from mundane talents to paranormal abilities), and Skills. Players may also give their characters Drawbacks, negative Qualities that give players additional points to spend on their characters.

Some interesting rules that contribute to the tone in *CX* are Pulling Strings and Resource Points. Characters can put points into Qualities like Contacts and Pulling Strings to acquire certain favors or access to certain facilities, depending on their professional backgrounds and cover identities. Players may also gain ranks in the Influence quality in order to gain Resource Points for their cells, which they can spend on permanent locations (bases of operations), facilities, staff, equipment, weapons, and even top secret, extraterrestrial, super science, or supernatural objects.

When characters perform a test, the player rolls a d10 and adds the relevant Attribute and Skill ranks, plus any relevant modifiers, then tells the GM the result. The GM factors in any additional modifiers, and if the final result is a nine or better, then the character succeeds at the action. The die can explode in either direction, so rolls of 1 and 10 can yield particularly dreadful or fantastic results.

**Setting**

*CX* games take place in the modern world as we know it, but where that very normalcy is a lie that covers the too-prevalent uncertainty, danger, and horror of alien threats and otherworldly corruption. Player characters are agents of Aegis, a U.S. top-secret covert organization that investigates extraterrestrial, paranormal, and supernatural menaces to our nation and planet. As players learn more about the secret history of their world, they will discover how shadowy forces have shaped humanity, incidents that never appeared in textbooks or on the news. Aegis will likely send characters on dangerous missions with insufficient information against other shadowy organizations and unknown threats, all to keep humanity safe for one more day.

**Evaluation**

> Complexity: 2
> Popularity: 1
> Support: 2
> Completeness: 3; the few available sourcebooks add considerably to the game experience and options.
> Versatility: 3
> Emulation: 4

**Comments**

What if *Men in Black* wasn't played for laughs? What if *The X-Files* were even scarier? Recommend *CX* to teens that linger in the library aisles where you shelve books about psychic phenomena, government conspiracies, black helicopters, aliens, and horror novels.

Cost: $35 hardcover; $17.50 PDF; if you're unsure whether this game is right for your group, try the free *Conspiracy X 2.0* Introductory Game Kit, available through RPGNow or DriveThruRPG.

# *Deathwatch*

Owen Barnes et al.
Fantasy Flight Games, 2010
http://www.fantasyflightgames.com
Genre Tags: Science Fiction, Space Opera
Dice: d%/d100

## Introduction

In the grim future of the forty-first century, mankind is locked in perpetual warfare against alien forces that threaten to overwhelm the Imperium of Man. To combat the alien threat, the genetically modified super soldiers of the Space Marines seek to hold back the tide of darkness.

## System and Characters

Players create characters in *Deathwatch* (*DW*) using a hybrid of random generation and a point-buy system. Unlike other games, *DW* represents basic combat training as attributes rather than skills. The role of each character is further defined by the selection of a Chapter, a group of Space Marines who share a specific culture, and a specialty, a role the character fulfills within the Chapter. The Space Marines in this game all begin as fairly powerful combatants, with specialties giving a tighter focus to each Marine's abilities. In addition to their physical prowess, certain Marines are able to channel the powers of the Warp through the use of psychic abilities.

At its core *DW* uses a percentile system for determining success. *DW* uses this basic resolution mechanic for nearly all tasks, both mundane and psychic. There are some rules in this game that are noteworthy and show the game's lineage from a tabletop miniatures wargame. For example, Cohesion, a measure of how well the squad cooperates, and squad mode allow characters access to abilities that are distinct from, and in certain circumstances very beneficial to their individual skills. These two features of the game emphasize the ideals of the game, of cooperation and mutual aid within the unit, and provide mechanical benefits for doing so.

## Setting

The setting for *DW* is the forty-first century, when humans have spread across the galaxy to create a large empire founded firmly on scientific principles. In the past, a Dark Age caused the loss of much of humanity's technological knowledge. After emerging from this Dark Age, the Imperium conducted a crusade to reunify the old empire. The armies of the crusade were led by trans-human warriors called Space Marines who formed enormous legions, each influenced heavily by its leader. During this crusade, humanity came into contact with various alien races, most being inimical to mankind. It was also during this time that Chaos, supernatural forces in the Warp, or hyperspace, emerged and began exerting a corrupting influence over humanity. Several legions fell to the corruption of Chaos and nearly brought the Imperium to ruin once again. With the rise of Chaos, a cult of personality began to surround the Emperor, and by the forty-first century it is a fully formed religion.

This game focuses on the loyalist Space Marines who are dedicated to fighting the threat from various alien races. The Deathwatch is a Chapter made up of Marines from all the other Chapters who serve for a period of time before returning to their parent Chapters. The main setting for this game is the Jericho Reach, an area of space dominated by the threats from the Tau (aliens bent on assimilating others for the "greater good"), the Tyranids (genetically engineered aliens that consume all biomass on a planet for conversion into more Tyranids), and the forces of Chaos.

## Evaluation

Complexity: 4; based on a miniatures wargame franchise, and
 includes multiple subsystems

Popularity: 4

Support: 4; several supplements available detailing setting and culture
 of the Space Marines

Completeness: 4; complete rules in the core rulebook, other books add
 options for play

Versatility: 3

Emulation: 5; a faithful translation of a miniatures wargame to an
 RPG

## Comments

The tone of the game can vary from straight-up missions to combat an alien threat to more subtle missions involving other organizations of the Imperium, chiefly the Inquisition. The ideals of honor, brotherhood, and duty are major themes in the game, and with the variety of Space Marine Chapters and their varied outlooks, role-playing opportunities abound that will make this game more than just about exterminating a threat. Also, with the number of supplements available and some reworking of the rules, gaming groups could play out any period of Imperium history, from the Great Crusade to the game's default era. *DW* would work especially well with the game *Black Crusade*, which details playing the forces of Chaos, allowing a group to play during the forty-first millennium or the in-game historical period of the Horus Heresy, which is also a series of popular novels published by Games

Workshop, owner of the *Warhammer 40,000* franchise that forms the core of this game.

Cost: $59.95 in print; $30 in PDF

## *Doctor Who: Adventures in Time and Space, Eleventh Doctor Edition*

David F. Chapman et al.
Cubicle 7 Entertainment, 2012 [2009]
Genre: Science Fiction, Television, Time Travel, Younger Gamers
Dice: d6

### Introduction

Truth in advertising! This game serves to emulate the bizarre and wonderful adventures of Doctor Who and his companions as they fly through time and space. Something weird is going on, and it's the players' job to investigate (i.e., poke it with a stick and see what happens!).

### System and Characters

Every action in the game is resolved the same way. Players attempting an action try to roll high, adding a character's relevant Attribute, the Skill the character is using, and, if applicable, a bonus or penalty from a Trait to a 2d6 roll. The result is used to beat an opposed roll or a target number determined by the GM. The higher the roll beats the target number by, the more successful the action; correspondingly, the lower the roll is below the target number, the greater the failure.

Each character has a number of Story Points that act as a metagame currency in the game, enabling players to enhance their characters' performance. Players can spend Story Points to add dice to their characters' rolls at crucial moments, to lessen the severity of failures, and to absorb damage, among other things.

One of the brilliant aspects of this system is how, like the television show, it de-emphasizes combat as a means of conflict resolution and promotes more cerebral solutions. For example, initiative depends on what your character intends to do, with talkers going first and fighters going last every round; runners go second, so you can get away from those nasty laser guns; and doers—those attempting any action other than fighting, running, or talking—go third. In addition, the difficulty of the opposition, and the relatively frail nature of the human body compared to many alien foes, means that players will need to focus on gathering clues and coming up with ingenious solutions—just like in the television show!

Characters have Attributes and Skills to flesh them out, as well as a number of Traits that serve to individualize the characters. Attributes include Awareness (a measure of perceptiveness), Coordination (measuring agility and dexterity), Ingenuity (covering wit, intelligence, and general creativity), Presence (force of personality), Resolve (willpower), and Strength (physical brawn). The Skill list is small but comprehensive, and allows players to specialize within certain fields; for example, two scientists might have identical Science scores, but one might have an area of expertise in biology, and the other in physics. Traits allow for further modification. Good Traits, like Lucky or Tough, give the characters bonuses to some actions, and Bad Traits hinder the characters but help the players earn Story Points (see above). Special Traits can grant rather powerful advantages, emulating alien abilities or psychic powers, and even allowing the character to be a Time Lord like the Doctor!

Players can play the iconic characters from the show or create their own. When using the characters from the series, the game creators recommend that the players rotate characters every session, so everyone has a chance to play the Doctor.

If players choose to create their own characters, then they can be aliens, psychics, or simply everyday humans. Since most of the Doctor's companions are human throughout the series, there's no disadvantage to being a scientist or simple shop girl. Ultimately, players can be as creative as they like. The key, regardless of the kind of character played, is to get into the spirit of *Doctor Who*, which is to say, throw yourself into the adventure and have fun!

## Setting

The recent series of *Doctor Who* began in 2005, and the earliest episodes of the franchise extend back to 1963. Fifty years of programming allow for a vast amount of material available for players to watch, read, research, and mine for adventures and ideas—far more than any group is likely to exhaust no matter how long it plays. Even better, the adventures of the Doctor and his companions range all across the universe to any point in time or space, so if you can imagine it, then it can happen in your game!

Even better, Cubicle 7 has recently begun putting out sourcebook supplements for each of the previous doctors as well, so you can set your *Doctor Who* game in any era you choose, or even have the various incarnations of the Doctors meet! (Wait, isn't that a bit dangerous, timey-wimey wise?)

## Evaluation

Complexity: 4
Popularity: 4, thanks to the franchise
Support: 3
Completeness: 4
Versatility: 3
Emulation: 5

## Comments

Given the popularity of the television show, this game is certain to meet with approval from many teen geeks. Players who tend to like lots of combat might be less enamored with this game, but many GMs, librarians, and teens who agree with renowned author Isaac Asimov, who wrote that "violence is the last refuge of the incompetent," might enjoy the challenge of a game that emphasizes nonviolent solutions and peaceful reconciliations whenever possible. (Then again, when the alien antagonists refuse to listen to reason, the Doctor has dispatched more than a few to their doom . . .)

Also, while GMs running this game may be automatically self-selecting their players—an already existing fan base—there are always those who haven't seen the show and could be introduced to it through this game, so make sure your library has some seasons of *Doctor Who* for lending!

One warning: There are a *lot* of extra pieces to keep track of in the boxed set, including chits (representing Story Points), dice, equipment cards, and several booklets. You will likely want to catalog it as a kit, and be ready to do some counting when patrons return this item!

Cost: $59.99 in print; $30 PDF

## *Dragonraid*

Adventures for Christ, 1984
http://www.dragonraid.net
Genre Tags: Christian, Fantasy
Dice: d8, d10 (dice provided in boxed set)

## Introduction

*Dragonraid* is an excellent example of an RPG designed for a specific pedagogical reason. The goal of *Dragonraid* is to teach the players, typically teens, how to be stronger Christians, accomplished by the characters going on adventures in a fictional world that has been overrun by dragons and their servants.

**System and Characters**

Character creation in *Dragonraid* uses an attribute and ability system. The seven primary attributes, called character strengths, model the seven heavenly virtues, and secondary attributes are calculated based on these virtues. This method of random character generation with its heavy reliance on the primary attribute could lead to unplayable characters. The game addresses this issue and allows players to create new characters if the total of their attributes is below a certain number.

*Dragonraid* is designed to be played with a battle map and miniatures, which are provided. The system for *Dragonraid* at its most basic is a simple roll over, percentile system. The target number is determined by using a chart and cross-referencing the character's ability score with the difficulty number set by the GM.

Being a Christian game, each of the attributes has a name taken from the Bible, and they are collectively referred to as the Armor of God. The characters, by dint of special training, have six special secondary attributes that are applied as bonuses to certain actions or to resist specific attacks, both physical and spiritual. Attacks of a spiritual nature, called sin enchantments, are perhaps the more troublesome as they not only impact the character directly, but they also apply penalties to each of the other characters as well. Players can, however, break sin enchantments through role-playing.

Most characters in RPGs have special powers, and *Dragonraid* characters are no different, though the resolution mechanic is very novel. As part of the pedagogical goal of this game, the players need to memorize and recite certain Bible passages to activate the WordRunes and TeamRunes in *Dragonraid*. Each Rune has a requirement for use and can either be read from the card granting the bonus or memorized, granting the bonus plus Maturity Points. Other limitations apply as well, as the more experienced, or mature, a character becomes, the more difficult the Runes they must use, and if the Runes are read rather than memorized, then only three can be used in a day.

Character advancement is handled by using Maturity Points. Unlike most games where experience points are used to either advance in level or are spent to improve specific scores, players accumulate and apply Maturity Points to specific character strengths based on the character's actions. Characters can also lose Maturity Points by falling victim to enchantments, which may in turn cause the associated strength to drop in value as well, reducing the overall effectiveness of the character.

**Setting**

The setting in *Dragonraid* is the continent of Talania on the planet EdenAgain. It is a fairly typical RPG setting with the continent's climate resembling that of North America. Each of the regions receives a brief description in the *Lightraider Handbook*, and the game leaves much detail for individual groups to fill in. The roles the characters play in *Dragonraid* are those of Lightraiders, specially anointed and trained servants of the OverLord of Many Names, who travel from the small beleaguered Liberated Lands, across the Peaks of the New Beginning, and into the Dragon Lands to destroy evil creatures and rescue dragon slaves, people seduced by the power of the dragons.

## Evaluation

Complexity: 4; while the die-rolling mechanic is fairly straightforward, the WordRune system can be complicated.
Popularity: 1
Support: 2; several adventures have been published.
Completeness: 5
Versatility: 1; no options are presented to play other types of stories.
Emulation: 5

## Comments

For a game that was first published in the mid-1980s and has seen little or no revision since, it has held up well over the years. We think the simple system and narrow focus has kept the game from feeling too dated, and it should still appeal to modern gamers' system sensibilities. The boxed set is also complete, including battle maps, miniatures, and dice.

Obviously, this game has a specific goal and purpose, and will appeal to Christian players, parents, and church groups.

Cost: $30 boxed set

## *Earthdawn, Third Edition*

Carsten Damm et al.
Redbrick Limited, 2009
http://earthdawn.fasagames.com
Genre Tags: Fantasy
Dice: d4, d6, d8, d10, d12, d20

## Introduction

*Earthdawn* is a game set in a world that is reemerging from a time of magical catastrophe. The characters are beings able to tap the magic of the world to enhance their abilities. Using these abilities, they will pit themselves against the lingering magical Horrors and against the expansionist, slave trading Theran Empire.

### System and Characters

Characters in *Earthdawn* are adepts, especially talented people who, through training and magical talent, can push themselves beyond typical human achievements. Players create their adepts using a combination of point buy and class-and-level system. Separate pools of points are spent improving the character's six attributes and various talents and skills. The character's race determines the starting attribute scores, with different races holding advantages in certain attributes. Players purchase skills and talents (special training) as well, with the character's discipline determining the talents available to them. A discipline is much like a class in other RPGs, as it embodies the professional training and philosophical outlook for a character.

The *Earthdawn* system uses a slightly different take on the standard die pool. A skill rank is added to an attribute step, which is then compared to a table to determine the type of dice rolled. The results are totaled, and if greater than the target number, the roll is a success. Modifiers can alter the target number and in special cases can add to the dice rolled. A unique feature of this game is that the writers made a conscious effort to make the rule vocabulary as much a part of the setting as possible; for example, characters in *Earthdawn* would not be out of place asking others what their disciplines are, while in other fantasy games asking a character's class would break the fourth wall.

### Setting

The setting of *Earthdawn* is our world approximately 14,000 years ago in the region of Ukraine and the Caucasus. The world has recently emerged from a time of isolation due to the presence of powerful supernatural creatures called Horrors. In order to escape the Horrors the Namegiver races built magically defended underground fortresses called *kaers*. Not all of these kaers survived, and many lie in ruins. The presence of the Horrors altered the landscape as well, giving the region a much more tropical climate and rearranging some of the mountain chains. In keeping with these changes the visuals of the *Earthdawn* game are significantly different from those of most other fantasy RPGs. This game draws its visuals from Mesoamerican, sub-Saharan African, and South Asian art, while incorporating its own unique features rather than simply copying actual civilizations. The game maintains a fairly optimistic tone and is written with the assumption that the characters will seek to improve themselves and the region whether by hunting the Horrors, resisting the Theran Empire, or helping the nascent nations come into their own power.

Barsaive, the region detailed in the core books, is populated by several Namegiver races, and in an interesting twist the dwarfs are the most well organized and dominant race. Humans, like in most games, can be found all over the region and readily adapt to local conditions. Elven settlements are typically deep in the wilderness and live in close community with the natural surroundings. Orks are passionate and freedom loving (being the only race enslaved by other Namegivers in the past) and live either in tribes of mounted nomads or in the newly formed nation of Cara Fahd. Trolls, tall and honor bound, live in the high mountains and chiefly make their living as raiders of other troll tribes or surrounding communities. Obsidimen are a genderless race that appears to be made from living rock. They are introspective and deliberative, and are greatly admired by the trolls. The T'skrang are a race of reptilian humanoids with a flair for the dramatic. They live along the major rivers of Barsaive and serve mainly as merchants along the rivers.

### Evaluation

Complexity: 4; the step system can be tricky to understand, and there are several subsystems to the game as well.

Popularity: 3

Support: 3; many supplements have been published for the various editions.

Completeness: 3; the advancement of adept Disciplines are only covered to the 8th Circle (level), so additional books are need to advance to the maximum Circle.

Versatility: 3; a variety of campaigns can be played using this game depending on what setting themes a group wishes to focus on.

Emulation: 5; this game was written to "rationalize" in the setting all of the common tropes and vocabulary of fantasy RPGs, and thus the setting and system are closely intertwined

### Comments

This game requires two books, the *Player's Guide* and *Gamemaster's Guide*, to play. The *Player's Guide* contains the rules needed to create characters, including skills, talents, and spells, and to run the game. The *Gamemaster's Guide* goes into greater depth on the setting, has chapters on adventure and campaign creation, and contains an extensive bestiary. Other supplements are available, and the majority of these are focused on expanding the setting rather than simply adding more rules. There are also two official variations of the game available that use the *Savage Worlds* rules and *Pathfinder* rules. These versions attempt to capture the feel of *Earthdawn* through the medium of their respective rules sets, with the *Savage Worlds* version being much more successful.

While FASA is the current owner of the *Earthdawn* game, the company hasn't done much with the rules system since acquiring it. Thus, this review covers the still-available third edition rules.

Cost: $39.95 print; $23.99 PDF

## *Faery's Tale Deluxe*

Patrick Sweeney et al.
Firefly Games, 2007
http://firefly-games.com/
Genre Tags: Fairy Tales, Fantasy
Dice: d6

### Introduction

*Faery's Tale* is a game about the small faeries and their existence in a magical world of high adventure and dark obstacles.

### System and Characters

Characters in *Faery's Tale* are one of four diminutive types of fae: pixies (whimsical pranksters), brownies (industrious souls), sprites (valiant and honorable), and pookas (feral shapeshifters). Each fae has its own way of accessing magical abilities—for example, pixies use glittering dust. The fae characters are ever-vigilant guardians of the world and seek to keep the dark fae, twisted reflections of the characters, from overrunning the world. They must also contend with other magical beings, including witches, dragons, and other mythic creatures. Mechanically, characters are defined by three attributes, essence (magical power), and gifts. The simplicity of a character makes it very easy for a GM to create new character types for the game based on player desires and the needs of the story.

*Faery's Tale* uses a dice pool system of d6s versus a target number. Players roll a number of dice based on which attribute is tested; even numbers are successes, and sixes explode, counting both as a success and an additional die to roll. Opposed rolls are handled in a similar manner, where the character with the most successes wins the exchange. Gifts work in a variety of ways, including giving static bonuses to attributes and allowing certain magical effects with the expenditure of essence.

### Setting

The base setting is Brightwood, an archetypal enchanted woodland with hardworking peasants, soaring castles, witches, and magic. Fortunately, a goodly portion of the book is aimed at GMs, detailing how to create adventures; there is even a short sidebar on what types of stories will interest different age groups. The book also contains three adventures based on familiar fairy tales.

### Evaluation

Complexity: 2
Popularity: 1
Support: 1
Completeness: 5
Versatility: 3
Emulation: 4

### Comments

This game is especially geared toward younger players, with sidebars offering advice on running the game for this audience. *Faery's Tale* could easily be set in other time periods, allowing groups to play anything from traditional fantasy to urban fantasy, and should be able to emulate stories in the children's and young adult sections of libraries. Acquiring a print copy of this game will be a bit of a challenge, as it has been long out of print and commands fairly high prices in the secondary market, though a PDF copy can be easily found from the publisher.

Cost: $10 PDF

## *Fate Core System*

Leonard Balsera et al.
Evil Hat, 2013
http://www.evilhat.com/home/
http://www.faterpg.com
Genre Tags: Multigenre
Dice: Fate dice (see below)

### Introduction

*Fate* is a fantastic multigenre system with rules that reinforce the narrative aspects of RPGs. If you want your RPG to run and feel more like a collaborative story, then *Fate* is the game you want to use.

### System and Characters

The *Fate* system uses Aspects, Skills, and Stunts to mechanically model characters. Aspects are words and phrases that best describe the narrative facets of the character and derive from the character's concept. Each character has a core concept Aspect, like "Knight of the Ebony Blade" or "Half-Vampire Private Investigator." Each character also has a trouble Aspect that usually works against the character or lands the character in difficult predicaments, like "Too Curious for Her Own Good" or "If It's Not Nailed Down, It's Mine. If I Can Pry It Up, It's Not Nailed Down." Each player then creates a quick notable incident in the character's past and derives an Aspect from that, like a young warrior recalling his father's mentorship to inspire the Aspect "Born to the Sword." For two more Aspects, players then form ties between their characters and one of the other player's characters—two players collaborate, make up a brief encounter/adventure they had together in the past, and derive Aspects from those mini-stories for their characters.

Each player then has a number of slots they fill with Skills from the book. The Skill list is a good representation of those found in many genres, and enterprising GMs and players can easily modify them for different genres, or create new ones if necessary. Initial Skill values range from +4 for the character's paramount Skill, to +1 for Skills where the character has only basic training.

Players can then create Stunts that enable their characters to use Skills in unique ways specific to those characters. Stunts can add bonuses to specific actions, let the characters ignore or make exceptions to certain rules within narrow parameters, or modify how a Skill works—the rules give extensive advice on building and balancing Stunts.

In *Fate*, players make checks using specialty dice, called Fate dice. Fate dice are cubes, with two sides showing a + (plus) symbol, two sides displaying a - (minus) symbol, and two sides that are blank. When players attempt an action, they roll four Fate dice, total the symbols, and add that result to their Skill. They compare the final result to a target number or opposed roll to determine success. Thus, if a player made a check and rolled [+] [+] [-] [blank], then the result of the roll is a +1 (one plus is cancelled out by one minus, leaving me with a blank that adds nothing, and a final plus), and the player would add that to the Skill used in the test. Fate dice results range from +4 to –4, but tend to average toward the middle, zero, which means that a character is usually as good at a task as the character's Skill rank indicates. (If you don't have Fate dice, some games that use the *Fate* system go with a d6 minus d6 roll, yielding a range of –5 to +5.)

*Fate* uses a metagame currency called Fate Points, which players can use to influence events and give advantages to their characters. Characters can spend a Fate Point any time to gain a +1 to a roll. If a circumstance comes up where a character's Aspect is relevant, then players can spend a Fate Point to invoke that Aspect, giving the player a +2 to the action, or enabling the player to reroll a failed test. Players can also use Fate Points to compel the Aspects of other characters. For example, if through interacting with a villain a player surmises that the character might have an Overconfident Aspect, then he or she can spend a *Fate* point to compel that Aspect and creatively narrate a situation to take advantage of that Aspect, and get a bonus against that villain.

When a *Fate* character suffers injury, the player marks off Stress boxes to indicate damage, whether Mental Stress or Physical Stress. However, *Fate* also gives players more agency over their characters' fates by mitigating damage through Consequences—players may take Consequences of varying severity that act as negative Aspects (like "twisted ankle" or "fear of spiders") that mirror the kind of damage taken and its source, and hinder the character, but relieve Stress that the character might have accrued. If a character's Stress boxes fill up completely, and it can't take any more Consequences to compensate, then that character is "Taken Out"—with the antagonist/opponent deciding the character's outcome (which may be death, or may be capture at the center of a deathtrap). However, players can concede conflicts before their characters are taken out, and can then have a say in what happens to their characters.

## Setting

*Fate* doesn't have a specific genre attached to it, as by design it is a multigenre game. However, the *Fate Core System* does suggest a number of settings through the art and examples, and even has rules to help gaming groups collaboratively create their settings.

## Evaluation

Complexity: 2; the core mechanic is simple, but players may need plenty of examples to grasp the use of Aspects, how to build Stunts, etc.

Popularity: 4; *Fate* is quickly becoming a very popular base system for a variety of gaming groups and published material.

Support: 3; there are a number of games that use variations on the *Fate* system, and Evil Hat has offered up a goodly amount of material for free, including the core game!

Completeness: 3; the game stands on its own well, but players who want to modify the game for themselves should check out the *Fate Toolkit* as well.

Versatility: 5; there are few games and settings that can't be run with *Fate*, either as-is or modified to a given group's taste.

Emulation: 4; *Fate* can handle most genres and settings with aplomb.

## Comments

If you are at a loss as to a system on which to run your shiny new idea, then be assured that *Fate* can probably handle it. In addition, as the system description indicates, *Fate* puts a lot of agency into the players' hands, and gives the characters far more survivability and capability than in many other RPGs.

Evil Hat has offered up electronic versions of the *Fate Core System*, as well as a faster, introductory game called *Fate Accelerated*, for free at http://www.faterpg.com/resources/. In addition, the *Fate Roleplaying Game SRD* site (http://www.fate-srd.com) has *Fate Core System*, *Fate Accelerated*, and the *Fate System Toolkit* available in html versions. Of course, if you like the games and want physical copies, or simply want to support Evil Hat, then you can purchase electronic and physical copies of the books, as well as Fate dice, at the Evil Hat online store, http://www.evilhat.com/store/.

Cost: $25 for hardcover + PDF; free PDF

## *Feng Shui: Action Movie Roleplaying*

Robin D. Laws
Atlas Games, 1999 (formerly Daedalus Entertainment, 1996)
http://blog.atlas-games.com/
Genre Tags: Action (specifically, action movies in a wide variety of genres and subgenres); Fantasy; Science Fiction; Time Travel; *Wuxia* (Chinese martial arts/fantasy)
Dice: d6

## Introduction

If your players like action films, then *Feng Shui* will knock their socks off. No, we're not talking about geomancy or furniture arrangement. We're talking about an RPG that is designed to emulate the blend of furious fight scenes and melodrama found in Hong Kong action cinema and in American films like *The Matrix* or the James Bond 007 franchise. This isn't a game of navel-gazing introspection and everyone getting along; this is the game where your character jumps out of airplanes, trades gunfire with cybernetic henchmen, dispatches the demons eating your parachute, makes a perfect landing, and looks suave as he presses the detonator switch blowing all his enemies to the bad place. This is all about nonstop action and looking cool while doing it.

## System

The *Feng Shui* system is as simple as it gets, a d6-d6 system using two differently colored dice, one positive and the other negative. Subtract the negative die from the positive die, add the result of the dice roll to a skill or attribute number, and compare the total to a target number to determine success; the higher the result, the better.

To emulate the incredible turns of fortune that heroes experience, for better and for worse, if a player rolls a 6 on either of the dice, positive or negative, then that die explodes, generating an even better or worse result for the player. If both dice come up with a result of 6, then both are rolled again; if the negative die has a higher result, then the character experiences a setback, but if the positive die is higher, then something unusually good happens to the character.

Since *Feng Shui* emulates action movies, emphasis is placed on combat. Player characters tend to have powerful butt-kicking abilities and can take minor penalties to their dice rolls to perform the ridiculously impressive stunts you see in films. Instead of simply saying, "I try to hit the bad guy," a player can take a small penalty to a roll to say, "I axe-kick the poker table, and as the lip of the table smashes into one goon's face, I catch falling poker chips and throw them with deadly accuracy into the onrushing gangsters." And yes, just like in action movies, if the players can roll high enough, then the heroes will be mowing down nameless mooks with wild abandon.

## Setting

The setting of *Feng Shui* is as weird and wild as a gaming group could ever want. Chi, the mystical energy that infuses the universe, accumulates at key feng shui sites (hence the name of the game), and these sites are the currency of power. Different factions, with names like The Eaters of the Lotus, The Architects of the New Flesh, and The Ascended, are fighting a Secret War to gain control of the world, including its history and its future. That's right—this game has time travel! The heroes, who belong to a faction called The Dragons, can access a bizarre region called the Netherworld and travel through time to fight factions in different eras. They may confront cackling eunuch wizards and their demonic minions in 69 A.D., or cybernetic monstrosities and mad scientists in an Orwellian 2056 A.D. If any faction gains the upper hand by controlling the most key feng shui sites, then they can reshape the entire world—past, present, and future. With stakes like these up for grabs, it's up to your heroes to secure the most feng shui sites and foil the other factions' diabolical plans!

## Characters

*Feng Shui* players begin the game with ultra-competent characters, including reformed gunslingers, martial artists, ninjas, soldiers, cops, thrill-seeking thieves, spies, sorcerers, cyborgs, monsters, and more. To aid them in their endeavors, heroes have various Shticks, special powers like mystical kung-fu powers, arcane technology, spells, insane abilities with weapons, and more. *Feng Shui* uses archetypes to get the group playing as quickly as possible. The players can pick their favorite character types, take a few minutes to customize them according to the instructions given for each archetype, pick their Shticks, and begin playing within fifteen to thirty minutes of sitting down!

## Evaluation

　　Complexity: 2
　　Popularity: 2
　　Support: 4
　　Completeness: 3
　　Versatility: 4
　　Emulation: 5

## Comments

While many people might look down on action films, one of the key aspects of good librarianship is to respect and encourage your patrons' interests. And believe you me—teens like to see things go boom. Most teens will respond *very* well to having time-traveling, monster-stomping, bad-guy-whomping, ultra-cool alter egos, and the system is built to encourage them to cinematically and exuberantly describe their characters' actions.

If the teens are up for a fun experiment, then tell them to watch the movie *Big Trouble in Little China*, one of the finest and cheesiest action films ever, to get them in the spirit. In fact, *Feng Shui*'s author, Robin Laws, gives a pretty extensive filmography at the back of the book. However, if you think that they'd respond better to more modern films, then try movies like *The Bourne Identity*, *Pirates of the Caribbean*, and *Sucker Punch*. Animated features like *Avatar: The Last Airbender*, *Bleach*, and *Naruto* can also provide excellent ideas for action stunts, as can many of the computer games your teens already enjoy playing!

As of this writing, there is a revised edition of *Feng Shui* in the works, but who knows when that will hit the shelves? Don't wait! Your teens want to kick bad guy behind right now!

Cost: $37.95 hardcover; $18 PDF

# *Firefly Role-Playing Game Core Book*

Monica Valentinelli et al.
Margaret Weis Productions, 2014
http://www.margaretweis.com
Genre Tags: Science Fiction, Space Opera, Television, Western
Dice: d4, d6, d8, d10, d12

## Introduction

The *Firefly* RPG, based on the television show by the same title, is a cinematic science fiction game that faithfully emulates the tone, action, adventure, and drama of the source material.

## System and Characters

*Firefly* characters have three basic Attributes—Mental, Physical, and Social—that come into play depending on the kinds of actions that they take, from practicing medicine, to shooting, to bluffing their way into the bad guy's lair. Characters also have Skills (abilities derived from knowledge and training, with a few Specialties that enhance particular skills), Distinctions (Professions, Personalities, and Backgrounds, each with special abilities specific to them, and triggers that bring them into play), and Signature Assets (like having your own ship, or a special gun named "Vera"). Attributes and Skills are ranked by die type—the more sides on the die, the better that trait is.

Players can elect to play the signature cast members or create their own unique characters for adventuring in the 'Verse—the core book has rules for coming up with your own distinctions. And since one of the most important aspects of gaming in the *Firefly* 'Verse is travel, groups can start out with their own ship—the core book has rules for building that ship and keeping her flying.

*Firefly* uses the Cortex Plus system (the house system for games from Margaret Weis Productions), a roll-high system versus an opposed roll. When making checks, players assemble a dice pool consisting of an Attribute die and a Skill die, with more dice possible depending on if Specialties, Distinctions, Signature Assets, and other factors come into play. The GM rolls a dice pool that sets the stakes, the target number the player must beat. A player rolls the dice, takes the two highest dice, and totals them; if the player successfully raises the stakes (beats the target number), then the player succeeds. Players can also earn Plot Points (*Firefly*'s metagame currency) and Big Damn Hero dice to help them out.

The core book has extensive GM advice for creating Complications (situations that help determine the stakes and increase drama and tension in the game), building GM characters that range from annoyances to worthy opposition and nemeses, and constructing adventures that reflect the cinematic and dramatic nature of the source material. The core book also has an introductory adventure to launch players into the 'Verse.

### Setting

The *Firefly* RPG takes place in the 'Verse, during the time of the television show and before the events in the film *Serenity*. Humanity has spread out across the stars, far from Earth-That-Was, but hasn't yet encountered any sentient alien species.

Of course, humanity can't seem to get along with itself any better in the future. The Unification War ended only six years ago and settled the matter of interplanetary authority. Browncoats, those who fought for independence from the Alliance, lost the war and must find new causes to fight for and new ways to make a living out on the fringes of Alliance territory. Unfortunately for the ex-rebels, the Alliance seems to be expanding its territory all the time.

Alliance Core planets have all the benefits of civilization and high technology, but the border worlds are newly terraformed and colonized, and tend to have a "space Western" frontier look to them, blended with an Asian influence on clothing, culture, and language. (The two most prominent spoken languages appear to be English and Chinese.) Out on the Rim, the very edge of humanity's reach, there's plenty of opportunity for profit and adventure, along with plenty of crime, danger, and other sorts of terminally fatal situations. Who knows what humanity may yet discover in the depths of space?

Plenty of weirdness abounds in the space lanes. Reavers, insane communities of berserk men and women, hunt for prey out in space, and there are rumors that some humans have developed psychic abilities. The Alliance denies such things, of course. (You do trust your government, don't you?)

The *Firefly* RPG has an extensive episode guide, so that GMs and players who haven't seen the television show and film *Serenity* will know of the signature crew's encounters and adventures. Even better, the episode guide comes with gaming examples, demonstrating how events in the show might have played out at the table, so GMs can see how to adjudicate a number of situations. The core book also has an extensive guide to the 'Verse, lots of write-ups for GMCs, and even a small guide to pronouncing Chinese words and a few choice phrases.

### Evaluation

Complexity: 3

Popularity: 1; the *Firefly* RPG is a new game, but it will surely find an audience thanks to the *Firefly* fandom, and may become more popular over time.

Support: 2; this RPG iteration of the franchise is brand new, but there are already several adventures for sale in PDF form.
Completeness: 4
Versatility: 4; the Cortex Plus system serves as the engine for several other genre games.
Emulation: 4

## Comments

There are plenty of *Firefly* and *Serenity* fans still around, and while there are currently no more television episodes or films, comics, conventions, and cosplay help keep the show alive. Librarians should have related DVDs and comics on hand for interested players, and to target fans for games. Margaret Weis Productions also publishes the *Cortex Plus Hacker's Guide*, so players who want to dig into the intricacies of the system can do so more easily and come up with a variety of new ideas for their games.

Cost: $49.99 hardcover; $19.99 PDF

## *GenreDiversion 3E Manual*

Brett M. Bernstein
Precis Intermedia, 2008
http://www.pigames.net
Genre: Multigenre
Dice: d6

## Introduction

The third edition of the *GenreDiversion* system (*GD3E*) hits an excellent sweet spot of affordability, adaptability, playability, and simplicity. *GD3E* is simple to use and easy to teach to new players, with a host of inexpensive supplements that allow gamers to play in a variety of settings.

## System and Characters

Abilities, Pursuits, and Gimmicks define the player characters. Abilities are raw attributes including Fitness (overall health, strength, and agility), Awareness (perception), Creativity ("affinity with spiritual and artistic aspects of life"), Reasoning (intellect), and Influence (charisma and presence). Pursuits are learned skills that characters possess. Gimmicks are either advantages or disadvantages, like Fearsome or Glass Jaw, that help to define the player characters further and make them unique. Different settings might call for additional Gimmicks and an easily applied layer of additional rules, depending on the game's genre.

The *GD3E* system is a simple 2d6, roll-high mechanic. Players determine an appropriate Ability for a task, add any bonus or penalty they might have from Pursuits or Gimmicks, then roll two six-sided dice and total the results. Players try to beat either a difficulty number or an opposed roll. If a player rolls higher than necessary, then the excess is called "overkill" and is a measure of player success.

*GD3E* includes rules for equipment and gear and for conflict and combat, a complete magic system, rules for vehicles, and a bestiary. It also includes conversion rules for sourcebooks and settings tied to the previous version of *GenreDiversion* (*GenreDiversion i*), making those materials easily backward compatible and simple to convert to *GD3E*.

**Setting**

*GD3E* includes a modern horror setting called *Unbidden & Forsaken*. In this setting, players take on the roles of Unbidden, characters whose lives have been torn away from them as they engage in a secret war against forces of darkness. Unable to go to the authorities for aid (who would believe the characters' stories of nightmarish and horrific monsters?), the characters only have their special supernatural powers (called Endowments and Lores) and each other to depend on.

Other, separately published compatible games and settings include:

*HardNova 2*, a space opera setting where characters can jet around the galaxy, explore new life and new civilizations, and fight alien menaces.

*Ghostories*, a supernatural mystery setting, where players can investigate possessions and hauntings, and may even have supernatural psychic abilities to aid them in their adventures.

*EarthAD.2*, a post-apocalypse setting, complete with mutants, robots, sentient animals, lost science of the world-that-was, and a cataclysmic world to explore.

*Coyote Trail*, a classic Wild West setting of cowboys, gamblers, and lawmen, where skill with a six-gun determines if a character is among the quick or the dead.

*Mean Streets*, a classic film noir setting filled with hardboiled detectives, femmes fatale, and G-men ready to take on gangsters and corruption.

*Bold & Brave*, a superhero setting with registered heroes, unlicensed vigilantes, and dangerous supervillains.

Even better, with a minimum of effort, all of these settings are compatible with *GD3E* and each other. Mix and match them, and you can easily emulate already existing media properties or create a variety of weird and wild subgenre mash-ups.

**Evaluation**

Complexity: 2; very simple to use, with additional layers of rules for various genres and settings

Popularity: 2; while not many gamers seem to be aware of this gem, it could certainly suit many gaming tables quite well.

Support: 3; *GD3E* has plenty of additional published compatible material.

Completeness: 3; *GD3E* includes one sample setting, but many groups will want one of the additional settings, or will have to do a bit of work to flesh out their own unique setting.

Versatility: 4; *GD3E* has an excellent track record of working within a variety of genres and power levels.

Emulation: 2/4; alone, *GD3E* may require some work by the gaming group to fit it to a particular genre, but if the group uses one of the other compatible settings, then it won't have any trouble.

**Comments**

*GD3E* is an excellent introduction to gaming for new players, is easily adaptable to other genres, and has a wealth of published material and settings available for purchase and use. Its easy to run, fast and stripped-down rules system easily allows for additional layers of rules, either from settings or invented by players, to adapt it to the feel of a given genre and the needs of a given group. For groups that have a strong "do-it-yourself" aesthetic, this basic rules engine will serve as an excellent foundation.

Cost: $19.95 softcover; $9.95 PDF

## *GURPS, 4th Edition*

Steve Jackson et al.
Steve Jackson Games, 2014
http://www.sjgames.com
Genre Tags: Multigenre
Dice: d6

## Introduction

*GURPS* (*Generic Universal RolePlaying System*) is one of the older RPGs on the market today. It was one of the first games that did not seek to emulate a specific genre, but instead chose to be a universal system. The basic set of *GURPS* is contained in two books: *Characters* and *Campaigns*. *Characters* contains all the information players need to make characters for any *GURPS* game. The *Campaigns* book is for the GM and has more advanced rules, GM guidelines, and setting information.

## System and Characters

Character creation in *GURPS* is point based. The GM sets the number of points available for character creation based on the power level of the campaign. A list of point ranges and power levels is provided in the *Campaigns* book. Players spend points on all aspects of a character, from attributes and skills to wealth and social status. A wide range of advantages and disadvantages allows players to add unique details to their characters. The GM plays an important role in guiding players to pick appropriate advantages, disadvantages, and skills for the type of game being run. Overall character creation can take some time, but all the work is front-loaded, requiring little calculation during play.

The basic system in *GURPS* is a roll-low dice pool. Players need to roll a fixed pool of dice and score below their modified skill rating. In many RPGs with skill systems, if a character does not have a specific skill, then he or she cannot attempt that action. In GURPS a character can potentially perform the action using a different skill or attribute, but at a penalty provided in the skill's description, with the penalty severity depending on the applicability of the substituted skill. There are still some skills, usually magical or highly technical, that a character cannot attempt untrained.

## Setting

The default setting is the Infinite Worlds. This setting showcases the universality of the *GURPS* rules as the characters typically play dimension-hopping agents trying to thwart another dimension-hopping government bent on controlling as much of the multiverse as possible. The Infinite Worlds is briefly discussed in the *Campaigns* book of the basic set. This book also provides rules for differing technology levels, including what gear is available and how various technological items interact with the rules. The *Campaigns* book also provides rules for more tactical combat, adding an optional layer of complexity for groups who desire it.

Infinite Worlds is by no means the only setting available. In fact, much of the work of designing the game elements for various historical periods and literary genres has been done in a plethora of supplements for previous editions of *GURPS*, with many still available in print and virtually all available electronically. These setting books range from the historical, for example, *GURPS Vikings* or *GURPS Napoleonic*, which discuss differing levels of realism in a setting (i.e., mythic vs. historical Vikings), to the genre books like *GURPS Steampunk*, *GURPS Dungeon Fantasy*, or *GURPS Horror*.

### Evaluation

Complexity: 4; once character creation is complete, *GURPS* is a simple system, but effects-based character creation can be overwhelming to new players.

Popularity: 4

Support: 5; a wide variety of supplements is available for both mechanics and settings.

Completeness: 4

Versatility: 5

Emulation: 5

### Comments

*GURPS* provides a solid generic system that, when coupled with the various high-quality supplements, will provide a group with many sessions of enjoyable play. Many of the flaws of the previous editions have been worked out or mitigated, leading to a well-balanced system. *GURPS* is also available in a short PDF booklet (*GURPS Lite*) or a single page (*GURPS Ultra-Lite*) for groups to download and use as introductory rules. *GURPS Lite* is available in several languages, with Steve Jackson Games working on even more translations.

Cost: $49.95 for *GURPS Characters* in hardcover ($29.99 in PDF); $34.95 for *GURPS Campaigns* in hardcover ($24.99 in PDF); free for *GURPS Lite* and *GURPS Ultra-Lite* in PDF

## *Hero Kids*

Justin Halliday
Justin Halliday, 2012
http://heroforgegames.blogspot.com
Genre Tags: Fantasy, Younger Gamers
Dice: d6

### Introduction

*Hero Kids* features a simplified system to get young gamers in on the action as early as possible!

## System and Characters

Characters in *Hero Kids* are pre-generated and cover a wide range of fantasy archetypes. After a few sessions of play, the simplicity of the system will foster the confidence to change and create new character types without unbalancing the system, even with fledgling GMs. Also, with play experience, more tactically complex options could easily be added as well.

This game uses a basic d6 dice pool system with contested rolls. The rules for combat follow the recent trend in fantasy games by using a map and paper fold-up miniatures. Maps are included with the adventures published for *Hero Kids*, though any map with a one-inch grid drawn on it will work for this game. The initial focus of the game is on combat encounters, allowing players to get a firm grasp of the system. Over time more exploration and role-playing elements can be added, depending on the comfort level of the group.

## Setting

The setting is a small village in a valley surrounded by a monster-infested wood and mountains. There is little detail provided, allowing the players to easily customize the setting or to abandon it completely for something of their own creation.

## Evaluation

Complexity: 2
Popularity: 2/3; more popular if restricted to RPGs for young children
Support: 3; several adventures are available.
Completeness: 5
Versatility: 4
Emulation: 5

## Comments

At its core, *Hero Kids* is a fusion between early editions of *Dungeons & Dragons (D&D)* and a pared-down version of *D&D 4th edition*. *Hero Kids* could easily be used as an introduction to that style of fantasy game, especially for children too young to understand the complexities of *D&D*. All of the adventures written for *Hero Kids* have average play times and difficulties included. This is of great help to GMs for planning how much can be accomplished in a specific time frame and can facilitate the running of adventures in small time increments.

Cost: $11.99 in print; $5.99 in PDF

# High Valor

Tim Kirk
Silver Lion Studios, 2010
http://silverlionstudios.com/
Genre Tags: Fantasy
Dice: d10

## Introduction

*High Valor* is a less rules-intensive game that places a strong emphasis on character choice and the attendant consequences. The characters are heroic in nature and live in a world that has been living in relative peace after a war with the forces of darkness. A recent meteor impact has broken the gate that keeps the Fane-Lords at bay, and the world once again teeters on the brink of war and an encroaching darkness.

## System and Characters

Characters in *High Valor* are chiefly differentiated by race and can be of several different ones, including humans (made up of several nationalities), elves, and dwarves. Two standout races are the Sidhain, a race of humans tainted by sorcery, and Formoradgh, a race of beastmen who once served the Fane-Lords as warriors. Little cultural detail is given about the races, which gives the players plenty of room to customize them as fits the needs of the game. Each description gives a trait and challenge and some notes on how to play a typical member of that race. In addition to a character's race, players also choose a profession, with each race having a separate list. Characters are defined by three attributes and a number of traits.

The base mechanic of this game is a dice pool rolled against a target number determined by the GM. The number of dice rolled is determined by which of the three attributes are being tested. The dice can explode in a limited manner. Applicable traits give a flat bonus to the dice roll total. Unlike many other RPGs that focus on a blow-by-blow account of combat, this system focuses on the overall outcome, greatly reducing playtime spent resolving actions.

## Setting

*High Valor* is a game set in a high fantasy world loosely modeled on the historical Dark Ages. The various player races have banded together to oppose the Fane-Lords and their hordes of monsters. One aspect that makes *High Valor* stand out is the use of monotheism. The vast majority of fantasy RPGs have a pantheon of gods that the characters may venerate, while this game has the Church of the Martyr as the central religion that characters follow.

## Evaluation
Complexity: 3
Popularity: 1
Support: 1
Completeness: 5
Versatility: 3
Emulation: 4

## Comments
*High Valor*'s rules system is fairly nonintrusive. Unlike other games with the same amount of focus on character-driven play, it does not have intrinsic personality mechanics. Characters' personalities are drawn out during play, where the stories will be defined by what the characters stand for. While there is a large threat to the setting, every game does not need to focus on the defeat of the Fane-Lords—the focus is on the personal struggles of the characters and what is important to them.

Cost: $35 hardcover; $9.95 in PDF

# *Icons: Superpowered Roleplaying, the Assembled Edition*
Steve Kenson et al.
Green Ronin Publishing and Ad Infinitum Adventures, 2014
http://www.greenronin.com/
http://stevekenson.com/ad-infinitum/
Genre: Comics, Superhero
Dice: d6

## Introduction
*Icons* is a quick and versatile superhero RPG. Players can create their own superheroes within minutes, or easily recreate their favorite heroes from the comics using the rules presented. The rules are simple enough that most players will grasp them quickly, and the group can start playing within thirty minutes of sitting down.

## System
*Icons* uses a variant of the popular Fate system. The rules define characters by their Abilities and Powers, each ranging on a scale from 1 (feeble) to 10 (mightiest superhuman potential), as well as Specialties and Qualities.

A character's Abilities tend to be a good gauge of his or her overall competence in most areas, and they include Prowess (deftness at close combat), Coordination (agility, hand-eye coordination), Strength (physical power and endurance), Intellect (ability to reason and learn), Awareness (perceptiveness), and Willpower (strength of mind and personality). Powers, of course, put the "super" in superhero, with broad categories covering a majority of the powers you might see in comics, cartoons, and movies. Specialties are essentially skills, areas of expertise and knowledge, and add to a character's relevant Ability when using that Specialty—for example, a Specialty in computers would add to a character's Ability to hack into a villain's security system.

Qualities, however, really round out a hero by defining those intangibles that measure the best and worst traits in the character. They include personality aspects, catchphrases, relationships, weaknesses, and faults. Some examples of Qualities include Superman's weakness around kryptonite and the Incredible Hulk's catchphrase, "Hulk Smash!" All characters have a pool of points, called Determination, a metagame currency that represents the extra "oomph" heroes need when the chips are down and the supervillain is gloating. When one of a character's negative Qualities comes up in play, the GM awards the player one or more Determination points to soften the blow. When players are in a circumstance where a positive Quality might come into play, the players can spend Determination points to enable the characters to push beyond their limitations

To determine the success of a character's actions, players roll 1d6 and add it to their relevant Ability, plus any modifiers. The GM determines the opposing difficulty or Ability, and adds it to a roll of 1d6. The opposing total is subtracted from the player's total to determine the outcome.

## Characters

By default, players roll up their characters, randomly using the charts in the book, then find a creative way to tie the characters' origins and attributes into a cohesive whole. However, GMs could just as easily allow players to pick and choose their powers for a more coherent concept. Using inspiration from comics, graphic novels, movies, and television, players can come up with just about any kind of superhero they can imagine.

## Setting

There is no default setting for *Icons*, though the range of supervillains provided in the back of the book as enemies for the characters suggests a setting that is wild, wacky, bizarre, and silly. While the art and array of bad guys is definitely kid-friendly, it would be easy to modify the tone of the game and produce villains and a setting that is more mature if the group consists of older teens and adults who desire something more along the lines of the television show *Heroes*, for example.

**Evaluation**

> Complexity: 2
> Popularity: 2
> Support: 2; previous sourcebooks can be used seamlessly with the
>     current edition
> Completeness: 4
> Versatility: 4
> Emulation: 5

**Comments**

With the popularity of graphic novels and comics, blockbuster movies, and even novels that feature superheroes, a game of *Icons* should be an easy sell to a group of creative tweens, teens, and adults. Younger players will enjoy the power fantasy, even as canny librarians and GMs introduce underlying themes from those same popular comics (like the outsider status and bullying prevalent in *Spider-Man* comics, and the prejudice against mutants in the *X-Men* titles).

The advantage of *Icons* lies in the simplicity and elegance of its design, its ease of use, and the speed with which groups can comprehend the rules and begin playing. We highly recommend *Icons* for new players, for one-shot games where you want to get players into the action as quickly as possible, and for experienced groups who like a freer hand to define for themselves what is or is not possible in the course of a game. Gamers who like a more substantial system to tinker with, however, will likely want to try *Mutants & Masterminds* (see entry later in this chapter).

Cost: $34.95 hardcover; $15 PDF

## *In Nomine*

> Derek Pearcy
> Steve Jackson Games, 1997
> http://www.sjgames.com
> Genre: Horror
> Dice: d6

**Introduction**

*In Nomine* is a game about the earthly conflict between the forces of the Christian God and Lucifer. The characters strive for one or the other side in an effort to win the existential war that has been fought for millennia.

## System and Characters

There are several character options available in *In Nomine*. The ones that receive the most attention are angels and demons, the celestials. These are the most powerful types of characters from the start of play. Celestials are subdivided into Choirs (for angels) and Bands (for demons); these divisions fulfill certain roles within celestial society. Soldiers, in the spiritual sense, and the undead form the next tier in power level, followed by normal mortals, rounding out the character types available to play in the core book.

All characters use the same three attributes and skills. Characters with access to the supernatural can also use Essence and Songs. Essence is the magical fuel used to power Songs, which are powers grouped along themes, such as Song of War or Song of Flowers. Angels and demons can also choose roles, guises they take on to blend into the mortal world and prevent some of their action from affecting the Symphony; use artifacts; and have servitors.

The base system for *In Nomine* is the d666 system. Here three six-sided dice are rolled with two added together to determine success and the third used to measure the level of success. The catch is that if either a 111 or 666 is rolled, then higher powers take an immediate interest in the action being performed. On a result of 111, the divine intervenes in the character's favor, whether or not doing so actually helps the character, and the converse is true if a 666 is rolled, when the infernal realms act.

## Setting

*In Nomine* is set in the modern world; therefore, most of the setting information deals with Heaven and Hell. These receive minimal coverage and do not stray from the traditional portrayals of these places. The realms of dreams, called the Marches, or ethereal realms are not discussed at all. (The Marches are where all the pagan beings retreated after Archangel Uriel waged war against them.)

Another key setting element involves the Archangels and Demon Princes discussed in this book. These beings give guidance (or direct orders) to the celestials that serve them. Each character serves one of these superiors at the start of the game. There are thirteen superiors for each side in the core book. Each one embodies a word (e.g., stone, war, gluttony, technology), and in addition to waging the greater war also seeks to promote his or her word in the world. The superiors grant their servants attunements, or themed abilities; although celestials can learn the attunements of others, their superiors typically frown upon that action.

**Evaluation**

> Complexity: 3; the game has a strange dice pool, and GMs must become more nuanced in their adjudication.
>
> Popularity: 2
>
> Support: 3
>
> Completeness: 3; published supplements added setting details and additional mechanical options.
>
> Versatility: 3; can explore many themes within the core concept of angels vs. demons.
>
> Emulation: 3; *In Nomine* takes a more comical approach than the French language game it is based on.

**Comments**

*In Nomine* is an irreverent look at a celestial war between the forces of the Christian God and the Devil. While the subject matter may seem a bit risqué, it's also that very irreverence that will attract the game's target audience. Older teens that enjoy books like *Good Omens* by Neil Gaiman and Terry Pratchett would enjoy this game, as might readers of the *Sandman Slim* series by Richard Kadrey.

Cost: $16.99 in PDF; hardcover currently out of print

## *Kuro*

> Neko et al. (English translation by José Luis Porfirio)
> Le 7ème Cercle, 2012 [2010]
> http://www.7emecercle.com/website/
> Cubicle 7 Entertainment has the license to translate and distribute
> *Kuro* in the United States.
> http://www.cubicle7.co.uk/
> Genre Tags: Cyberpunk, Horror
> Dice: d6

**Introduction**

*Kuro* is a magnificent mash-up of low-level cyberpunk and Japanese-style horror films like *The Ring* (*Ringu*) and *The Grudge* (*Ju-On*). The evocative near-future setting and relatively simple rules make this a good choice for teens. (Note: There is a bit of swearing in the book's text.)

**System and Characters**

*Kuro* has a selection of archetypes/templates for players to choose from, including Fixer (quasi-criminal information and services broker), Student,

Cop, Media Idol, Private Investigator, Occultist, and Overclocker (quasi-legal technology and robotics expert). This selection represents the most common types of characters likely to engage players with the cyberpunk noir/horror setting of *Kuro*, which elicits an atmosphere of the mundane touching the supernatural, and the mundane crossing the boundaries of legality and criminal behavior. However, the creators provide these templates for convenience, so groups can start running games as quickly as possible; the archetypes do not represent the full range of possible character options, and *Kuro* uses a point-buy character creation system for players who want more control over constructing their characters.

*Kuro* characters have eight primary characteristics—four physical (Dexterity, Strength, Stamina, Reflexes) and four mental (Intelligence, Perception, Charisma, Willpower)—with several secondary characteristics and skills. *Kuro* is a roll-high system; when performing tests in-game, *Kuro* players roll a number of six-sided dice equal to the rank of the appropriate characteristic (typically ranging from 1 to 3 at character creation), and add the dice total to either twice the characteristic rank (for a characteristic check) or the appropriate skill rank (for a skill check) to get a final result. Rolling dice has one clever exception: as the Japanese word *shi* could mean either "four" or "death," any die that shows as a 4 is not counted at all toward the total; effectively, if the face of a die shows a 4, then it's actually 0. Fortunately for players, any dice that show 6 on a roll act as exploding dice. Most checks are made against either a target number, or compared to an opposed roll (highest roll wins).

*Kuro* also has an interesting variety of high-tech gear for players to have, including weapons, transportation, robots, and implantable biotechnology or nanotechnology, as well as a blend of scientific and mystical enhancement called occultech. *Kuro* also has a section of nasty supernatural creatures for characters to investigate and encounter, and a section on GMing *Kuro*, including how to get a group together, how to build adventures and campaigns, and the stylistics of Japanese horror stories. An introductory adventure and further potential sources of inspiration round out the book.

**Setting**

As with their games *Qin* and *Yggdrasill*, the authors do an excellent job of describing the setting such that players and GMs will feel at home and better able to immerse themselves in play. *Kuro* takes place in the near future, Japan in the mid-twenty-first century. After an accidental Chinese nuclear missile launch, one of the missiles simply disappears in an electromagnetic storm over Japan. The rest of the world assumes that Japan has broken its treaties, and has both nuclear weapons and a secret antimissile technology that places it in a superior military position. An international alliance enforces an embargo on Japan, and alliance ships prevent any air traffic from leaving or entering Japanese airspace. Japan is effectively isolated and in dire need of supplies, due to the embargo; international tensions are on a razor's edge; and since the incident, supernatural horrors have returned to the island nation.

*Kuro* continues with a rundown of Japan's social situation, from its socially dominant Genocracy to the poor and disenfranchised. *Kuro* then details Japan's capital city, renamed Shin-Edo, and all its neighborhoods and important locations (including its shadier side) and daily life for the Japanese citizens of 2046, along with terrifying whispers and rumors that are becoming more frequent.

### Evaluation

Complexity: 2

Popularity: 1

Support: 1

Completeness: 4; while *Kuro* does well as a stand-alone game, the book details additional supplements that expand the setting, although as of this writing the English translations of those supplements are still forthcoming.

Versatility: 2; the system does what it does well, but has a rather particular purpose.

Emulation: 4; this is a creative combination of science fiction and horror.

### Comments

If the teens at your library enjoy manga, anime, and "J-horror" movies, then give this game a try. The horror begins subtly, but the characters will almost certainly be running for their lives all too soon.

Cost: $34.99 hardcover; $19.99 PDF

## *Lady Blackbird*

John Harper

One Seven Design Studio, 2010

http://www.onesevendesign.com

Genre Tags: Steampunk

Dice: d6

## Introduction

*Lady Blackbird* is a small product that packs a big punch, providing rules, a flavorful setting, and absolutely fabulous first adventure—all in sixteen pages!

## System and Characters

Players choose characters from those provided, including the eponymous Lady Blackbird and her associates. Player characters have Traits, aspects of the character like "Noble" or Athletic," and each Trait has a collection of Tags, skills, and abilities linked to those Traits (e.g., "Acrobatic" might be a Tag under the Trait "Athletic"). Characters also have Secrets (powers specific to those characters) and Keys, character-specific behaviors that players should try to emulate when playing that character. Character Conditions that indicate various adverse mental and physical states, like "Injured," "Angry," or "Trapped," fill out the bottom of the character sheet. Finally, all players have special Pools of seven dice that they can add to their characters' rolls when necessary; these Pools can be depleted through use or refreshed by role-playing the character's Keys.

*Lady Blackbird* uses a roll-high dice pool system. During play, characters will encounter obstacles that challenge and confound them. When players want to attempt action to overcome obstacles, they get a single die for free, and get additional dice for any Traits and Tags that are relevant to the situation. They may also spend dice from their Pool. Players roll their dice and every die that shows a result of 4 or greater is a hit. Players total their hits and compare their result to a target number. If the roll is successful, then players discard their dice and narrate the outcome. If the roll is unsuccessful, then players narrate the outcome and keep their collection of dice, and get an additional die to add to their Pool—they may get another chance to roll, depending on the circumstance. Failure may also lead to the GM imposing a Condition on the character.

*Lady Blackbird* emphasizes the narrative portion of RPGs. For example, when a player successfully "hits a Key"—engages in behaviors specific to that character's Keys—the player may take an additional Pool die, or take an experience point that the player can later spend on advancement, gaining additional Traits, Tags, Keys, and Secrets. Players can also run short "refreshment scenes"—in-character dialogs to learn more about one another, or flashback scenes that reveal a part of the character's background—to regain Pool dice. Additionally, entire fight scenes that take considerable time in other games, sometimes hours, can be played out in moments by assigning the opposition an obstacle number, making the roll, and narrating the events afterward.

## Setting

*Lady Blackbird* largely implies, rather than explicitly describes, most of its setting, but does so more skillfully than many other games that spend dozens of pages on setting chapters and supplements. Adventures take place in the Wild Blue, where a host of worlds float in a breathable sky and circle a small star. People traverse the Wild Blue in skyships that run on steam technology and risk the attention of sky pirates. Some characters have sorcerous powers they derive from their bloodlines and that may be powered by the star's energy, or Essence. An Empire rules a portion of the Wild Blue, opposed by a collection of Free Worlds.

The Wild Blue has its hazards, including the Lower Depths, a corrosive fog below the Wild Blue's sky that is dangerous to ply, but desperate ships sometimes hide there from enemies. The Remnants, a collection of world fragments like an asteroid field, is nearly unnavigable, and may be the hiding place of the Pirate King!

As mentioned earlier, the game is also a beginning adventure. *Lady Blackbird* thrusts characters directly into the action, as the eponymous Lady Blackbird and her crew have been captured by Imperial Forces, on their way from helping Blackbird escape an arranged marriage and delivering her to her lover, the Pirate King.

So we have an Empire, an alliance of Free Worlds, a dastardly Count (Blackbird's betrothed), pirates, skyships, steampunk, high adventure, swashbuckling, and sorcery. Essentially, players quickly read their character sheets, the GM presents the situation, and the game says: GO! PLAY! NOW!

## Evaluation

Complexity: 2
Popularity: 2
Support: 1
Completeness: 3/4; while the core game is essentially a one-shot adventure, the *Lady Blackbird Companion*, written by a fan of *Lady Blackbird*, does a lot to flesh out the setting, and the game itself is simple and complete.
Versatility: 4
Emulation: 4

## Comments

*Lady Blackbird* is one of those games that immediately captures the imagination and demands to be played. Even after groups complete the adventure, the Wild Blue and setting of *Lady Blackbird* cry out for further exploration. Fortunately, as mentioned above, a fan of *Lady Blackbird*, Tim Adamson, created a twenty-seven page "appendix" to the game called the

*Lady Blackbird Companion* or *Tales from the Wild Blue Yonder*. This companion, as well as other hacks, variants, and modifications of *Lady Blackbird* can be found at http://mightyatom.blogspot.com/2010/03/lady-blackbird-hacks.html.

We should note the Lady Blackbird system appears to be based on another game, *The Shadow of Yesterday*, by Clinton R. Nixon and CRN Games (http://crngames.com).

Cost: Free PDF at publisher's website

## Legend of the Five Rings Roleplaying Game, 4th Edition

Shawn Carman et al.
Alderac Entertainment Group, 2010
http://www.alderac.com
Genre Tags: Asian, Fantasy
Dice: d10

### Introduction

In *Legend of the Five Rings* (*L5R*), players take the role of samurai, shugenja (mystics), and courtiers, representing their clan in the Emerald Empire. Intrigues between the clans and external threats from monstrous horrors threaten the kingdom, and characters must make difficult choices in a setting where honor must be stronger than steel.

### System and Characters

*L5R* character creation is a combination of class and point-buy. Players select which of the Rokugani clans their characters belong to, and a particular family from within the clan. Each of the clans has its own distinct personality, like the mighty Crab clan that keeps monstrous creatures from overrunning the Empire, or the Scorpion clan that keeps the other clans divided so that none may challenge the Emperor. Each family within a clan is responsible for an aspect of the clan's well-being, and its descendants tend to have particular roles: for example, the samurai family and the shugenja family.

Characters have five traits that define them, named after the rings from *The Book of Five Rings* by Miyamoto Musashi. The Air ring governs Reflexes and Awareness, Earth governs Stamina and Willpower, Fire governs Agility and Intelligence, Water governs Strength and Perception, and Void determines the number of Void points (metagame currency) for the characters. Players gain skills, advantages, and disadvantages to round out their characters. Players then play a game of "Twenty Questions" with the GM, where their answers help to breathe life into the character's personality. Characters also have ranks in Honor, Glory, and Status, and increase in Insight (experience points) to advance their abilities.

*L5R* uses a unique roll-high system called the Roll and Keep System. Players making checks add the ranks of the appropriate ring and skill involved. Players then keep only a number of dice equal to the ring, total those numbers, and compare the results against a target number. Players may gamble on even greater success in a roll by declaring Raises before the roll; for every increment of 5 the player rolls above the target number, the character gains a Raise, which can translate into truly impressive successes.

## Setting

Rokugan and its Emerald Empire are pan-Asian fantasy settings primarily influenced by Japanese folklore, history, and culture. Rokugan has a rich history and mythology, where the clans trace their bloodlines to the children of the gods themselves. Characters are honorable servants of the divine Emperor, where samurai meet on battlefields and courtiers wage wars no less deadly at court, using words and whispers instead of blades. Rokugan's physical world must live in harmonious conjunction with the spirit world or risk calamity, and it depends on its shugenja to keep the balance. Even worse, Rokugan must contend with the Shadowlands, a physical manifestation of evil that breeds corruption and monstrosities that threaten the whole Empire.

Unlike many fantasy RPGs where characters simply wander about looking for trouble and loot, the players will need to immerse themselves in the setting and culture of Rokugan, as their ability to play their roles in this unique setting affects both the narrative and mechanical aspects of the game. Fortunately, the book has a long section detailing Rokugan, its people, its culture, its government, and its spiritual beliefs. While the setting has grown and altered considerably over the game's lifetime and editions, and thus has considerable detail to digest, the rulebook has guidelines for easing players into the game and setting.

## Evaluation

Complexity: 2/4; *L5R* has a relatively simple resolution system but also includes subsystems and details that may require players to do some digging into the rules.

Popularity: 4; *L5R* has been a fan favorite for nearly twenty years.

Support: 4; *L5R* has plenty of support material.

Completeness: 3; while *L5R* is a relatively complete game, the many
supplements add a host of options for players and GMs, and
flesh out the setting even further.
Versatility: 3
Emulation: 4

## Comments

Players fascinated by Japanese culture and folklore, and who enjoy
samurai films and manga, will be eager participants in deciding the fate of
the Emerald Empire. Librarians can recommend classics like *The Book of
Five Rings* by Miyamoto Musashi, manga like *Lone Wolf and Cub* and *Vag-
abond*, and films by Akira Kurosawa.

Cost: $59.99 hardcover; $34.99 PDF; *Legacy of Disaster* (free quick-start
rules and introductory adventure) available at publisher's website

## *Lords of Olympus*

The RPGPundit
Precis Intermedia, 2012
http://www.pigames.net
Genre Tags: Diceless, Fantasy, Mythology
Dice: None!

### Introduction

*Lords of Olympus* is a game about Greek mythology, intrigue, power,
and being a hero or godling in the Greek Pantheon, one of the most dysfunc-
tional families of all time.

### System and Characters

PCs are quite powerful entities in the era of Greek myths and legends,
the children of the gods themselves. *Lords of Olympus* is a point-buy, diceless system that eschews randomizers.

PCs have four primary Abilities: Ego, measuring will, psychic ability,
and degree of omniscience; Might, measuring physical strength; Fortitude,
measuring a character's endurance; and Prowess, measuring a character's
skill in combat as well as an ability to think strategically. Abilities are ranked
on a scale of Mortal, Heroic, and Numbered (not all gods are created equal,
after all). Mortal and Heroic ranks are penalties that players can choose to
get more points to spend on powers or other character options, whereas

Olympian is the baseline, and Numbered Abilities make the character notable even among gods.

Players create their characters using a unique bidding system. The GM calls out the first Ability to bid on, and players make their initial bids secretly, after which the GM tells the group the highest bid, and players can continue bidding until everyone is satisfied. Since players have a limited number of points to spend on Abilities as well as other powers, players must manage their resources carefully.

After bidding on Abilities, players may purchase powers like immortality, Olympian magic, the ability to walk between the various worlds and realms of Greek myth, metamorphosis, and unique magical artifacts. Any remaining points go into Luck, an Ability that demonstrates how much the Fates smile upon the character. Players may take negative luck as a source of points to spend elsewhere but shouldn't make this decision lightly, as it may come back to haunt their characters later.

Before or as players create their characters, they should consider their characters' backgrounds carefully. Who is the character's divine parent? What is the character's background or profession, and what skills might that character have?

Character tasks, including combat, center on the character's relevant ability and rank, and whether said rank is sufficient to the task. A character with Olympian-class Prowess would likely have no trouble with a few bandits but might think twice before taking on an entire army (in which case the character's Might and Fortitude would certainly also come into play). Fortunately, *Lords of Olympus* has a clear and helpful chapter on adjudicating conflicts in a game without randomizers, such that GMs have some structure and rules scaffolding to help them make their decisions.

## Setting

*Lords of Olympus* details the various realms of the Multiverse that characters might visit, including Olympus, Hades, Tartarus, Atlantis, and the mortal realm—including Classical Earth and, if GMs want, Modern Earth as well. *Lords of Olympus* has a nice section on monsters and mythical beasts that heroes might encounter, as well as a huge section detailing and describing the gods, goddesses, titans, primordials, and other named entities of Greek myth. Along with this Who's Who list, *Lords of Olympus* discusses Olympian culture and the influence that family will have on every aspect of a character's life—after all, if your father is Zeus and your mother isn't Hera, then you're likely going to have one miserable childhood, and an even more problematic adulthood.

## Evaluation

Complexity: 3; while the system is actually rather simple, there is some complexity in mastering the nuances of a diceless system.

Popularity: 1

Support: 1; then again, how much support does this game need beyond a visit to the local library?

Completeness: 5; this book could second as an encyclopedia of Greek gods and goddesses.

Versatility: 4

Emulation: 4

## Comments

Considering how many students have to do a classical mythology project every year, teachers might consider running this game in their classrooms! If you have teens and youth interested in Greek mythology, then definitely hand them a copy of *Lords of Olympus* along with Edith Hamilton's *Mythology*. Fans of Rick Riordan's *The Lightning Thief* and the other Percy Jackson/Olympians books will also want to try this game.

The system for *Lords of Olympus* was first used in the *Amber Diceless Role-Playing Game* by Erick Wujcik, which was in turn based on the Amber novels by Roger Zelazny. If players like *Lords of Olympus*, then they may also enjoy visiting Amber for a while. Alternately, the system is also used in the *Lords of Gossamer and Shadow* RPG, so interested gamers should check out that game as well.

Cost: $29.95 black-and-white softcover; $49.95 color softcover; $12.95 PDF

## *Monsterhearts*

Joe Mcdaldno
Buried without Ceremony, 2012
http://buriedwithoutceremony.com/
Genre Tags: Horror, Mature Audiences, Paranormal Romance
Dice: d6

## Introduction

In *Monsterhearts*, players take on the roles of high school students and play out their messy and convoluted lives. This game dives wholeheartedly into the teen paranormal romance genre with a strong focus on the characters' social lives.

**System and Characters**

Character creation is very streamlined. There are several Skins, pre-generated roles, each embodying a specific supernatural archetype. These Skins have four abstracted stats, which are rated on a scale that is both positive and negative, with human average being a 0. These stats grant all characters basic Moves—general headings that cover actions the character can take—while each Skin has a set of specific Moves that the player can choose from. Skins also have a Sex Move, which is a game effect that occurs after the character engages in sexual activity. Finally, each Skin has a unique Darkest Self ability; this ability is triggered when a specific condition is met and is used to compel a character to indulge in less positive, and life-complicating, behaviors. In addition to a trigger, an end condition is listed as well. After the mechanical parts are assigned, each of the players reads the background story for the Skin and fills in details with input from the other players. This should result in all of the characters being linked to at least one other character before play begins.

The system for *Monsterhearts* (an adaptation of the *Apocalypse World* engine taken from the game with the same title) is very straightforward. Two d6s are rolled; a stat is added and any conditional modifiers. A result above a 10 is a complete success and 7–9 is a success with a complication. An example of a conditional modifier is a String. Strings are emotional or social holds that characters have on each other or on nonplayer characters (NPCs). These Strings can be used to gain bonuses to rolls or to use certain Move powers. This game has a particularly well-written GM advice chapter covering not only how to teach and run the game but also how to modify or create Skins and genre-appropriate adversaries.

**Setting**

The setting for *Monsterhearts* is left intentionally vague. Other than the fact that the characters are high school–age people there is very little predefined. This allows the setting to be tailored to the specific needs of the group and story. There is an element of intercharacter rivalry in this game.

**Evaluation**

Complexity: 2
Popularity: 2
Support: 1; one expansion of additional characters and one adventure series has been published.
Completeness: 5
Versatility: 1
Emulation: 4

## Comments

This game explores the genre of teen paranormal romance and has a strong emphasis on teen relationships and sexual dynamics, both healthy and unhealthy, including heteronormative and queer relationships. Thus, it's also a game that may generate some controversy if placed in a library's collection. That said, the rules accurately emulate an extremely popular genre of teen fiction, fiction that is certainly on the library shelves already. Thus, while it might not be the best choice for adults to run with teens, you can bet that older teens will be interested in having the game available to run for their own groups.

Cost: $25 softcover + PDF; $10 PDF

## *Mouse Guard Roleplaying Game*

Luke Crane
Archaia Studios Press, 2008
http://www.archaia.com/
Genre Tags: Animals, Comics, Fantasy
Dice: d6

## Introduction

*Mouse Guard* is a game where noble mice defend their settlements in the wild against the predators that threaten their home.

## System and Characters

The system used in *Mouse Guard* is a modified version of the system used in *Burning Wheel*. Unlike *Burning Wheel*, *Mouse Guard* does not use lifepaths. In this game players use a narrative approach to character creation by answering questions posed by the GM and picking traits based on the narrative choices made. Task resolution uses a dice pool of d6s based on the trait the GM determines is needed to pass the obstacle, with the target number set by the GM based on how difficult the task is.

Some of the more mechanically interesting parts of *Mouse Guard* characters are beliefs, instincts, and goals. A belief is an ethical stance taken by the character. An instinct is an inherent reaction, either instinctive or from training, that a character will perform without thinking. Unlike beliefs and instincts that will change only rarely over the course of a campaign, a character's goal will change from session to session. These elements use in-game rewards to drive a character's actions without overruling player creativity. Another advantage of these elements is that they allow the players to tell the GM what types of stories they would be interested in participating in, thereby avoiding players making "useless" characters. Using these three elements in play will grant the character fate and persona points, which can be spent in-game to grant bonuses to a character's die roll.

## Setting

The setting for *Mouse Guard* is based on the eponymous comic book written by David Petersen. The characters are members of the Mouse Guard, an organization that serves as border patrol, search and rescue, and law enforcement for the far-flung mouse communities in the Territories. The Territories themselves are a large forest made up of dense and rugged terrain. The communities of mice exist in relatively isolated conditions. Each of the major settlements has a brief description, with a list of minor settlements and guidelines on creating your own. The rulebook details several challenges for players and provides the GM with several plot hooks.

Unlike many other RPGs, the seasons play an active part in *Mouse Guard* and have a chapter dedicated to them, discussing activities undertaken by mice during the season, plants and animals encountered, and environmental challenges.

## Evaluation

Complexity: 3; simplified version of the *Burning Wheel* mechanics
Popularity: 2
Support: 1
Completeness: 5
Versatility: 4
Emulation: 5

## Comments

This game would provide an excellent introduction to role-playing, especially for middle school–aged children. The system strikes a good balance between intuitiveness and complexity, with a strong emphasis on narrative. While it has a background story, it is not imperative that all the players be familiar with it before playing, and the background is contained in the *Mouse Guard* graphic novels that many libraries have on their shelves. This game may also go over well with fans of the *Redwall* series of novels by Brian Jacques.

Cost: $69.95 boxed set; $34.95 core book; $19.99 PDF of the core book

# Mutant Future, Revised Edition

Daniel Proctor and Ryan Denison
Goblinoid Games, 2010 [2008]
http://www.goblinoidgames.com
Genre Tags: OSR, Post-Apocalypse, Science Fantasy
Dice: d4, d6, d8, d10, d12, d20, d%/d100

## Introduction

Imagine blending movies like *The Road Warrior* and *Mad Max: Beyond Thunderdome* with *The Planet of the Apes*, then mix in all those weird comics like *Kamandi* and cartoons like *Thundarr the Barbarian* that posited a far-future (yet strangely recognizable) Earth devastated by nuclear war, filled with bizarre life forms mutated by radiation, and littered with the super science of the past, waiting to be rediscovered. That's *Mutant Future*. Because as we all know, comic book science says that copious amounts of radiation give you gonzo superpowers.

## System and Characters

*Mutant Future* uses a type of class and level system, where the classes are actually five character types: androids, pure (nonmutated) humans, mutant humans, mutant animals, or mutant plants. Pure humans tend to be hardier, smarter, and better looking, and all the groovy scientific ruins, robots, and technology typically respond better to them. Androids can have special abilities connected to their original design and robotic bodies. Mutants of every sort can have special powers or debilitating hindrances that reflect their original genetic stock and the vagaries of centuries of irradiated evolution.

*Mutant Future* is an "old school" game (see "Old School Renaissance" in the glossary) that uses a variant of the system designed for older versions of a very well-known fantasy game with an alliterative title. Thus, PCs have variations of the classic six attributes (Strength, Dexterity, Constitution, Intelligence, Willpower, and Charisma), saving throws (target numbers to avoid or mitigate—"save against"—various hazards), hit points, and an armor class rating that varies based on armor worn and a given character's reflexes.

Players with characters that get powers or mutations roll randomly to determine how many and which abilities they receive. As players gain experience, they get various bonuses to their characters, from increased attributes to better combat skill. Players purchase gear for their characters, and then it's off to the savage wastelands and adventure!

The remainder of the book has rules for various super science and pre-apocalypse technology that the PCs might find and salvage, a whole bestiary of bizarre monsters and antagonists, advice for the GM ("Mutant Lord") on how to create adventures, a sample adventure, and rules for mashing up this game even further with other fantasy retroclones.

## Setting

*Mutant Future* posits an absolutely and delightfully unrealistic post-apocalyptic world that is ready-made for adventuring. Humans, robots, and mutants form enclaves and attempt to rebuild civilization, or rule over its ashes. Player characters explore ruins, from ancient cities to missile silos to shopping malls, surviving from day-to-day, engaging in picaresque adventures, and stumbling across the high-tech remains of Earth-that-was. Characters might find incredible and wondrous devices left over from a previous age, learn their uses, or utterly mishandle them and blow themselves up—it's all part of the fun of living after the bomb!

## Evaluation

Complexity: 2
Popularity: 2
Support: 3
Completeness: 4
Versatility: 4
Emulation: 5

## Comments

The teens that played this game *loved* it. Every adventure was deadly, dashing, uproarious, and hilarious by turns. The bizarre nature of the setting meant that they never knew what they might find next, and yet they were generally competent and powerful enough to deal with the unknown—or enjoyed rolling up new characters, if luck turned against them.

Librarians might try offering *Mutant Future* fans books like *Orphans of the Sky* by Robert A. Heinlein, *Hiero's Journey* by Sterling Lanier, and *Non-Stop* and *Hothouse* by Brian Aldiss. Even better, given the popularity of dystopias and post-apocalypse fiction among teens, any one of the societies they read about in books like *The Hunger Games* or *Divergent* might be an enclave of civilization that their characters can encounter . . . and likely up-end!

Cost: $23.95 softcover; $30.90 softcover + PDF, $6.95 PDF (with art); free no-art version PDF

# *Mutants & Masterminds Deluxe Hero's Handbook, Third Edition*

Steve Kenson
Green Ronin, 2013 [2011]
http://www.greenronin.com
Genre Tags: Comics, Superhero
Dice: d20

## Introduction

When *Mutants & Masterminds* (*M&M*) first hit the shelves in 2002, it was a revolutionary game that used the Open Game License (OGL) for something other than *D&D* fantasy and took the RPG world by storm. Now in its third edition, *M&M* is still the first choice for many gamers when it comes to superhero RPGs, and has as an added bonus a license for the DC Universe.

## System and Characters

*M&M* is a roll-high, point-buy system that also uses levels. The beginning level of the character (default is level 10) determines how many points players get in order to buy Abilities (Strength, Stamina, Agility, Dexterity, Fighting Intellect, Awareness, and Presence), Skills, Advantages, and, of course, Powers. PCs also get Complications, like motivations for living the superhero lifestyle and other options, like a secret identity or the existence of a substance that robs your hero of its powers (e.g., kryptonite), which make life more interesting for your character. The advantage to Complications is that, when the GM uses them against you, you can gain Hero Points, *M&M*'s metagame currency, and Hero Points give your character many ways to shine by improving rolls, enabling the character to recover faster or gain temporary abilities or insight into a problem, and generally to act even more heroic.

Most checks take the form of a d20 roll plus modifiers versus a target number, with different types of rolls having different modifiers from Abilities, Skills, etc., and different target numbers based on some characteristic of the opposition or circumstance.

*M&M* actually has three methods of character creation. The first is the point-buy option, where players can select Abilities, Skills, Advantages, and Powers, and even apply Extras and Flaws to their powers, modifiers that enhance or limit the character's superhuman abilities, to get exactly the character the player wants. However, generating your own character so thoroughly can take a substantial amount of time, and the complexities of the system might overwhelm a new player. Fortunately, *M&M* also has ready-made archetypes based on common types of superhero characters, from the Battlesuit wearing hero (e.g., Iron Man) to the Crime Fighter (e.g., Batman) to the Paragon (e.g., Superman) to the Speedster (e.g., Flash), and many others. Players can choose an archetype, make a few modifications to fit the characters to their vision, and begin playing quickly. The third method of character creation involves randomly rolling up a character, which could result in some interesting combinations!

*M&M* also has rules for gadgets, vehicles, secret lairs, and bases to round out characters, as well as a section on GMing *M&M*, with guidelines on how to create adventures and campaigns for the heroes.

### Setting

The default setting for *M&M* is Emerald City, but unfortunately that setting is detailed in a different supplement by the same name. Still, superhero comics and cartoons are sufficiently ingrained into the popular culture that most players know what a superhero world is supposed to be like.

Groups could, of course, create their own settings from scratch, or simply adapt *M&M* to an existing franchise, like DC Comics. Green Ronin has the DC Comics RPG licensing rights and has already adapted *M&M* with its *DC Adventures Hero's Handbook,* with setting and character information in the supplements *DC Adventures Universe* and two volumes of *DC Adventures Heroes & Villains*.

### Evaluation

Complexity: 3/4; while players may quickly learn what they need to run their characters, players who want to dig into the point-buy will likely need to take time to master the system.

Popularity: 3

Support: 5; with a GM guide, the Emerald City supplement, and a huge amount of PDF material on the market, gaming groups have plenty to keep them busy if they like this game.

Completeness: 4

Versatility: 5; superhero games are the ultimate kitchen sink of genres, so if you can use a system to run supers, then you can likely use it to run just about anything else.

Emulation: 4

### Comments

*M&M* is a solid choice for GMs and gaming groups who want an RPG that can emulate a range of superhero games and don't mind rolling up their sleeves and digging into the system. For gaming groups who want a simpler system with plenty of flavor, try *Icons*, another game by creator Steve Kenson (see entry earlier in this chapter).

Cost: $39.95 hardcover; $20.00 PDF

## Night's Black Agents: A Vampire Spy Thriller

Kenneth Hite
Pelgrane Press, 2012
http://www.pelgranepress.com
Genre Tags: Horror, Spy, Thriller
Dice: d6

### Introduction

In *Night's Black Agents* (*NBA*), characters are spies working in the shadows, conducting clandestine operations for secret masters . . . who happen to be vampires. It's *The Bourne Identity* meets Bram Stoker!

### System and Characters

Player characters have abilities that represent their wide variety of skills. In *NBA*, there are two classes of abilities: general, including most physical abilities; and investigative, the technical, academic, and interpersonal skills, knowledge, and expertise that characters need when conducting investigations. As *NBA* is a point-buy system, players spend points on one or more backgrounds that depict various covert and quasi-legal professions that characters had before they went solo, and get the abilities listed under those backgrounds. Players then spend additional points to enhance those abilities or purchase ranks in others. In *NBA*, it helps to have a wide spread of abilities, especially since investigative abilities always succeed—that's right, no roll necessary, although you may spend ranks of an ability to get an even higher success.

The reason that investigative abilities succeed automatically is because *NBA*'s core system, GUMSHOE, is designed to keep investigative games flowing, so characters don't miss important clues; the emphasis is on players putting the clues together, following leads, and figuring out the mystery, so the action doesn't stall.

General abilities, however, do require rolls, which is when *NBA* becomes a roll-high system versus a target number, although players may spend ranks in their general abilities before they roll to increase their final result.

In order to enhance the espionage feel and flavor of the game, *NBA* has wonderful abilities like Preparedness, to simulate the ability for smart spies to always have the gear they need, and Network, which represents characters' contacts wherever they happen to be in the world—spies do get around, after all.

This game shines even brighter on the GM's side of the screen. *NBA* allows for four different kinds of vampires—supernatural, damned, alien, and mutant—with a full set of rules for building them with traditional, bizarre, or unique powers, so players never know what you'll be throwing at them. *NBA* also has four modes of play that vary the style and tone of the game: Dust mode allows for lower power cinematic thrillers; in Stakes mode, your characters will be driven to great risk and greater reward; in Burn mode, characters may suffer psychological trauma from their missions; and in Mirror mode, characters never know whom they can trust.

And because investigative games need to make sense backward and forward, *NBA* provides GMs with the Vampyramid, a method of detailing all the plot connections in an adventure and an escalating response from the antagonists!

The book rounds out with rules on "building" your cities, the settings where much of your action takes place. The rules give a few examples of taking cities from around the world, peopling them with monsters, and preparing them for conspiracy stories and making them new again, so that GMs can convey the right tones of exoticism and danger. The book ends with an introductory adventure to launch characters into the fray against the vampire conspiracy.

## Setting

*NBA* emulates the shadowy world of espionage thrillers and spy stories—with a twist. Thus, depending on the mode that gaming groups use, PCs could be neck deep in James Bond– or Bourne-level action, or they could be playing the smooth, nerve-wracking chess-like long game of a John le Carré novel. Once the characters discover the vampire conspiracy, they will need to work hard to stay alive, investigate the conspiracy, uncover the vampires' weaknesses, and eventually bring the bloodsuckers down.

## Evaluation

Complexity: 2
Popularity: 2
Support: 2
Completeness: 5
Versatility: 4
Emulation: 5

## Comments

Spies versus vampires? Sign us up! We don't know if Hollywood has contacted Mr. Hite yet, but if they haven't, they should! The closest thing we can think of to this mash-up is the short-lived British television series *Ultraviolet*. Nonetheless, run this game for teens who want to enter the world of espionage—at least in their imaginations—and who think that vampires are monsters, not viable dating partners.

Cost: $44.95 hardcover + PDF (from the publisher's website); $24.95 PDF

## *Numenera*

Monte Cook
Monte Cook Games, LLC, 2013
http://www.montecook.com
Genre: Post-Apocalypse, Science-Fantasy
Dice: d6, d20, d%/d100

### Introduction

*Numenera* is a science-fantasy game set in the "Ninth World," a time eons distant from our own. Players take the roles of martial Glaives, wily Jacks, and knowledge-seeking Nanos exploring a bizarre future world where science seems like sorcery.

### System and Characters

*Numenera* features a variation on class-and-level systems that allows for a wide variety of diverse characters within a few simple parameters. When creating a character, players complete the simple concept sentence of "I am a [Descriptor] [Type] who [Focus]." Players take on the roles of one of three Types: warriors, called Glaives; rogues, rascals, and ne'er-do-wells called Jacks; and Nanos, who command the seemingly sorcerous science of a new age. A character's powers and abilities might derive from grueling training, psychic abilities, genetic or technological enhancements, or all three.

Players do nearly all the dice rolling in *Numenera*, which features a d20 roll-high system, against a target number assigned by the GM that reflects the difficulty of the feat or toughness of the opponent the character faces. Character traits include Might (physical strength and endurance), Speed (nimbleness and quickness), and Intellect (a combination of intelligence and charisma). Players assign points to each of these traits and can spend these points in-game to lower the target number. Players also decide on their characters' skills, which also serve to lower target numbers assigned to actions associated with those skills. As players gain experience, they spend those points to rise in tiers and gain additional abilities.

In order to add diversity to the basic types, *Numenera* characters get a Descriptor like Tough or Swift or Clever that grants additional benefits and some drawbacks to add flavor to the character. Finally, players choose a Focus for their characters, like "Bears a Halo of Fire" or "Fuses Flesh and Steel," which grants even greater powers and specializations to the character.

As a final bit of fun, *Numenera* characters will often come across unique bits of technology (called cyphers, artifacts, and oddities), flotsam and jetsam bits of advanced science that add flavor to the setting and grant one-shot powers to their wielders.

## Setting

*Numenera* emphasizes exploration and presents a massive sandbox for characters to travel and discover. The key to understanding the Ninth World is that the setting takes its cue from author Arthur C. Clarke's "Third Law": "any sufficiently advanced technology is indistinguishable from magic." This far-future world blends seemingly high-fantasy tropes, like dragons, medieval governance, monsters, and magic, with science fiction; various races and creatures are, in fact, alien extraterrestrials and ultraterrestrials, or the results of genetic alteration; and sorcery is actually a process of controlling nanotechnology and far-future, but little-understood, science. *Numenera* then combines these elements with weirdness (one notable NPC is a flying koi) and a touch of the post-apocalyptic, including bizarre mutations and the goal of rebuilding a new civilization from the remnants of the old. *Numenera* benefits from magnificent art that illustrates a unique setting; it has the striking visual spectacle of a widescreen summer blockbuster and compels players to explore its mysteries and discover its bizarreness and beauty. *Numenera's* Ninth World has a wide scope and breadth; the rulebook spends most of its pages describing the various lands, major characters, rumors, unique technologies, and unearthly creatures. That said, *Numenera* also leaves a great deal of its vast setting open for individual GMs to add their own towns, societies, creatures, and super-science weirdness, and to give each group's Ninth World its distinctive stamp.

## Evaluation

> Complexity: 2; while the resource management aspect of *Numenera* is uncommon, the basic mechanics are easy to comprehend, and players should quickly grasp the rules.

> Popularity: 2; *Numenera*, while the result of a massively successful Kickstarter campaign and written by one of the biggest names

in RPGs, is still a very new game. However, we expect that its popularity will grow.

Support: 2; Monte Cook Games is moving quickly to make supporting material for *Numenera*, and as of this writing the company has already published a series of adventures, supporting fiction, a bestiary, a player's guide, and cards with monsters and cyphers to use in-game.

Completeness: 4; *Numenera* is a very complete game in itself (dice sold separately, of course), and while support materials will enhance the experience, the material in the main book could fuel years of play.

Versatility: 3; while the game is very specific to the Ninth World, there are a great many types of campaigns that groups can enjoy within that vast setting.

Emulation: 4; *Numenera* has one of the most fully realized and game-able science-fantasy settings we've seen in a long time.

**Comments**

This game appeals to the players' sense of wonder and promises new strangeness around every corner. Players will enjoy the stunning visual art that works fantastically well to give shape and definition to the Ninth World and encourages rather than limits the imagination of what adventurers might encounter. Librarians familiar with Anne McCaffrey's *Pern* novels, where seemingly fantasy tropes are actually the result of forgotten advanced science, might use that knowledge as a read-alike suggestion, but Monte Cook has a sizeable list of inspirations from books, comics, films, and animation for further exploration. A set of adventures at the end of the book is a great resource for new GMs, or GMs new to this type of science-fantasy blend, as they feature advice on how to structure adventures and the various types of adventures possible in the Ninth World, from "adventurers come to town and solve a problem" to intrigue to "dungeon-crawl" exploration.

Cost: $59.99 hardcover; $19.99 PDF

## *The One Ring: Adventures over the Edge of the Wild*

Francesco Nepitello
Sophisticated Games and Cubicle 7, 2011
http://www.cubicle7.co.uk/
Genre Tags: Fantasy
Dice: Specialty dice (see below)

## Introduction

*The One Ring* (*TOR*) is a game set in J.R.R. Tolkien's Middle Earth shortly after the events in *The Hobbit*. Characters face the remaining evils from the reign of the Necromancer and Smaug, and seek to improve the lot of their people in the region.

## System and Characters

Characters in *TOR* use a fairly loose class and level system, called callings. Characters are primarily defined by the cultures they are from. Each culture has six backgrounds to choose from, though GMs could easily create new backgrounds. The backgrounds the players select define their characters' beginning skills and starting attributes. Numerically, characters are defined by three base attributes and eighteen common skills; weapon skills are listed separately.

This game uses a dice pool consisting of one d12 and a number of d6s, depending on the character's skill rating. The dice that come with the game have special icons on some of the faces indicating certain levels of accomplishment. The rulebook includes instructions for groups that do not have the proprietary dice, and may only have the PDF, as initially the dice were only available with the boxed set. Characters have Hope points that can be spent to improve die rolls, which represent a character's positivity and spiritual strength, and have an effect on how much misery a character can suffer before succumbing to the Shadow.

Character advancement in *TOR* is handled a bit differently than in other RPGs. It is presumed that a group of characters goes on one adventure per calendar year, and after that adventure is concluded, they spend the rest of their time at home improving their abilities and helping their people.

## Setting

*TOR* is set in the northern half of Middle Earth, chiefly Eriador and Rhovanion (Wilderland), five years after the events of *The Hobbit*. The various peoples of the region, including sylvan elves, dwarves, and various human cultures, are beginning to cooperate again in trying to lift the region out of the shadow it was under. A strong emphasis is placed on community, and while the characters are set apart by going forth on adventures, they can still earn rewards and benefit from belonging to and cultivating ties with various communities, as remaining apart from people makes resisting the Shadow more difficult.

In other RPGs the map, and by extension a wilderness setting, is primarily used to provide travel times and rough spatial relations between adventure locations. In *TOR*, in emulation of Tolkien's works, the map and wilderness are more central to the game. The entire area is divided into regions that are given two types of classifications: the first is ease of travel, and the second the degree of settlement, and therefore safety. Traveling through less settled lands is hazardous and sets a greater challenge to the group. A narrative map is provided for the players and looks like a map the characters may actually possess, while a second map marked with travel and safety regions is provided for the GM.

## Evaluation

Complexity: 3
Popularity: 2
Support: 2
Completeness: 5
Versatility: 2
Emulation: 5

## Comments

*TOR* does an excellent job of capturing the feel of Tolkien's works, not only in the way the characters are portrayed but also in the tying of Middle Earth themes into the game, chiefly through the use of the Hope and Shadow mechanics. Unlike other licensed RPGs, this game also provides enough invented material that groups should not feel bound to simply recreate either characters or plots of the *Lord of the Rings*. By placing the setting between the *Hobbit* and the *Lord of the Rings*, *TOR* also avoids the pitfall of having the characters' actions take place at the same time as the written stories. Other games use the explanation that the characters are doing important things, just in a different location, but this explanation rings false; if the PCs' actions were just as important, then they would have been mentioned in the lore alongside Bilbo's and Frodo's journeys.

Cost: $59.99 in print; $29.99 in PDF

## *Pathfinder Roleplaying Game Core Rulebook*

Jason Bulmahn et al.
Paizo Publishing, 2009
http://paizo.com/paizo
Genre Tags: Fantasy
Dice: d4, d6, d8, d10, d12, d20, d%/d100

## Introduction

*Pathfinder* is a refinement of Wizards of the Coast's *Dungeons & Dragons, 3.5 edition* (*D&D 3.5*). Utilizing *D&D*'s OGL, Paizo addressed some of the more awkward rules while maintaining backward compatibility with *D&D 3.5*.

## System and Characters

Characters in *Pathfinder* use a class and level system. The process for making a character follows six steps, beginning with attributes. *Pathfinder* uses the "classic" six attributes of *D&D* (Strength, Dexterity, Constitution, Intelligence, Wisdom, and Charisma) and offers several different methods of determining scores, leading to a wide range of character competency. These scores are arranged to favor a specific class, as the bonuses provided by high scores are substantial. Race, technically species, and class are chosen next, with a character's class being the most important selection made during character creation as it defines the majority of the character's abilities. Skills, training in certain broad subjects, and feats, very specific training that grants special abilities, round out the character and define what a specific character is good at.

*Pathfinder*, being derived from the OGL, has the archetypical fantasy races available for characters: humans, elves, dwarves, gnomes, half-elves, half-orcs, and halflings. The classes are taken from the OGL as well and include: barbarian; bard; cleric (warrior-priest); druid (nature protector, shapeshifter, and ecological mystic all in one); fighter; monk (martial artist); paladin (holy warrior); ranger (wilderness adventurer); rogue (thief and rascal); wizard (gains arcane power from study); and sorcerer (gains arcane power from a particular bloodline). These classes have undergone significant revision, as the designers of *Pathfinder* felt that the classes did not provide enough options to facilitate interesting play at all levels. The classes, in general, get more options and uses of their abilities than an equivalent character in *D&D 3.5*. Also certain class abilities underwent radical changes; for example, basic clerics cannot turn undead but can channel divine energy in certain ways depending on which feats are chosen. *Pathfinder* also expands the number of feats available to characters, as well as the rate at which characters attain them.

The core resolution system for *Pathfinder* is the same as all recent editions of *D&D*; a d20 is rolled, modifiers are added, and the result is compared against a target number. Like its predecessor, this game requires a map and miniatures to play, as there is a heavy emphasis on positioning during combat. *Pathfinder* incorporates two new traits that assist in making combat a bit less complicated. Combat Maneuver Bonus and Defense scores eliminate the need for multiple consecutive rolls in determining the success of a special attack in battle. Unfortunately, being derived from *D&D 3.5*, *Pathfinder* suffers from some of the same design flaws, specifically that the spells of wizards and other spell casters have a damage value that is dependent on the level of the character, while the fighter, or other weapon-using class, has a fixed damage value. This leads to the obsolescence of melee-based characters around tenth level, or one third of the way through a character's progression.

### Setting

There is no explicit setting provided in the *Pathfinder* core rules. There is, however, an officially supported world, Golarion, that is the setting of numerous supplements and adventures and should appeal to most fans of high fantasy. The advantage to the wide variety of cultures in this setting is that groups should have little challenge finding one, or more, that suit their preferences.

Paizo produces series of linked adventures, called Adventure Paths. These are six-part adventures that form long story arcs and are set in different parts of Golarion. Beyond these adventures, Paizo also produces a living campaign, called the Pathfinder Society. In this campaign, players can use their characters at any game that is a sanctioned Pathfinder Society event. These events can vary from home games to worldwide conventions like Gen Con. To keep the game experience equitable to all players, Paizo publishes the adventures that can be run for the Pathfinder Society.

### Evaluation

Complexity: 3; while the basic core mechanic is easy to learn, *Pathfinder* greatly rewards system mastery, which can take considerable time.

Popularity: 5; *Pathfinder* gaming groups exist just about anywhere.

Support: 5

Completeness: 3; while the core rulebook contains all the core rules, a group will likely need to have at least one of the bestiaries to create adventures.

Versatility: 3; *Pathfinder* exemplifies the very popular type of high fantasy that many gamers find familiar, and the rules could be adapted to other fantasy subgenres.

Emulation: 4; *Pathfinder* captures the high-fantasy feel it strives for.

### Comments

The *Pathfinder* core rulebook contains everything a group would need to get started playing. GMs would benefit from the *Bestiary*, as it provides stats for many of the monsters the characters will encounter. The *GameMastery*

*Guide* provides guidance to dungeon masters on running the game. Recently, Paizo produced a *Pathfinder Roleplaying Game Beginner Box*, designed to be a simplified introduction to the game that includes everything a group would need to begin play.

Cost: $49.99 hardcover; $34.99 beginner box; $9.99 PDF

## *Primetime Adventures: A Game of Television Drama, Second Edition*

Matt Wilson

Dog-Eared Designs, 2006

http://www.dog-eared-designs.com (Note: The website seems to be rather out of date, is missing links, and advertises a third edition of *Primetime Adventures* that, as far as we know, never saw print. We've provided an alternate link under "Cost" below if you desire to purchase the PDF.)

Genre Tags: Diceless, Multigenre, Television

Dice: This game uses a standard deck of playing cards instead of dice.

### Introduction

*Primetime Adventures* analyzes the structure of engrossing television shows and examines what makes these serial entertainments work, then turns that examination into a brilliant story game that will capture the emotional involvement of your players.

### System and Characters

Like many games, *Primetime Adventures* uses its own jargon to describe the game's elements and participants, but since its terms are evocative of television entertainment, we'll cover them briefly. The GM is called the Producer, and the player characters are Protagonists. Each session of play is considered an episode of your television show/game and is broken down into scenes. Story arcs track the personal issues of a character over the course of a season of episodes.

Once the players have decided on a concept and setting, they develop Protagonists that work within that setting. Players determine the story arcs for their characters by deciding on which personal issues each character grapples with. Groups determine the length of a season (how many episodes/sessions they will run), and each character has an amount of star power in a given episode that determines which character's issues get the most focus. The characters' star power gets distributed equitably over the course of a season, so everyone has moments as background or center-stage characters, and this structure helps Producers plan for future sessions.

Players decide on particular Traits that define their characters, which could range from the mundane (Retired Cop) to the superhuman. Traits act as shorthand to all the knowledge, skills, background, obligations, knowledge, connections, and abilities of the characters. Players also choose Connections for their Protagonists, NPCs that serve as permanent supporting cast for the show. To round out the characters, players choose Personal Sets for their characters (someplace in the setting connected to the character) and an optional Nemesis, if appropriate. A Nemesis doesn't need to be a supervillain, mind you; it could simply be a romantic rival for a character's affections.

Finally, Protagonists have Fan Mail, a metagame currency that fuels the game's system economy. Over the course of the game, players earn fan mail from one another for their role-playing and character portrayals.

In an episode, players, including the Producer, take turns creating scenes for their characters based on the meaningful dramatic actions they want their characters to take; players must declare the scene's focus, agenda, and location. Good scenes require conflict, and players talk through the situation and determine which characters are involved and the stakes of the conflict—something fundamental that matters to the Protagonists involved. The Producer spends up to five points from a budget determined by how many characters are in an episode and their star power; each point purchases the Producer a card. Protagonists in the scene get a number of cards equal to their star power, and may gain more by spending any Traits appropriate to the scene and Fan Mail. When all players have their cards, they reveal them, and the player with the most red cards (hearts and diamonds) wins the conflict and narrates the result of the scene, taking into account the stakes.

We know that's quite a lengthy description of *Primetime Adventure*'s system, but its unique resolution mechanics demand a lengthier explanation. As you can see, the emphasis of the game is on conflicts, and while these might be fistfights or laser battles, they could just as easily be attempts to win another's heart or gain social status. Over time, the Protagonists may become defined by the conflicts they win or lose, and thus they will change over the course of a season, possibly growing or becoming destroyed by their issues. In any event, sessions are likely going to be exciting and involving!

## Setting

*Primetime Adventures* spends a considerable number of pages describing what makes great television work, then goes on to develop a number of sample television shows to serve as examples for gaming groups.

*Primetime Adventures* encourages players to collectively come up with the concept, premise, and tone of their setting, so that all the players, including the Producer, explicitly buy in to the game. This process is one method of making the social contract of the game more explicit, and helps ensure that all the players get an opportunity to declare what they want from the game.

Even better, given the way *Primetime Adventures* works, players may desire to go beyond the more traditionally gameable genres into areas they may not have considered, like soap operas, strictly historical fiction, and more! Rest assured, though: *Primetime Adventures* can handle action, adventure, fantasy, science fiction, horror, and all the other genres you love as well!

## Evaluation

Complexity: 3
Popularity: 1
Support: 1
Completeness: 5
Versatility: 5
Emulation: 5

## Comments

Any player who has ever become engrossed in a favorite show can now make that experience happen at the table with *Primetime Adventures*. This game will help your players bring their A-game to the table. One word of caution: smaller groups might work better with this game, at least until the Producer learns to juggle all the steps and mechanics involved.

Cost: $12 PDF; interested parties can purchase this game at the Indie Press Revolution website, http://www.indiepressrevolution.com/xcart/home.php

## *The Prince's Kingdom*

Clinton R. Nixon
CRN Games, 2006
http://crngames.com
Genre Tags: Fantasy, Younger Gamers
Dice: d4, d6, d8

## Introduction

*The Prince's Kingdom* is a game in which the characters are children of a king; they travel about the kingdom solving various problems. This game focuses on discovery, exploration, and adventure and is heavily geared toward play by children. This game has a strong moral component to it that is not typically found in most RPGs.

## System and Characters

Characters in *The Prince's Kingdom* are created using a narrative framework with numerical values added at the end. Characters are chiefly defined by their age. The age of a prince determines the number of qualities that the prince may have, which are divided into strong and troublesome. Qualities grant the character bonuses to perform certain actions and can range from the mundane to the magical. They also help set the tone of the game, giving the GM an idea as to what kinds of stories the players would like to encounter. Relationships are also very important in this game and, like qualities, are divided into strong and troublesome. The last major defining feature of a character is the equipment it carries.

The base system of *The Prince's Kingdom* uses pools of three different types of dice: d4, d6, and d8. The number of dice rolled is determined by the age of the prince and any applicable relationships or equipment. Unlike typical dice pool systems, this game uses the dice values in a bidding match to determine which side succeeds. Lengthy examples accompany the discussion of rules, giving sufficient guidance to new GMs.

## Setting

The default setting is an archipelago with a distinctly South Asian/Arabian appearance based on the cover art and in-character dialog. This default is easily adjusted by the GM and can be altered to fit any cultural milieu. As one of the main emphases of the game is on exploration, this general level of detail is sufficient.

There is a chapter with advice to help the GM create islands for the characters to encounter, including the types of conflicts that an island could suffer from. These problems are listed in the order in which they are developed on the island from the least serious (conceit) to the most serious (killing). Each type of conflict may be added to an island, creating more complex problems and taking more game time to solve. Another chapter discusses the creation of citizens (NPCs). Each citizen in the game starts out with a brief narrative description. Game stats are added later with the use of proto-citizens, which can be used to stat out individuals and groups.

## Evaluation

Complexity: 2
Popularity: 1
Support: 1
Completeness: 5
Versatility: 3
Emulation: 4

## Comments

Although the game is titled *The Prince's Kingdom*, there is no restriction on the gender of the characters or the type of kingdom. This game's rules and type of play are influenced by the beliefs of the American Friends Service Committee.

Cost: $19.96 softcover; $9.99 PDF

## *Prose Descriptive Qualities (PDQ) Core Rules*

Chad Underkoffler
Atomic Sock Monkey Press, 2004
http://www.atomicsockmonkey.com
Genre Tags: Multigenre
Dice: d6

## Introduction

*PDQ* is a perfect little game engine to use when you have an adventure clearly in mind and need a quick and easy system to run it in.

## System and Characters

Players create characters by assigning them qualities, which can be anything from professions to descriptors of their notable physical, mental, or social traits to talents. Each quality reflects an ability to perform, knowledge about the quality, and social connections linked to the quality; if your character has the quality of "weightlifter," then it reflects your character's strength, perhaps size and endurance, as well as knowledge of how to remain fit, and contacts at the local gym. Qualities have ranks listed from Poor (for negative qualities, or weaknesses) through Average, to Good, Expert, and Master, and each rank has a modifier ranging from –2 to +6, increasing in increments of 2 for each rank. When a particular quality comes into play, players make a check by rolling 2d6 and adding the relevant quality's modifier, then comparing the total to a target number or against an opposed roll.

Players can attempt to gain additional bonuses by describing their characters' actions in very vivid and flavorful detail, corresponding with the setting's tone and genre.

In a conflict situation, the difference between the opposed rolls determines the amount of damage the losing character takes, expressed in temporarily lost ranks of qualities, to be deducted from whichever qualities the losing player chooses. The conflict resolution system can represent physical combat but can also represent duels of wits, exchanges of insults, debates, and other forms of mental and social conflict as well. Thus, the type of "damage" dealt will vary depending on the conflict, ranging from bruises and wounds to loss of face at a social gathering to possibly failing an important negotiation.

## Setting

*PDQ* is a multigenre system that groups can use for a wide variety of games. It is a good "pick-up" system that players can use when they feel like gaming on the spot; so long as the GM has a clear idea of the setting and situation, then players can create characters in minutes and get into the adventure.

## Evaluation

Complexity: 2

Popularity: 2

Support: 2; the core system is free, and there are several games that use *PDQ* ranging from superheroes (*Truth & Justice*) to comedic fantasy (*Questers of the Middle Realms*), sword-and-sorcery (*Jaws of the Six Serpents*) to pirate swashbuckling fantasy (*Swashbucklers of the 7 Skies*).

Completeness: 3; whatever the core game doesn't include, players can create themselves using the base rules.

Versatility: 4

Emulation: 4

## Comments

*PDQ* is a versatile gem of a game with a short learning curve and a lot of playability. Atomic Sock Monkey also offers a free variant, called *PDQ Sharp* (*PDQ#*), which is optimized for swashbuckling play and acts as the core system for *Swashbucklers of the 7 Skies*.

Cost: Free PDF from the publisher's website

## *Psi\*Run*

Meguey Baker
Night Sky Games, 2011
http://www.nightskygames.com
Genre Tags: Science Fiction, Younger Gamers
Dice: d6

### Introduction

In *Psi\*Run*, the player characters are Runners, amnesiac psychics with incredible powers who have just escaped their keepers. While the characters make a run for freedom, they are pursued by Chasers, agents of a shadowy organization, who want to recapture the Runners for unknown, but likely nefarious, reasons.

### System and Characters

Since the Runners have amnesia, players only assert a few facts about their characters when they start playing, including the characters' names, their powers, and what the characters look like. Players then write down a quick list of four to six questions, like "Why do I have a bus ticket stub in my pocket?" or "Where's Joe? Wait, who's Joe?!" that help to guide play and drive the characters to solve the mystery of their identities and the agenda of the mysterious Chasers. Like the Runners, the Chasers, played by the GM, have only a very rudimentary description at first—appearance, methods, and technology—but are fleshed out during play. (The GM has a few additional facts kept secret from the characters.)

Play progresses as the Runners decide what they want to do. During the game, the GM uses index cards or sticky notes to note the characters' trail—where they go immediately after escaping—that the Chasers will follow. When a Runner takes significant actions, the number of dice the player rolls is determined by the nature of the action and the nature of the character's risk, typically four to six dice. Each die is assigned to a particular aspect of the risk (does the action lead the character closer to his or her goal, does the character use his or her power, is the character risking being harmed?). The results of each die are then compared to a chart, called the Risk sheet, which determines the result of each action.

As play progresses, the rules determine whether a player or GM has "first say" in what occurs, but the rules also emphasize that the whole group should feel free to contribute its energy and ideas to each scene to make play that much better. Likely, the players will want to follow the rules of improvisation, including going with the flow, not shutting others down, and using phrases like "Yes, and . . ." or "Yes, but . . ." to keep the game moving. Ultimately, the game ends when one of the players' character sheets has all the questions answered.

## Setting

The setting is a very general, undefined modern or near-modern time and place; as the PCs have amnesia, they may have to discover where they are. However, players and GMs will likely flesh out the setting as play progresses.

## Evaluation

Complexity: 2
Popularity: 1
Support: 1
Completeness: 4; beyond the dice, the game does need tokens and sticky notes or index cards, but most households will have these items handy.
Versatility: 2; the game could be adapted to other kinds of "on the run" stories.
Emulation: 5; *Psi\*Run* perfectly emulates "people with powers who are on the run" kinds of stories.

## Comments

*Psi\*Run* is a fantastic little story game that is intended for about five hours of play, either in one session or broken up over two to three sessions. Teens are likely already familiar with this kind of story and will enjoy getting to exercise their full creativity to affect their own and the other players' fates. This game is also an excellent opportunity to introduce, recommend, or reinforce the love of books like James Patterson's *Maximum Ride* series, the novel *Jumper* by Steven Gould (or the film by the same title), and *X-Men* comics, graphic novels, and films.

Cost: $23 softcover + PDF if shipped in the U.S.; $25 softcover + PDF if shipped elsewhere; $10 PDF

## *Qin: The Warring States*

Neko et al. (English translation by Marcus M. Birch)
Le 7ème Cercle, 2005
http://www.7emecercle.com/website/
Cubicle 7 Entertainment has the license to translate and distribute
*Qin: The Warring States* in the U.S.
http://www.cubicle7.co.uk/
Genre: Alternate History, Asian, Fantasy, Historical, *Wuxia* (Chinese
martial arts/fantasy)
Dice: d10

### Introduction

*Qin: The Warring States* allows players to place themselves in the *wuxia* genre, where the martial artists and knights errant of Chinese film and literature soar across the landscape, experience epic and tragic love affairs, and defend the helpless in a never-ending battle against corruption. Fans of films like *Crouching Tiger, Hidden Dragon*; *Hero*; *House of Flying Daggers*; and *Red Cliff* will love this game!

### System

The system uses a "yin-yang" d10-d10 dice mechanic using two differently colored dice; corresponding with the Chinese symbol, the yin die is black, and the yang die is white. When players roll the dice, whichever die's number is lower is subtracted from the higher die, and the result is added to a character's relevant traits, ability score, and skill. Players compare the total to a difficulty number or an opposed roll to determine the success of a character's actions.

Ability scores, called Aspects, are patterned off the traditional Chinese elements, and each governs a different domain: Fire governs personality and charisma; Water denotes physical health and agility; Metal covers martial actions; Wood reflects the reason and intellect; and Earth handles actions of a mystical nature.

Each character also chooses from a selection of skills, weapon proficiencies, and most importantly the Taos, here meaning special abilities of sorcery, divination, or mystic martial disciplines.

### Characters

*Qin* does a remarkable job of guiding new players through its setting (see below) and character creation. The core rulebook gives a wide and varied list of potential adventuring professions found in Chinese history and lore, from exorcists and diviners, to thieves and spies, to bandits and chivalrous martial artists, and more. Each character type gives a list of skills important to that profession, and suggestions of that type's role in Chinese society.

## Setting

As the title of the game suggests, *Qin*'s setting is the Warring States period of China, when the Qin Empire is poised to conquer all of its fellow states and unify China under one rule. This history, however, is viewed through the lens of Chinese myth, folklore, and mysticism. The authors do an amazing job of covering the history of China from the time of its creation and the First Sovereign Emperor through the time in which the characters live, naming the relevant gods, demons, and dynasties as they go.

In fact, to ease players' transition into the setting, as well as to set the scene for prospective GMs, the authors spend about two-thirds of the book covering the history and culture of Warring States China. They handle just about every relevant topic, including what life is like in each of the states (along with the important historical figures), religion, morality, family life, food, work, the arts, settlements and dwellings, the calendar and seasons, the reigning philosophical schools of thought, and more. In short, the authors excel at immersing players and GMs in the history and culture of Warring States China, and then give them a huge setting to play and adventure in. To cap it all off, the game has a very nice initial adventure that puts the cultural context into practice, along with a trade city for players to explore and interact with.

## Evaluation

Complexity: 2
Popularity: 2
Support: 2/3; decent support is available in the native French, the game's original language, but less support is available in English.)
Completeness: 4
Versatility: 2
Emulation: 5

## Comments

Games this accomplished are rare, and the creators should be lauded and applauded for their work. Not only do they use a very simple system that players and GMs can easily grasp, but they also make every effort to ease their audience into what might otherwise be an intimidating and alien setting and help readers and gamers feel completely at home. The color art depicting the adventuring professions is stunningly beautiful, and the black-and-white line art ably depicts the details of the setting. While *wuxia* literature isn't easy to find in the English language, we recommend using this game in conjunction with movie nights featuring any of the films mentioned in the introduction above to get players in the mood. If your gamers are interested in the *wuxia* genre, then *Qin* is the game you need.

Cost: $44.95 hardcover + PDF; $24.99 PDF

## *Reign: A Game of Lords and Leaders*

Greg Stolze
Schrodinger's Cat Press, 2007
http://www.gregstolze.com/reign/
Genre Tags: Fantasy
Dice: d10

### Introduction

*Reign* is a game that shifts the focus from the actions of individual characters to a broader stage. This system lets a group control organizations of varying sizes, from mercenary companies to entire nations. An interesting variation of the dice pool mechanic allows conflicts to be resolved in a single die roll.

### System and Characters

Characters in *Reign* are defined by six attributes and thirty-four skills that are divided among the attributes. Players can create characters using either a point-buy system or by rolling 11d10 and using random tables to generate scores and backgrounds. In addition to individual characters, *Reign* has rules for creating Companies, which are groups defined by a common goal. Companies can be nations, religious organizations, trading companies, mercenaries, or any other type of group the players can think of.

*Reign* uses the One Roll Engine (ORE) system, with a dice pool of d10s as its core mechanic. Unlike other games, which may use multiple rolls to determine turn order, combat, defense, and damage, ORE keeps resolution to one roll per participant. A player assembles a character's dice pool by totaling the scores in a character's skill and attribute. The dice are rolled, and the results are generated by looking for sets within the pool, such as pairs, three of a kind, four of a kind, etc. The number of dice in a set, or the width, grants certain benefits as does the value of the set, or the height. Generally a wide set goes before a narrow set, and a high set is more effective than a low set. The dice are only rolled for tasks where the result is in doubt (or contested) and has some bearing on the story.

## Setting

*Reign*, as written, has a broadly described fantasy setting. This is not the typical pseudo-European or Tolkien-inspired setting that many other fantasy RPGs use. It consists of two continents, Heluso and Milonda, shaped like a man and woman lying on their sides in a partial embrace. The sun and moon are two stationary, lantern-like objects that increase and decrease in brightness to mark the day.

This unique setting lends itself to the different cultures discussed in the book. The cultures are depicted fairly broadly and follow general types: the rigid decedent Empire, the militant Dindavarans, the hard scrabble Truils, and the meritocracy of Uldholm. Each culture has a chapter in the book describing its values, culture, and political situation, with enough detail to allow players to feel comfortable but granting groups room to add details during play. The entire setting upends some of the more common assumptions ingrained in fantasy settings. For example, characters in the setting believe that riding astride a horse renders a man impotent, so all cavalry are either women or eunuchs. Also the material culture and physical appearance of the people have interesting reversals of certain racial assumptions.

## Evaluation

Complexity: 3; the width and height mechanic has a learning curve to it.

Popularity: 2

Support: 3; Greg Stolze's website has numerous free PDF supplements for *Reign*.

Completeness: 5

Versatility: 3; the ORE system is used in conjunction with several genres and games, but *Reign* is tied to a specific setting. The *Enchiridion,* mentioned below, is much more generic.

Emulation: 3

## Comments

*Reign* is available in two forms. The first is the *Reign* rulebook, described above, and the second is *Reign Enchiridion*, which contains all the rules from the core book but none of the setting. *Enchiridion* also has rules for creating new esoteric and martial disciplines.

Cost: *Reign* $37 softcover; $19 PDF; *Reign Enchiridion* $9.99 PDF

## *Risus: The Anything RPG (Version 2.01)*

S. John Ross
Cumberland Games and Diversions, 2013 [1993]
http://www222.pair.com/sjohn/cumberland.htm
http://www222.pair.com/sjohn/risus.htm
Genre: Multigenre
Dice: d6

### Introduction

*Risus* (which means "laughter" in Latin) is a free, fast-playing, easy-to-learn RPG. It's perfect for new GMs and players, and groups can learn the rules—which are only four pages long—and begin playing in minutes.

### System and Characters

*Risus* is a roll-high system that uses a handful of six-sided dice to resolve the actions of characters. Results are judged against an opposed roll by an antagonist, or a target number set by the GM.

Introductory characters are constructed with four "clichés," aspects that define the character, such as "Bold Northern Barbarian" or "Smooth-talking Con Artist." Clichés can be just about anything, relating to the character's species, profession, powers and abilities, talents—anything that defines who the character is or what the character does. Each of these clichés is assigned a number of six-sided dice, the best getting 4d6, the next best getting 3d6, etc. Characters have whatever gear, equipment, and abilities the clichés suggest. If a situation comes up in the game where a particular cliché is useful, then a player rolls the number of dice associated with that cliché.

### Setting

*Risus* doesn't come with a setting. Living up to its name as "The Anything RPG," it can emulate a number of genres fairly well, from fantasy to science fiction, horror to superheroes, and even comedy and romance. However, the GM will have to do a bit of work beforehand by deciding on the genre, setting specifics, and coming up with an adventure. That said, there are some solo adventures on the publisher's website for prospective GMs to run through themselves and get a feel for how to construct RPG adventures for their players. In addition, since *Risus* is so adaptable, GMs and players can use existing IPs that they are already familiar with—television shows, movies, books—and run adventures using those characters and story lines.

## Evaluation

Complexity: 1; *Risus* is just about the easiest RPG to learn that we've ever come across.

Popularity: 3; *Risus* has a loyal fan base that is active in providing and sharing new content for groups to use.

Support: 3; *Risus* has a host of free support on the Internet, from material written by S. John Ross to adventures and supplements written by other fans.

Completeness: 3; *Risus* is fairly complete in its four pages—a remarkable achievement for an RPG.

Versatility: 4; *Risus* can, and has been used to, play just about anything you can imagine.

Emulation: 3; Because *Risus* uses so sparse a system to achieve its goals, its ability to emulate a given genre is largely dependent on the GM and players to immerse themselves in the game.

## Comments

*Risus* is an excellent tool for introducing new players of any age to RPGs. In addition, because it is so adaptable, it can easily tie in with other programming going on at your library. For example, a group that has just finished a book discussion or movie night might want to use *Risus* to further explore the setting, even using the same characters from the story or film. And if your patrons enjoy this game—and we think that they will—then you should definitely consider purchasing the *Risus Companion* from the publisher. The *Risus Companion* is a fantastic expansion that opens up this simple game system to a whole host of possibilities, has great GMing advice, and even includes a "Big List of RPG Plots!"

*Risus* has been translated into a number of languages and was voted Best Free RPG in the 2001 RPGnet Awards.

Cost: Free PDF. *Risus* can be downloaded for free at http://www222.pair .com/sjohn/risus.htm

## *Savage Worlds Deluxe Explorer's Edition*

Shane Lacy Hensley
Pinnacle Entertainment Group, 2012
http://www.peginc.com
Genre Tags: Multigenre
Dice: d4, d6, d8, d10, d12, occasionally d20

## Introduction

*Savage Worlds* is a solid multigenre game engine that is perfect for high action and high adventure genres and settings; or, as the publisher likes to say, *Savage Worlds* is "Fast! Furious! Fun!"

## System and Characters

*Savage Worlds* characters have five primary attributes: Agility, Smarts, Strength, Spirit, and Vigor. Attribute ratings use die types (e.g., Strength d8), and the higher the die type, the better the trait (so a d10 is better than a d8). Skills are also rated by die type. Most characters get a free advantage, called an Edge, at character creation; Edges allow characters to break or ignore certain rules in *Savage Worlds*, or gain extra abilities and benefits, like the ability to cast spells or use psionics. Players may give their characters Hindrances, disadvantages like Overconfident or Clueless, and gain points for additional Edges or other benefits.

When performing tests, players roll a trait die and a wild die against a target number or, less often, an opposed roll; players use the best result on either the trait die or wild die. Rolls in *Savage Worlds* are open-ended, and all of the dice explode for both trait rolls and damage rolls, which can lead to some fantastic successes! For every increment of 4 a player rolls above the target number, the player gains a "raise" to the roll that can translate into even greater degrees of success.

*Savage Worlds* also makes use of a metagame currency called bennies. Players may spend bennies to reroll failed tests, or make tests to soak damage from opponents, turning potentially dire wounds into forgettable scrapes and bruises. GMs may award players with bennies in-game for excellent role-playing.

As *Savage Worlds* campaigns progress, characters gain experience that they use to gain levels. When characters attain a new level, the players can choose to increase attributes and skills, gain additional Edges, or even gain new spells and powers, depending on the game's genre and setting.

The core book has additional rules for creating your own alien/fantasy species, vehicle chases, and combat; handling mass battles between armies; and using powers in your game, whether they're defined as magic, psionics, mutations, or simply weird science devices. The book also has a bestiary of monsters and antagonists, and five sample adventures that GMs can use to challenge their players.

Perhaps best of all, because *Savage Worlds* is designed to handle games in a variety of different genres, the rulebook has a very helpful GM advice section on how to modify the game rules for different settings, and how to adapt existing settings and IPs to the *Savage Worlds* system.

## Setting

The *Savage Worlds* core rulebook is a multigenre game that GMs and players can adapt to nearly any setting they can imagine, and they can use the tools of the game to make that setting playable and bring it to the table. That said, Pinnacle Entertainment Group has a large number of setting rulebooks that cover a wide variety of genres and genre mash-ups, and these will likely scratch just about any adventuring itch no matter how strange. Thanks to Pinnacle's licensing agreement, many third-party publishers use *Savage Worlds* as the system for their games.

Here are just some of the game settings available for *Savage Worlds*:

*Deadlands: Reloaded*: The Civil War is over, and an even more sinister, secret war has begun. When the Native Americans performed their Ghost Dance to oppose the white invaders, horrors returned to the world, and history was changed forever. Now, the Union in the North squares off against an equally strong Confederate South that won its independence, California fractures into a variety of waterways, and everyone is heading West to find Ghost Rock, that strange substance that mad scientists use to power their infernal contraptions. Worst of all, horror is slowly spreading across the land, and those areas entirely given over to fear become Deadlands, patches of Hell on Earth. Players can take the roles of gunslingers, magic-using hucksters, mad scientists, Native warriors and shamans, holy-rolling miracle-making Blessed, and other characters who know that the real danger is far worse than any human conflict. Civil War buffs, Western fans, and horror aficionados will all be ready to enjoy this game. You can pair this setting with books like *Gone to Texas* by Forrest Carter, *Killer Angels* by Michael Shaara, and the Weird Western novels of Joe R. Lansdale.

*50 Fathoms*: A trio of vengeful witches cursed the land of Caribdus, drowning it under fifty fathoms of water. Your heroes, either natives of Caribdus or drawn from Earth's own Age of Sail, must lift the curse and save the world! If your teens are huge fans of the *Pirates of the Caribbean* films, then this is the setting you need! Players can be humans, or one of several strange races like the giant crab-like Scurillians, walrus-like Grael, dolphin-like Doreen, or shark-like Kehana.

*Necessary Evil*: The superheroes are gone, wiped out by a massive alien invasion. Now there's no one left to oppose the alien overlords . . . except the supervillains! Are you going to let these aliens take your place as rightful ruler of the planet? Take on the role of superpowered bad guys and show the alien invaders what a menace you really are! Like the tagline says, "The fate of the world lies with the scum of the Earth!" If your players enjoy superhero comics, then they will absolutely love this setting!

*Rippers*: Victorian England is a setting filled with elegance, learning, beauty . . . and terror! Mad scientists create patchwork monsters in old forgotten keeps, vampires rule the night, warlocks and witches assemble in secret covens, and werewolves howl deep in the forests. Who will save civilization from these fearsome foes? You and your heroic band of monster hunters, that's who! With the advent of Ripper technology, you can even steal the creatures' powers and, using strange alchemical techniques, graft their special abilities into your own body! But beware, lest you become more horror than human! Players interested in gothic horror will eat this setting up, and you can recommend novels like *Frankenstein*, *Dracula*, *The Invisible Man*, and *The Strange Case of Dr. Jekyll and Mr. Hyde*.

In a last note about *Savage Worlds* settings, many are built around the "Plot Point" concept (https://www.peginc.com/savage-worlds-plot-points/). Essentially, Plot Point campaigns have a string of adventures for players to follow that provide an epic campaign, but they are also designed to act as sandbox settings that the characters can simply wander and explore, allowing for both plot-directed and player-directed styles of games.

**Evaluation**

Complexity: 2/3; the basics of the game are very easy to grasp, but the nuances of the powers and combat may take time to master.

Popularity: 4; There is a wide network of *Savage Worlds* players.

Support: 5; Between Pinnacle Entertainment Group and third-party publishers, groups will have no problem finding material to suit them.

Completeness: 2; in addition to dice, the game is designed to use miniatures, tokens, and playing cards, at the least. (Of course, you could just raid game components from board games that you already own.) Players and GMs may also want to get the various genre-specific books, the *Savage Worlds Fantasy Companion*, *Savage Worlds Science Fiction Companion*, and *Savage Worlds Super Powers Companion, Second Edition*.

Versatility: 4; if you want a game with furious action for any genre you can think of, then *Savage Worlds* delivers.

Emulation: 4; *Savage Worlds* is easily adaptable to a variety of settings and can do most of them very well.

## Comments

We've already commented on the variety of settings and potential crossovers with books and films above. Beyond that, we would like to point out the fantastic price-point of the *Savage Worlds Deluxe Explorer's Edition* rulebook: ten bucks. Ten dollars for a full-color, digest-sized, almost two-hundred-page rulebook that can handle nearly anything you ask it to do? Can we say: "Best value for your buying dollar?"

Cost: $9.99 softcover; $9.99 PDF

## *Seven Leagues: A Fantasy Roleplaying Game of Faerie*

Hieronymous
Malcontent Games, 2005
http://malcontentgames.com
Genre Tags: Fairy Tales, Fantasy
Dice: d12

## Introduction

*Seven Leagues* is a game that seeks to emulate the wonder, beauty, adventure, and even horror of fairy tales, myths, legends, and folklore.

## System and Characters

PCs, called protagonists in *Seven Leagues*, consist of seven components. The first is an Aspect, a few words that define your character, like "proud dragon-slayer" or "lucky good-natured fool." A protagonist's Virtues are the character traits of Head (the character's mental attributes like intellect and perception), Heart (the character's emotional and spiritual attributes like courage and empathy), and Hand (the character's physical attributes), all of which have a rating of 1 to 7. Players then choose Charms (some form of supernatural gift) and Taboos (supernatural hindrances) for their characters. Characters also have Fortune, in the form of Luck (bonuses) or Curses (penalties) that they accrue through adventuring. Finally, players will write Legends for their characters, short passages regarding their histories and abilities (determining, for example, if that high Hand score relates to the swiftness of a child of the wind, or the brute strength and vitality of an ogre), and give their characters Names.

*Seven Leagues* uses the Roll 13 system; essentially, a player rolls a d12, then adds an appropriate Virtue score and any modifiers to determine success. When two or more characters are in conflict, then the GM and players determine success through a series of steps: players vie for a Courage roll (a Heart check) to determine who gets to narrate the conflict first; they define conditions of victory for their characters; they embellish and vividly narrate their characters' actions, and each embellishment can earn positive or negative modifiers for the characters; and then, finally, players and GM make opposed checks, with the highest result determining victory.

*Seven Leagues* further details various antagonists and hazards that protagonists might encounter, and gives GMs good advice on how to adjudicate conflicts, depending on the various ideas and narrating skills that players bring to bear.

### Setting

While *Seven Leagues* explicitly brands itself as a game of Faerie, this description also includes heroic legends and sagas, myths of gods and goddesses, and even urban fantasy tales like those of Charles de Lint, Neil Gaiman's *American Gods* novel and *Sandman* series of comics, and television shows like *Beauty and the Beast* (both the series from the 1980s and the current series that began in 2012).

*Seven Leagues* does have a wonderful chapter detailing a variety of fantastical realms for players to adventure in and the significant allies and antagonists that make their homes in these provinces. The book ends with three different adventures in the domains of Faerie that GMs can run for their players.

### Evaluation

Complexity: 2/3; while the dice mechanic is simple, GMs and players with better storytelling skills will find the system easier to manipulate than less loquacious players.
Popularity: 2
Support: 1
Completeness: 5
Versatility: 3; this system can handle a variety of stories beyond traditional fairy tales.
Emulation: 5

### Comments

*Seven Leagues* is an excellent game that will interest fans of fairy tales, folklore, and myths, as well as readers of urban fantasy. In addition to the authors mentioned above, hand these players fairy tales by the Brothers

Grimm and Hans Christian Andersen, *Bullfinch's Mythology*, and Edith Hamilton's *Mythology*. Since *Seven Leagues* is highly adaptable to tales from nearly any culture, the librarian has an opportunity to introduce stories from around the world into his or her games. For adventure inspiration and read-alikes, look to the books in the Pantheon Fairy Tale and Folklore Library (http://www.surlalunefairytales.com/boardarchives/2003/oct2003/pantheonfairytales.html). In fact, given the nature of *Seven Leagues*, you could likely use it to run games set in Oz, Narnia, and similar settings.

Also, the writer uses a lot of lovely public domain artwork to illustrate his RPG, but only the PDF version is in color.

Cost: $21.95 softcover; $13 PDF

## Spears of the Dawn

Kevin Crawford
Sine Nomine Publishing, 2013
http://www.sinenomine-pub.com
Genre Tags: African, Fantasy, OSR
Dice: d4, d6, d8, d10, d12, d20, d%/d100

### Introduction

*Spears of the Dawn* is a pastiche of mythic Africa, where the characters are the eponymous Spears of the Dawn, tasked to combat the evil remnants of a prolonged war with a supernatural evil.

### System and Characters

Character creation in *Spears* follows the same model as most other Old School Renaissance (OSR) games (i.e., a class and level system). The character's attributes are randomly generated and provide a bonus to the various die rolls in the game. Before picking a class, players need to choose a concept and origin. The concept is a general idea of the character, the why and how he or she became a Spear of the Dawn. The character's origin provides a list of skills that the character has a familiarity with. *Spears* offers a wide array of origins divided among five nationalities. Each nation gets a brief description along with a list of specific origins that range from peasants to merchants to warriors to nobles. Fortunately, these origins do not force a player into choosing a specific class. The classes follow familiar classic archetypes that have appeared in fantasy games for decades: Griot (bard), Marabout (cleric), Nganga (magic user), and Warrior.

The basic system for *Spears* uses a d20 roll, with bonuses or penalties from modifiers, against a target number. Skill checks use 2d6 against a target number, with appropriate bonuses and penalties applied. Characters might also make saving throws to avoid various magical and environmental effects. A useful inclusion is a section on converting *Spears* from its core system, based on *Stars without Number*, to other systems. Many of the OSR games share the same antecedents, so translating to different systems is fairly straightforward. The spell lists for the magic-using classes are fairly short, harking back to older games. This is a good design choice as GMs and players can add new spells as desired, and new players are not overwhelmed with long spell lists.

## Setting

The Five Kingdoms are currently recovering from a long war against Deshur, a kingdom ruled by evil immortal kings. After the defeat of Deshur, the Five Kingdoms had no common enemy to unify them and have reverted back to a tenuous peace with numerous border wars and skirmishes. These struggles have left some areas uncontrolled by any of the nations and have allowed the Eternal, the immortal kings of Deshur, to begin rebuilding their strength and influence throughout the Kingdoms. Spears of the Dawn must navigate this fractious political situation as they assume the task of fighting against the evils of the Eternals.

The setting chapter includes discussions of various aspects of society in the Five Kingdoms. Each section is fairly short, making it easily digestible and open enough for groups to add details as wanted. Players can find a brief write-up on the individual Kingdoms in the character creation section under Origins, and a longer treatment on each of them later in the book. *Spears* also details the religion of the Five Nations, including write-ups on the various gods in the setting. True to its pastiche origins, the pantheon of gods is an amalgamation of several different African pantheons.

There is a large section on GM advice, including several series of tables for random adventure creation, allowing even novice groups to begin adventuring fairly quickly. Rounding out the GM advice chapter is a bestiary with a good mix of familiar and pastiche-Africa-specific monsters.

## Evaluation

Complexity: 2
Popularity: 1
Support: 1
Completeness: 5
Versatility: 3
Emulation: 4

**Comments**

This game is a breath of fresh air in the fairly uniform pseudo-European OSR landscape. As with most fantasy RPGs, this game does not seek to emulate any specific culture or time period. With the reviving popularity of the Sword and Soul fantasy subgenre (sword and sorcery fiction set in Africa), this game gives GMs a ready-made setting, able to incorporate most of the literature available.

Librarians should be ready with books by Charles Saunders to hand interested readers, and they may consider anthologies like *Griots: A Sword and Soul Anthology* and *Steamfunk*. For another take, keep an eye out for *Ki-Khanga: The Sword and Soul Role-Playing Game*, currently in development by author Balogun Ojetade.

Cost: $39.99 hardcover + PDF; $29.99 softcover + PDF; $9.99 PDF

## *Star Wars: Edge of the Empire Beginner Game* and *Star Wars: Edge of the Empire Roleplaying Game Core Rulebook*

Jay Little et al.
Fantasy Flight Games; Beginner Game, 2012; Core Rulebook 2013
http://www.fantasyflightgames.com
Genre Tags: Science Fiction, Space Opera
Dice: Special proprietary dice (see below)

**Introduction**

It's dangerous to underestimate the power of the Dark Side . . . and it's just as difficult to overestimate the popularity of the *Star Wars* franchise. Fantasy Flight Games is the third publisher to gain the *Star Wars* license and release a tabletop RPG based on George Lucas's famous films, and it's likely that this game will find a welcoming audience among fans.

For clarity's sake, the *Star Wars: Edge of the Empire Beginner Game* is a boxed set with abbreviated rules that is geared toward introducing new players to the game. It comes with an adventure book, a rulebook, a set of the special *Star Wars* proprietary dice, pre-generated characters, a map, and cardboard character tokens to visually represent characters on the map.

The *Star Wars: Edge of the Empire Roleplaying Game Core Rulebook* is a rather large tome, more than four hundred pages in length, with the complete rules, but is a stand-alone product—libraries (and/or players) will have to purchase the special proprietary dice separately.

## System and Characters

*Star Wars: Edge of the Empire* (*EoE*) takes as its starting point the period just after the Rebel Alliance destroys the Death Star in *Star Wars: A New Hope*. The main characters in this game are scoundrels and rogues living on the fringes of the Empire's control, trying to make their way through a galaxy in turmoil.

Characters have six characteristics (Agility, Brawn, Cunning, Intellect, Presence, and Willpower). Players choose a species (human, droid, or one of the various alien species), career, and specialization; thus, *EoE* does have a class system component, if not a level system. Careers are the characters' professions, and include options like Bounty Hunter, Colonist, Explorer, and Technician, among others. Each career has a few specializations that determine the character's core skills and which Talent Tree the character will use to advance in experience; talents act like advantages or feats in other games, and give the character special abilities specific to his or her career and specialization.

Characters also have an Obligation (like a duty to a particular person or organization, or a bounty on their heads) that ties them to the setting and makes life interesting, and a Motivation, that serves as a reason to be out adventuring among the hyperspace lanes and a guide to the characters' behavior.

*EoE* has special dice specifically for use with this game, and the dice are used differently than in other games. Each type of die has a given number of sides, its own color to distinguish that type from others, and various symbols on the die that represent success, failure, or some other possibility. Some dice types (Boost dice, Ability dice, and Proficiency dice) represent the positive factors in any given check. Other dice types (including Setback, Difficulty, and Challenge dice) represent the negative factors in any given check. One type of die represents the mysterious Force that affects characters' fates. The player decides the number and type of dice to roll based on characteristic ranks, skill ranks, the difficulty of the task, and any other factors, beneficial or detrimental, that are specific to the situation. Players roll all of these dice together and, depending on which symbols appear and which dice cancel each other out, determine if the character has succeeded or failed, and then narrate the results based on the dice. This unique system leads to some very interesting possibilities. For example, if a character was shooting at some Stormtroopers, then the dice may say that the character failed at the task, but some other beneficial situation comes into play. Thus, the player might narrate that while the character missed the Stormtrooper, he or she did hit some nearby steam pipes that give the group cover for their escape. This narrative dice system is an interesting way of prompting and formalizing players' ability to narrate outcomes for their characters, and while it may take a bit of getting used to, it can lead to a great deal of creativity at the table! Fortunately, *EoE* gives beginning players and GMs advice on interpreting the dice rolls.

The *Core Rulebook* also has excellent equipment and vehicle sections so characters can prepare for their adventures among the stars, although these sections are abridged in the *Beginner Game*. Both the *Beginner Game* and the *Core Rulebook* have introductory adventures; the beginning adventure in the *Beginner Game* is particularly good, as it gets groups playing quickly and walks them through all the basics of playing the game, including the activities common to scenes in *Star Wars*: conflict, combat, negotiation, infiltration, and spaceflight.

## Setting

Any people unfamiliar with the *Star Wars* universe probably aren't going to be reading this book anyway. However, seeing as the *EoE* rules are very specific as to their timeline and style of play, some explanation may be necessary. As mentioned earlier, *EoE* is set just after the destruction of the first Death Star. Player characters are typically scoundrels and mercenaries, the new Hans Solos and Lando Calrissians living at the edge of the Empire's influence, hence the name of the game. This can make for a slightly, or greatly, grimmer and grittier *Star Wars* universe, depending on the gaming group.

The *Core Rulebook* spends a large number of pages detailing various areas of the *Star Wars* galaxy, so players have plenty of places to explore and find adventures, and Imperial law and society, so players know when their characters are in trouble and when it's time to find a new planet to visit. And speaking of trouble, both the *Beginner Game* and the *Core Rulebook* have chapters on adversaries. Adversaries are rated as minions (cannon fodder or minor entities), rivals (more formidable enemies), and nemeses (with abilities equal to or greater than the player characters—possibly campaign-defining antagonists).

The time period of *EoE* also means that the players aren't going to be making Jedi characters. Yes, we can hear the collective groans and gripes of gaming groups everywhere—we made a few similar noises ourselves when we found out. Still, the *Core Rulebook* has rules for playing Force-sensitive characters, and further expansions to the game promise more options.

## Evaluation

Complexity: 3; the narrative dice work very differently from other game systems, and the layers of rules that differentiate and enhance characters, like talents, can increase the game's complexity.

Popularity: 4; shortly after Fantasy Flight Games released *EoE*, the game raced to become a bestseller.

Support: 3; while *EoE* is a relatively new game, Fantasy Flight already has an extensive list of supplements in the works, as well as additional rulebooks to expand the scope of the setting and the types of campaigns (see "Comments").

Completeness: 3; *EoE* is fairly complete in itself, with the exception of Jedi not being fully playable as character types (see "Comments"), but later supplements will certainly expand the gaming options. However, don't forget those proprietary dice!

Versatility: 3; while Fantasy Flight used a version of the narrative dice system with another game (*Warhammer Fantasy Roleplay,* 3rd edition), this is only the second game to use the system—but if it sells well, it probably won't be the last.

Emulation: 4; the narrative dice encourage gamers to be freer and more varied in their descriptions than with many other systems, and that can go a long way to capturing the feel of the *Star Wars* universe.

## Comments

Need we say it? We recommend this book for libraries where *Star Wars* is popular. *EoE* is just the first in (suitably) a trilogy of *Star Wars* RPGs from Fantasy Flight. As of this writing, Fantasy Flight will soon release the next boxed set, the *Star Wars: Age of Rebellion Beginner Game*, and the publisher seems determined to continue producing material for *EoE* as well. Fantasy Flight also has free adventures and pre-generated characters on their website, so be sure to download them.

And lest we forget, while some libraries might consider the proprietary dice to be an issue, interested players can also download a *Star Wars* dice app that will serve just as well, and the app is considerably cheaper than the physical dice sets.

Cost: $29.95 *Star Wars: Edge of the Empire Beginner Game* boxed set; $59.95 *Star Wars: Edge of the Empire Roleplaying Game Core Rulebook* hardcover; $14.99 *Star Wars: Edge of the Empire* dice set; $4.99 *Star Wars: Edge of the Empire* dice application for Android or IOS. (As of this writing, none of the purchasable materials are available in PDF.)

# Stars without Number (free and core editions)

Kevin Crawford
Sine Nomine Publishing, 2010
http://www.sinenomine-pub.com
Genre Tags: OSR, Science Fiction, Space Opera
Dice: d4, d6, d8, d10, d12, d20, d100

## Introduction

*Stars without Number* (*SWN*) is a science fiction game that manages to touch on several subgenres and elegantly ties them all to a single simple set of well-known rules.

## System and Characters

*Stars without Number* takes the time-tested rules of the world's best-known fantasy RPG and reworks them into a system for science fiction adventure. *SWN* is a class and level, roll-high system. *SWN* uses the classic six attributes (Strength, Intelligence, Wisdom, Dexterity, Constitution, and Charisma) with values ranging from 3 to 18, and has three classes: Experts (ranging from technicians to scientists, ambassadors to smugglers), Psychics, and Warriors. Unlike many science fiction games, the character default species is solely human, although players can choose to design robot characters as well. Players choose both background packages and training packages tied to their characters' classes in order to gain skills (typically ranked from 0 to 4), with Experts specializing in having the best noncombat skills, while Psychics possess mental powers, and Warriors are the best combatants. Players then use their characters' funds to purchase gear, including high-tech tools, armor, and weapons.

Combat rolls are a d20 check, adding the opponent's Armor Class (a lower armor ranking is better) and weapon skills to the die roll; if the roll totals 20 or above, then the character hits. Other skills rolls are made by adding a skill value to 2d6 and trying to roll equal to or higher than a target number determined by the GM.

As befitting a science fiction game, equipment can vary by technology (tech) level; items with higher tech levels are superior, and cost more. The author elegantly uses the core rules to model starships, cybernetics, robots, and mech suits, all without unnecessarily complicated and difficult-to-learn subsystems. Once you learn how ships work, you essentially know how mechs function within the system mechanics. And, yes, players can build robot/artificial intelligence characters that are no more complicated to run than the other PC options.

## Setting

As pleasing as the rules are, the setting material shines even more brightly. The author lays out a very general history for his far-future, in which a pan-galactic civilization dependent on its advanced psychic and technological sciences suffers a catastrophic event, called the Scream, that killed the majority of psychics, shut down the various Jump Gates linking humanity, and issued in a new dark age. Six hundred years later, humanity has recovered faster-than-light ship technology, and various sectors and pockets of civilization have begun to discover one another again.

From this point, *SWN* encourages GMs and gaming groups to truly make the game their own by offering an extensive setting-creation system by which GMs can create their own sandbox setting for PCs to explore. *SWN* includes rules for generating sectors of planets, complete with their societies, governments, and inhabitants (human and alien); potential allies and enemies; unique characteristics; and factions that may be at odds in these worlds, using a simple set of random roll tables and a little imagination.

## Evaluation

Complexity: 3
Popularity: 2
Support: 3
Completeness: 4
Versatility: 3
Emulation: 4

## Comments

*SWN* is not only an impressive game, but it's also free in PDF format. While the free version lacks a few features (primarily the robot and mech rules) that the for-pay "core edition" has, it's still a complete game that players can try out. If the group enjoys it, then librarians may want to consider purchasing the core edition, available in PDF and softcover.

An additional advantage of *SWN* is its compatibility with retroclones of the world's best-known fantasy RPG—GMs and players can reskin many of those modules, monsters, and more for the science fiction setting of *SWN*!

Use this game if you want a relatively simple science fiction RPG that offers a lot for long-term play and has a nice selection of science fiction books on hand to offer players as well.

Cost: $29.99 softcover + PDF (core edition); $19.99 PDF (core edition); free PDF (free edition)

# Swords & Wizardry Core Rules

Matthew J. Finch
Mythmere Games, 2008
http://www.swordsandwizardry.com
Genre Tags: Fantasy, OSR
Dice: d4, d6, d8, d10, d12, d20, d%/d100

## Introduction

*Swords & Wizardry* was one of the earliest OSR movement games published. It closely reinterprets the early editions of *D&D* with an eye toward compatibility with other editions of *D&D* and other OSR games. Like many of the OSR games, *Swords & Wizardry* has a very short rule set that provides basic guidelines for play rather than attempting to cover every conceivable situation with a specific rule, like many modern games do.

## System and Characters

Characters in *Swords & Wizardry* are made using a class and level system. Each character has the classic six attributes (Strength, Dexterity, Constitution, Intelligence, Wisdom, and Charisma), with the scores determined randomly. Fortunately, the bonuses and penalties for high or low scores are minimal, so characters with lower attribute scores aren't unduly penalized and unplayable.

The main defining characteristic for each character is its class, the profession that the character engages in. In *Swords & Wizardry* there are three "core" classes: Fighting-Man (or Fighter), Cleric (a holy warrior), and Magic-User, with three more optional ones, based on demihuman races in the book: Dwarf (basically a Fighter), Elf (a Fighter/Magic-User hybrid), and Halfling (a diminutive Fighter, or Thief, if the GM uses those rules). Two additional classes, the Thief and Monk (unarmed fighter), are provided in an appendix. The limits on the classes and the combinations of races and classes were present in the first edition of *A D&D*, though with the high level of compatibility between many of the OSR games, interested GMs can easily decouple the race-as-class options.

The system for *Swords & Wizardry* uses two main mechanics. The first is used chiefly during combat where a d20 is rolled, modifiers are added, and the result is compared to a table to see if an attack is successful. Players may also need to make Saving Throws, a d20 roll against a target number to avoid or mitigate—"save against"—various hazards. The vast majority of the other actions in the game are handled by GM adjudication. Like Gary Gygax stressed in the early editions of *D&D*, *Swords & Wizardry* instructs the players and GMs that these rules are guidelines and simple enough that house ruling will not break the game, a perspective that frees up groups to improvise both rule and setting information.

## Setting

There is no explicit setting in *Swords & Wizardry*, though there is an implicit setting, that of the megadungeon. The megadungeon harkens back to the origins of fantasy RPGs, and is a multilevel labyrinth of various rooms (both natural and man-made), traps, and other obstacles, with each subsequent level containing, generally, more and more challenging encounters.

The game provides basic guidance on the creation of a megadungeon and gives a brief example of a small dungeon level for GMs to use. In addition to the dungeon environment, the book has a short section that discusses the creation of a campaign setting. Most of this advice is very general, and a GM wanting more detail or advice should look to the many online forums discussing such topics.

## Evaluation

Complexity: 2

Popularity: 4; one of the more popular OSR rules sets.

Support: 4; several different iterations of the rules and a multitude of adventures are published by Mythmere and third parties.

Completeness: 4

Versatility: 3; primarily focused on dungeon delving, but supplements and other iterations of the system expand beyond this basic activity

Emulation: 5

## Comments

*Swords & Wizardry* comes in three versions. The first is the *Core Rules* reviewed above. The second is the *White Box*, which is an even smaller rule set. The third version is the *Complete Rulebook*, which decouples race from class and offers several more class options. *Knockspell* is a magazine published by Mythmere Games (available in PDF and softcover format) that supports *Swords & Wizardry* and other OSR games.

Cost: *Swords & Wizardry Core Rules* and *Swords and Wizardry Whitebox* are available as free PDFs at http://www.swordsandwizardry.com. *Swords & Wizardry Complete Rulebook* is available as a free PDF or as a $34.99 hardcover from its current publisher, Frog God Games (http://froggodgames.org).

## *Thou Art but a Warrior,* Second Edition

Anna Kreider
Tasty Bacon Games (now Peach Pants Press), 2012
http://browserbeware.com
Genre Tags: Historical
Dice: d6

### Introduction

In *Thou Art but a Warrior* (*TABAW*), the characters are Muslim knights living in the *taifas* of Al-Andalus. The characters can find themselves in myriad situations, from military to political to personal, as they struggle to prevent the fall of the *taifa*.

### System and Characters

The system is very different from most of the games discussed in this book. The chief difference is that the GM's responsibilities are distributed among all the players. Each player has an area of responsibility for every other character. The Heart is the player who controls the character, much like in traditional RPGs; the Infidel controls the environment and antagonist characters; the Star controls characters that have a hierarchical or social relationship to the Heart; and the Moon controls characters with an emotional or personal connection to the Heart.

Character creation is a collaborative process in which the players contribute ideas to each other's Cosmos, the aforementioned Heart, Star, and Moon, and ideally share some of these ideas with other characters. In addition to these elements, there are four attributes for a character; all of them have fixed starting values and will change during play. Aspects are used and organized by Theme: Offices (a character's function within the *taifa*), Blessings (specific items, animals, or people), Abilities (unique knowledge or talent), and Fate (shared by all of the characters).

Play begins with the speaking of a phrase that is used for every session and sets the tone for play. The system is framed around the use of certain key phrases to frame events and negotiate conflict. Each scene centers on one or more protagonists and their Infidel, who sets up a conflict. This conflict is played out using the key phrases, and any adjudication is done by the Moon and Star players of the protagonist. Unlike other games, experience in *TABAW* measures the character's growing world-weariness; it also is used as a time for the fall of the *taifa*.

## Setting

The setting of *TABAW* is the Iberian Peninsula after the fall of Al-Andalus and before the Reconquista. The rules have brief descriptions of the different classes of people that live in the *taifas*: the *dhimmi*, second-class non-Muslim citizens; *muladi*, non-Muslims who have converted to Islam; and Muslims, whether they are Arabs, Moors, or Berbers. A general discussion of what the culture was like and the role of the characters in the *taifas* are included as well. This gives the barest introduction to the complexities of the period, but it also gives enough for a group to play a game true to the idiom.

## Evaluation

Complexity: 2
Popularity: 1
Support: 1
Completeness: 4
Versatility: 2
Emulation: 3

## Comments

This game is quite different from most games in both system and setting. Its system is derived from the *Polaris RPG* and covers a historical period not touched by any other game we are aware of.

Cost: $20 softcover + PDF

## *Thousand Suns Rulebook*

James Maliszewski
Grognardia Games, 2011
Genre Tags: Science Fiction, Space Opera
Dice: d12

## Introduction

*Thousand Suns* is a science fiction game that hits the sweet spot at the intersection of exploration and adventure.

## System and Characters

*Thousand Suns* characters are quick and easy to generate with a combination of point-buy and lifepath character creation systems. Characters have traits called abilities—the primary attributes of Body, Dexterity, Perception,

Presence, and Will—and skills. Players spread a given number of points across their abilities and then choose their characters' species (which will affect abilities and skills, and may grant some special abilities) and Homeworld, which determines which general skills they gain from their upbringing. Players then pick three career packages, anything from Entertainer to Soldier, Pilot to Ambassador, and gain further boosts to abilities and their skills; packages may be taken more than once to demonstrate remaining within the same career.

Characters then choose five hooks that represent significant qualities they have gained throughout their lives (one for Homeworld, one for species, and three from their careers). These hooks can be character traits, people, events, anything that connects them to their larger world. Players also have action points that they can use either independently, to give a small bonus to rolls, or in conjunction with hooks; when a hook becomes relevant in play, a character can spend an action point to gain a greater bonus to a check, or reroll a check.

In the 12 Degrees game system that *Thousand Suns* uses, players roll 2d12 against a target number (typically determined by adding the character's ability and skill values and any modifiers, and trying to roll under that number) or by an opposed roll. In an opposed check, characters roll 2d12 and attempt to roll under their target numbers. One or both may fail, but if both succeed, then the one who gained the greatest degrees of success—determined by just how far under the target number the player rolled—is the victor. For example, if the target number is 13, and a player rolls a 6, then he or she has 7 degrees of success.

*Thousand Suns* also has rules for creating your own alien species and starships, lots of technology for your characters to use, psionic abilities (like telekinesis, telepathy, etc.), and rules for creating your own worlds and space sectors to adventure in!

## Setting

*Thousand Suns* takes place in what Maliszewski calls a generalized "Imperial" science fiction setting, emulating the popular space opera stories common to the 1950s, 1960s, and 1970s, which typically included mighty galactic empires and decadent republics. Maliszewski chose this type of science fiction because, unlike many later science fiction subgenres, the activities are well geared toward exploration, action, and adventure, and the tone communicates looking at the universe with a wide-eyed sense of wonder. The universe of *Thousand Suns* is actually more of a metasetting that is ready-made for players to adventure in but gives GMs plenty of room and opportunity to develop and change as they see fit.

## Evaluation

Complexity: 2
Popularity: 2
Support: 1
Completeness: 4
Versatility: 3; the 12 Degrees system also powers both the swords and sorcery game called *Shadow, Sword & Spell*, and the historical occult horror game *Colonial Gothic*.
Emulation: 5; *Thousand Suns* handles its chosen area of science fiction flawlessly.

## Comments

Fans of older science fiction space opera styles will love *Thousand Suns*. Librarians can use films like the new *Star Trek* movie franchise as an example of *Thousand Suns'* flavor of science fiction, and can use this opportunity to introduce readers to the work of science fiction luminaries like Isaac Asimov, Poul Anderson, Alfred Bester, and H. Beam Piper, and more current authors like Lois McMaster Bujold and David Weber.

Cost: $30 hardcover + PDF; $25 softcover + PDF; $10 PDF

## *Traveller Core Rulebook*

Gareth Hanrahan
Mongoose Publishing, 2008
http://www.mongoosepublishing.com/
Genre Tags: Science Fiction, Space Opera
Dice: d6

## Introduction

*Traveller* is a science fiction RPG that takes place in the far-future where humanity has spread across space and established a large Imperium. Typically the characters are free traders, either legal or not, looking to find work out in the Spinward Marches, *Traveller*'s default setting.

## System and Characters

Character creation in *Traveller* is a combination of randomly rolled attributes and a lifepath system. The lifepath system is chiefly career based, and dice are used to inject some randomness into a character's background. There are several careers covering the spectrum from military to government to entertainment to citizen, each with three specialties. Careers modify attributes and skills and can introduce complications through events and mishaps.

Players resolve tasks using a roll-high target number system. A roll typically consists of 2d6 plus any relevant attribute and skill modifiers. This roll is compared to a fixed target number. GMs will often use a second style of die roll, called the d66, to generate random encounters and incidents. The d66 is functionally identical to a d% roll, but uses two d6s instead. The author thoughtfully includes a table of probabilities based on a modified 2d6 roll, which allows GMs to have a finer control of the rate of success in a game without having to determine rates of probability on their own.

The *Traveller* main rulebook also includes rules for creating aliens, including aliens as PCs, designing spacecraft, and using psionics, should the gaming group want to have superhuman mental abilities like telepathy and telekinesis in their games.

While the trader style of campaign is most common, *Traveller* also supports campaigns that focus on military missions, espionage, exploration, and more.

**Setting**

The core setting for *Traveller* is the Spinward Marches of the Third Imperium. This is a border region of the Imperium and has the feel of a wild frontier where the control of the Imperium is fairly light. The region is vast, and the book provides rules and guidelines for creating sectors and subsectors of space. This process gives the group a sufficient number of planets to explore and places to visit, while not tying the group to a published set of planetary descriptions. Of course, not all planets are equally advanced, and guidelines are provided to describe the various technology levels, ranging from 0 (Stone Age), to 7 (Earth at the beginning of the twenty-first century), to 15, where super science is the order of the day and hyperspace travel is routine.

Two standout chapters discuss world creation and trade. The trade chapter contains random roll tables and system applications for characters to engage in legitimate trade or smuggling, and includes suggestions as to which products are available, and more importantly, desired, on which type of planet. This chapter meshes with the world creation chapter as world types, governments, environments, and infrastructures can be determined randomly or selected from a table. Fortunately, these tables are varied enough that *Traveller* does not fall into the space opera trope of monocultures or monoclimates on planets.

**Evaluation**
Complexity: 3
Popularity: 3
Support: 4
Completeness: 3
Versatility: 3
Emulation: 4

**Comments**
*Traveller* has a number of excellent supplements available that give more details on various facets of the game, focusing on character options, settings, alien species, adventures, and equipment. Fans of *Firefly* and *Serenity*, *Star Trek*, and classic science fiction will enjoy the simplicity of *Traveller*'s system, and its ability to handle vast and varied science fiction campaigns.

Cost: $39.95 hardcover; $23.97 PDF

## Weird West

Stuart Robertson
Robertson Games, 2011
http://robertsongames.com (which is really just a link sending you to the Robertson Games section of DriveThruRPG: http://rpg.drive-thrustuff.com/browse.php?manufacturers_id=3286)
Genre Tags: Horror, Western
Dice: d4, d6, d8, d10, d12, d20

**Introduction**
*Weird West* is a shining example of simplicity and cost effectiveness. This game is eight pages long, costs $1 in PDF form, and yet has sufficient material to inspire dozens of adventures in the Weird West!

**System and Characters**
*Weird West* is a class and level system with a touch of point-buy character creation. Players begin by distributing points among their characters' four attributes: Fighting, Grit, Magic, and Skill. Players can choose one of four classes, called paths: Adventurers (the Indiana Jones types with Skill and fighting prowess), the Gifted (jacks of all trades, with a bit of Fighting, Magic, and Skill); Fighters (guess what they do best), and Magicians (best with mystical powers); as characters gain levels, their attributes increase

depending on their specialties. Characters with Magic choose from a list of powers and unusual abilities. Combat is determined by comparing a character's Fighting attribute to an opponent's Defence [sic.] score on a chart, and finding a target number to beat on a d20 roll. Other tests require a d6 roll versus a target number determined by comparing the relevant attribute to the difficulty of the task.

## Setting

The implied setting of *Weird West*, taken from the ad copy and the list of strange powers available, is an American West where cowboys, Native Americans, Chinese immigrants (with kung-fu, of course), and mad scientists do battle with pulpy supernatural horrors and other malevolence. Currently there's no shortage of Weird Western material, as evidenced by recent books like *The Buntline Special* by Mike Resnick and *Shadows West* by Joe R. Lansdale, and films like *Wild Wild West* and *Jonah Hex*.

## Evaluation

Complexity: 2
Popularity: 1
Support: 1
Completeness: 4
Versatility: 3; if you can use this simple a system for so varied a
      subgenre like Weird Westerns, then imagine what else you could
      create!
Emulation: 4

## Comments

When you buy this game, you also get directions on how to print it out, and how to cut and fold the page so that it becomes a tiny little eight-page booklet you could slip into your wallet. With this booklet and a fistful of dice, you're ready to game anywhere! Even better, this game should inspire your players with its simplicity and utility, and could challenge them to create their own games.

Cost: $1 PDF

## *Werewolf: The Apocalypse, 20th Anniversary Edition*

Bill Bridges et al.

CCP, 2012. Also see original publisher White Wolf Game Studio
    (owned by CCP) and current publisher Onyx Path Publishing,
    which publishes White Wolf gaming material under license
http://www.white-wolf.com
http://theonyxpath.com
Genre Tags: Horror, Mature Audiences, Urban Fantasy
Dice: d10

### Introduction

*Werewolf: The Apocalypse* (*W:tA*) is a game of savage horror in a war against evil. The characters are the Garou, werewolves born with the blessing of Gaia and Luna, and raised by Tribes to wage an ageless war against the forces of corruption. The Garou must balance the inherent Rage in their hearts with caring for their Kin and the landscape, both physical and spiritual. Their Rage has led to rash decisions and has made the war against the Wyrm (the spirit of Entropy) more difficult; some would say unwinnable.

### System and Characters

This game uses the Storyteller system, but not the same one as *Werewolf: The Forsaken* (and the rest of the new *World of Darkness*; see next entry in this chapter). At its core the Storyteller system is a dice pool using target numbers or opposed rolls.

Character creation uses a point-buy system in which discrete pools of points are used to buy Attributes, Abilities, and Advantages. There are nine attributes grouped into Physical, Mental, and Social aspects. Certain Tribes and Auspices tend to emphasize one group over the others, but that tendency is not enforced mechanically and allows players to create characters against type without penalty. Abilities are divided into Talents (inborn abilities), Skills (learned through training), and Knowledges (learned through study). Advantages are Backgrounds, representing a character's connections, wealth, and social standing, and Gifts, which are magical abilities, learned by the character either from another Garou or a spirit.

There are two special attributes in *W:tA*, Rage and Gnosis. Rage is the anger that Gaia has given the Garou for fighting against the Weaver and Wyrm; while useful, in that Rage can allow a Garou to act quickly or perform feats of superhuman strength, it can also overwhelm a Garou and cause it to commit horrible deeds. Gnosis is the essence of the spirit world and represents the mystical connectedness and strength of a Garou.

Rage and Gnosis are used to power the Gifts and Rites of the Garou. Gifts are blessings and powers taught by spirits to the Garou who impress the spirits. Unlike Attributes and Abilities, Gifts are taught through different legacies, making them easier to learn by a certain Breed, Auspice, or Tribe (see "Setting" in this entry). While Gifts represent the connection between Garou and spirits, Rites represent the connections among Garou. They are rituals and celebrations used to, among other things, grant social status, punish, or mourn.

## Setting

The *World of Darkness* is a world very much like this one. A key difference is that the corrupting forces of greed and power have a will of their own. This corruption stems from the imbalance of the Triat. Gaia created three spiritual beings to embody the forces of existence: the Weaver is stasis, the Wyld is creation, and the Wyrm was balance. In the dim past the Weaver snared the Wyrm in its webs and drove the Wyrm mad, causing it to twist itself from maintaining balance into a force of corruption. The Wyrm is the main foe of the Garou, who strive against it and its minions until the final battle in the coming Apocalypse. The Weaver also poses a threat in that the stronger the Weaver becomes, the more difficult it becomes to access the spirit world; the Weaver's influence also deadens the emotions and empathy of mortals as well.

The Garou Nation is not a unified group, being divided into thirteen Tribes, each hailing from a different geographical region and reflecting its own culture. They are further divided by Breed: Homid (born of a human parent), Lupis (born of a wolf parent), or Metis (born of Garou parents). Garou choose the Tribe they wish to join, but their Auspices are determined by the phase of the moon they are born under. The Auspice defines the role the Garou plays in society from the Ragabash (No Moon trickster) to Ahroun (Full Moon warrior). Conflict arises between the Breeds as the Lupus blame the Homids for humanity's destruction of nature, and both shun the Metis for the sin of their parents' weakness—Garou are forbidden to mate with other Garou.

Tensions exist between Tribes as well; the ambitious Shadow Lords wish to replace the failing Silver Fangs as leaders of the Garou Nation, while the primal Red Talons push for more direct action against humans but are opposed by the pacifistic Children of Gaia, who want to reunite the fractured Nation and bring all back into harmony.

The battle against the Wyrm takes place not only in the physical world but also in the Umbra as well. The Umbra is an animistic spirit realm where the Garou can interact with the spiritual reflection of the physical world, or travel deeper into more symbolic Realms, such as the Aetherial Realm where the spirits of the planets and stars dwell and can be interacted with, or Wolfhome, a primal land where the divisions of Tribe fade and the Garou can be one nation again. Spirits inhabit this place and can cross over into the physical realm, typically by possessing physical objects, both living and inanimate.

## Evaluation

Complexity: 2
Popularity: 3
Support: 4
Completeness: 3
Versatility: 3
Emulation: 3

## Comments

First published in 1992, *Werewolf: The Apocalypse* was an attempt to play with the genre conventions of werewolf folklore, much like the other games in the original *World of Darkness* line did with other supernatural creatures, including *Vampire: The Masquerade, Mage: The Ascension, Wraith: The Oblivion,* and *Changeling: The Dreaming. W:tA* does carry a caution that it is for mature readers, so we recommend it primarily for older teens.

Cost: $104.99 color hardcover + PDF (premium); $99.99 color hardcover (premium); $69.99 color hardcover + PDF (standard); $64.99 color hardcover (standard); $54.99 black-and-white hardcover + PDF; $49.99 black-and-white hardcover; $29.99 PDF

## *Werewolf: The Forsaken*

Ethan Skemp et. al.
White Wolf Game Studios, 2005
http://www.white-wolf.com
Genre Tags: Horror, Mature Audiences, Urban Fantasy
Dice: d10

## Introduction

*Werewolf: The Forsaken* (*W:tF*) is a game set in the World of Darkness. Here the players take on the roles of the Forsaken, werewolves who are tainted by an ancient crime and are compelled to hunt to protect their territories. The Forsaken seek to maintain Harmony by fulfilling their ancestral duties, keeping the physical and spiritual worlds in balance while dealing with other werewolves that seek their destruction.

### System and Characters

This game uses the basic Storyteller system described in the new *World of Darkness* (*nWoD*) review (see entry later in this chapter). Additional rules are introduced in this book to deal with specific abilities of the Forsaken.

Character creation in *W:tF* follows the rules in the core *nWoD* book with the werewolf template applied. The template consists chiefly of three elements, with multiple sub-elements. The two most important are auspice and tribe. The auspice of a werewolf is determined by the sign of the moon under which it experienced its first change, and each of the five auspices plays a different role in Forsaken society. If the auspice is a character's inherent nature, then the tribe is a matter of external choice. The five tribes are groups of like-minded werewolves who form a loose organization based on shared interests. These selections will shape the choices of powers that the individual werewolf has. For example, the *Rahu*, or the Full Moon auspice, is that of the warrior, and their Gifts (supernatural powers) are oriented toward combat, while the *Ithaeur*, the Crescent Moon, is that of the mystic and will have Gifts that are focused on dealing with spirits. The other major element of rules introduced in *W:tF* are for the five forms a werewolf can take, ranging from normal human to wolf and including three intermediate forms.

The Forsaken also wield magical abilities reflecting their partially spirit nature in the form of Gifts and Rites. Gifts are just that, powers that are learned and granted by various spirits, after negotiating and paying the spirit in some way, depending on the types of Gifts to be learned. These are organized into different functional categories, such as Dominance, Evasion, or Insight, with each category having five Gifts of ascending power. Most of the Gift groups are able to be learned by any of the Forsaken, with only the auspice categories restricted. While Gifts are typically short in duration, and of focused power, Rites take longer to perform and typically have a more lasting effect.

### Setting

The World of Darkness is a dark, animistic world. As creatures half flesh and half spirit, the Forsaken can travel between the physical world and the spirit world, the Shadow. The Shadow is a spiritual reflection of the physical world where physical objects take on a symbolic resonance, and the strength of the spiritual reflection is based directly on the amount of emotional attachment and energy invested in a place or object. The spirits in the Shadow regard the Forsaken as traitors for slaying Father Wolf. This perceived betrayal has turned the majority of the spirits against the Forsaken, making the Shadow a dangerous place. In addition to the spirits, there are three Tribes whose ancestor did not aid in the killing of Father Wolf; these Tribes call themselves the Pure and seek to kill or convert the Forsaken one wolf at a time.

A typical game will have the characters seeking to defend their territory as a pack. They will have to deal with the local spirit world, the presence of the Pure, and if desired, other supernatural entities like vampires. Unlike *Werewolf: The Apocalypse*, there is no worldwide tribal culture, so the pack is free to create what traditions it sees fit.

### Evaluation

Complexity: 3
Popularity: 2
Support: 4
Completeness: 1; requires the *World of Darkness* core rulebook to
    play
Versatility: 3
Emulation: 3

### Comments

White Wolf's *World of Darkness* was once arguably one of the most influential RPG properties on the market, and it still retains a considerably loyal fandom. One of the reasons we included reviews of both *Werewolf* games, as well as the *World of Darkness* core rulebook, is to demonstrate some of the changes that took place between White Wolf's old and new *Worlds of Darkness*. In the near future, even this reimagined vision of *Werewolf* will undergo a revision, much like *Vampire: The Requiem*'s *Blood and Smoke*, with the working title of the *Idigam Chronicles*.

*W:tF* is intended for mature readers, so librarians may want to reserve running it for older teen patrons.

Cost: $19.99 PDF; free demo version in PDF

# Witch Girls Adventures: The Drama-Diaries Game of Modern Magic and Mischief

Malcolm Harris
Channel M, 2009
https://www.facebook.com/pages/
Channel-M-Publishing/171551682888514
Genre Tags: Supernatural
Dice: d2, d4, d6, d8, d10

## Introduction

*Witch Girls Adventures* (*WGA*) is based on the *Witch Girls Tales* comic books. In this game the characters are tween girls who practice magic, and the game is about their interactions with both the mundane and magical worlds. Much like other urban fantasy settings, the world of magic is hidden from the mundane world.

## System and Characters

Character creation is similar to *Savage Worlds* in that there are six attributes, each assigned a die type, and secondary attributes with values derived from the primary ones. The die types available are dependent on the clique the character comes from. Cliques represent the characters' upbringing and how immersed they are in the magical world. These cliques provide the base scores for attributes, magical skills, and education and a bonus to a type of magic. Skill points are divided into magic and mundane points. Traits are specialties divided into talents and heritages. These provide either a minor advantage or a major advantage and a drawback. Magic is divided into twelve types, and a character has a set number of points to assign to these groups. The default characters are tween girls, but the game does include rules for creating characters both younger and older than that.

Task resolution is based on skill rolls, derived from the attribute die plus skill rating, and rolled versus a target number or opposed die roll. Spells are cast using the Casting skill and must overcome the spell resistance of the target. The effects of spells are limited by the ranks a witch has in that type of magic. Experience points, voodollars, are primarily awarded for excellent role-playing.

## Setting

The setting of *WGA* is an occult modern fantasy setting with witches being the main focus; other supernatural beings exist but are not detailed in this book. The Witches' World Council serves as a supranational government overseeing witch society. It has established a series of laws governing witch behavior. The book covers further details of witches' daily life, including sports, entertainment, and schooling; there are a variety of magical schools, but the Willow Mist school in Maine receives the most detail.

Witches are descendants of Lilith, and only females can be witches. There are other types of supernaturals in the setting, collectively referred to as Otherkin. The main types are: Fae, descendants of Queen Mab; Immortals, descendants of Gilgamesh; and Nightlings (vampires and shapeshifters), descendants of Echidna. Each of these groups has its own worldwide organization, but they are all smaller in size and less powerful than the Witches' World Council, and most groups are subject to the council's rulings.

Normally an equipment chapter would not get mentioned in the setting section, but in *WGA* this chapter is particularly evocative and has many atmospheric items, noticeably lacking the arms and armor lists prevalent in many RPGs. Various familiars, potions, wands, brooms, and other useful noncombat magic items are available and reinforce the social aspects of the game.

A bestiary chapter is included with both magical and mundane threats listed. Also in this chapter is a rogues gallery of NPCs that GMs can use. The cast of NPCs includes potential patrons, foes, and some "historical" figures, including King Arthur and Vlad Dracul.

## Evaluation

> Complexity: 2
> Popularity: 1
> Support: 2; both rule expansions and adventures are available.
> Completeness: 5
> Versatility: 2
> Emulation: 5

## Comments

While based on a specific IP, this game could easily be adapted to emulate other settings, such as Harry Potter. This RPG is one of the only games we are aware of that caters specifically to girls.

Cost: $9.99 PDF

# The World of Darkness: Storytelling System Rulebook

Bill Bridges et al.
White Wolf Game Studio, 2004
http://www.white-wolf.com
Genre: Horror, Supernatural, Urban Fantasy
Dice: d10

## Introduction

The new *World of Darkness* (*nWoD*) is a fusion of recent urban fantasy and horror. The world is a dark and mysterious place, with horrors lurking in every shadow and mysteries wrapped in enigmas ready for the characters to unravel. (Note: The term *nWoD* stands for "new *World of Darkness*," as this is the second iteration of the shared world designed by White Wolf Game Studio.)

## System and Characters

Characters in *nWoD* have nine attributes and twenty-four skills, divided among physical, social, and mental abilities. Several other traits are derived from the scores in these attributes and skills. Players create characters using a point-buy system.

One mechanic pioneered by White Wolf is that of a numeric morality trait. The name of this trait and the hierarchy of transgressions (what the trait measures) vary depending on which *nWoD* game the group is playing. This trait can slowly drop or rise over time based on character actions, and it tracks a character's degeneration or enlightenment. Unlike a typical alignment system, the morality trait does not dictate a character's actions but is a reflection of them. Additionally the *nWoD* uses Virtues and Vices to guide a character's actions. Based on the traditional seven Virtues and deadly Sins, these have an in-game effect by interacting with the character's Willpower score. Finally the system of Merits and Flaws allows players to give their characters benefits and penalties that lie outside the normal rules.

The *nWoD* uses a dice pool mechanic based on d10s. The dice explode on rolling a 10, and may do so on a lower number depending on character abilities. Dice pools are based on the total of an attribute and ability plus any situational modifiers. Combat is given its own short chapter and additional dramatic actions in another. The system is intuitive enough that once the basics are learned a GM can adjudicate results with little reference to the rulebook.

## Setting

*World of Darkness* is set in the modern world seen through a dark lens. There is a distinctly modern gothic feel to the setting with an emphasis on the isolation and localism of the setting. The core rulebook is written with human protagonists as the main characters, with humans and ghosts taking on the roles of antagonists. Further expansions to the setting and additional supernatural denizens and powers can be found in the line of supplements from White Wolf, including *Second Sight*, *Inferno*, or *Mirrors*, or in one of the other game lines set in this world, such as *Vampire: The Requiem*, *Werewolf: The Forsaken*, or *Mage: The Awakening*. There are supplements that deal with other time periods as well, including *New Wave Requiem* for *Vampire* or *Mage Noir* for *Mage*.

**Evaluation**
> Complexity: 2
> Popularity: 3
> Support: 4
> Completeness: 2; the core rulebook is sufficient for mortal stories,
>> but other kinds of supernatural characters will require additional books.
> Versatility: 4
> Emulation: 4

**Comments**
> There is a strong focus on humans in the setting in the core rulebook. A wide array of various supernatural elements can be added through acquiring other games in the line, such as *Vampire: The Requiem*, *Werewolf: The Forsaken*, or *Mage: The Awakening*, or supplements for *World of Darkness* detailing specific facets of the setting, such as *World of Darkness: Second Sight*. This game is recommended for older teens.

Cost: $14.99 PDF

## *Yggdrasill*

> Neko et al. (English translation by Sarah Newton and Morgane
>> Guillemot)
> Le 7ème Cercle, 2012 [2009]
> http://www.7emecercle.com/website/
> Cubicle 7 Entertainment has the license to translate and distribute
>> *Yggdrasill* in the United States.
> http://www.cubicle7.co.uk/
> Genre: Alternate History, Fantasy, Historical
> Dice: d10

## Introduction

Imagine a setting where the sagas and myths of the Viking Age were manifest in the world. The characters are members of one of three kingdoms and engage in various heroic exploits. *Yggdrasill* is set in a legendary pseudo-historical Germanic Iron Age in Scandinavia.

## System and Characters

Using a point-buy system, players can create proud nobles, mighty warriors, wise sages with magical knowledge, travelers and emissaries, or even simple workers and farmers. (We suspect that warriors and sages will likely be the most popular choices.) Player characters have nine primary traits in three categories: Body (Strength, Vigor, Agility), Mind (Intellect, Perception, Tenacity), and Soul (Charisma, Instinct, Communication). Players roll a number of ten-sided dice equal to the rank of the primary trait, keep the highest two results, and add them together along with a relevant skill rank. Players then compare this number to a target number or an opposed roll to determine success.

The dice pool can be augmented by the use of *furor* dice, which represent the characters heroically exerting themselves. Players may also add dice to a roll through the use of runes. Each character has three runes randomly assigned to it during creation, and if an action fits within the meaning of a rune then a die bonus is applied.

Any character that wishes to use magic must take a specific trait and have training in any or all of the three magical skills. Each magical skill represents a different type of magic. *Galdr* (chants) include curses, illusions, and various charms. *Seidr* (sorcery) are learned spells—each has a single effect, and *Seidr* most closely resemble spell casting in other RPGs. *Runes* are the third type of magic, and as during character creation, each of them has a positive or negative effect.

Combat feats are available to all characters. Initially these feats are purchased with the same pool of points that players use to purchase spells, so as to balance out casters and noncasters. Combat feats have colorful names like "Boar's Charge" and "By Thor's Arm," and they grant special maneuvers or bonuses to characters during battle.

Significantly for a culture whose heroes are lauded in poetry and song, the rulebook also has systems for great deeds and renown, such that PCs may one day become legends themselves in their games.

## Setting

As with the game *Qin: The Warring States*, the authors spend a considerable amount of time describing and elaborating the myths, legends, and historical aspects of their Norse setting, Scandia, so that players can more fully immerse themselves in their roles and in the game.

The book begins with key cultural concepts that will enable players to better take on the roles of Norse characters, then details the cosmology of the Norse worldview, including Yggdrasill the World Tree, along with the Nine Worlds that the tree connects. The authors go on to describe the gods of the Norse pantheon, their aspects and personalities, and various religious rites important to the characters in their setting.

The authors then focus on the mortal world, the realm of Scandia, and the kingdoms of Denmark, Norway, and Svithjod in the mortal world. They emphasize the overall harsh, cold, and demanding environment that daily tests its peoples, and depict each kingdom's specific ruling families and significant personas, geographic features, and settlements. The authors spend an entire chapter on the practices of daily life, including work, travel, raiding and warfare, codes of law, social bonds, lifestyle, culture, festivals, arts, and even foodstuffs.

The setting has its own perils as well, including cunning adversaries, fearsome beasts, and mythic monsters, and the book even contains a sample adventure to start your characters' no-doubt legendary journeys!

## Evaluation

Complexity: 3
Popularity: 2
Support: 1
Completeness: 5
Versatility: 3
Emulation: 4

## Comments

If your players are interested in Norse adventure, perhaps through the various tales and myths, or through television shows like *Vikings* and films like *The 13th Warrior*, then this is definitely the game to play with them. The basic mechanics are simple enough to grasp, with combat styles and magic adding a layer of complexity. If there is sufficient interest, then we recommend also buying the supplement *The Nine Worlds*, which details the worlds beyond the mortal realms, to open up new areas of adventure.

For your adventurous readers, you might recommend books about Norse tales: *The Prose Edda*; *The Poetic Edda*; *The Saga of the Volsungs*, including the tales of Sigurd; and other Norse sagas.

Cost: $49.99 hardcover; $24.99 PDF

## Glimpses of the Future!

While the following games won't see release before this manuscript reaches print, we can give you brief glimpses of games to come given what has been published.

# *Dungeons & Dragons (fifth edition): D&D Starter Set and D&D Basic Game, version 0.1*

Mike Mearls et al.
Wizards of the Coast, 2014
http://company.wizards.com
Genre Tags: Fantasy
Dice Needed: d4, d6, d8, d10, d12, d20, d%/d100

### Introduction

*D&D*, the first RPG ever published, needs little introduction. Over the decades, it has expanded incredibly from the three original little booklets in a box to hundreds of published tomes, supplements, and adventures. For the game's fortieth anniversary, Wizards of the Coast is publishing the fifth edition of *D&D* (though it appears that the game's covers, advertising, and marketing are eschewing any mention of edition). The beginning boxed set, the *D&D Starter Set*, is available in stores, and the *D&D Basic Rules* are available for free in PDF from the publisher's website. The three core rulebooks, the *Player's Handbook*, the *Monster Manual*, and the *Dungeon Master's Guide*, will be published throughout the latter half of 2014.

### System and Characters

First, to clarify, the *D&D Starter Set* is a boxed set that contains an abbreviated 32-page rulebook, sufficient to begin play; a 64-page adventure book that prospective dungeon masters can use to kick off their campaigns; a full set of six dice; and five pre-generated characters with sufficient information to advance them from levels one through five.

The *D&D Basic Rules* (version 0.1) is a 110-page PDF document that includes the basic rules players need, as well as the character creation and advancement rules for the four core fantasy character races (human, elf, dwarf, and halfling) and four core classes (cleric, fighter, rogue, and wizard) from levels one through twenty. As the publishers receive feedback and publish errata, Wizards of the Coast will update the *Basic Game* as necessary. While these rules are sufficient for players, prospective dungeon masters will need to find the rules for monsters and other necessities in either already published *D&D Next* adventures available on RPGNow (http://www.rpgnow.com) or in upcoming volumes.

The latest edition of *D&D* remains a class-and-level system, and the four featured classes include: the cleric, a martial and spiritual warrior serving a religion or deity; the fighter, an iconic fantasy warrior; the rogue, a rapscallion, conniver, and thief; and the wizard, wielder of arcane magic. Characters also gain Backgrounds, enhancements like Soldier or Blacksmith, that flesh out the characters' origins and give them additional abilities and skills related to their pre-adventuring years. Backgrounds also suggest Personality Traits, Ideals, Bonds, and Flaws, aspects of the character that guide role-play and that players can use to gain Inspiration (*D&D*'s metagame currency) to gain advantage to their rolls (see below).

The system uses a roll-high mechanic, and checks require a d20 roll plus modifiers, usually against a target number called a Difficulty Class, although occasionally the system uses opposed rolls to resolve conflicts instead. The rules provide guidelines for assigning appropriate Difficulty Classes for various challenges. Certain circumstances may give a PC advantage or disadvantage on a check; if a character has advantage on a check, then the player rolls 2d20 and takes the higher result, whereas if a character has disadvantage, the player rolls 2d20 and takes the lower result. If due to various circumstances a player has both advantage and disadvantage on a check, then they cancel each other out, and the player simply rolls 1d20 for the check.

PCs still have the original six abilities of Strength, Dexterity, Constitution, Intelligence, Wisdom, and Charisma, with scores typically ranging from 3 to a maximum of 20. Depending on the particular ability's score, a player may have a bonus or penalty associated with any check using that ability. Each of the abilities has a list of common types of skills keyed to that ability; for example, using the Athletics skill is a Strength ability check, whereas Investigation is an Intelligence ability check. Saving Throws (checks to survive a variety of adventuring hazards) are now a type of ability check. A character may also have a proficiency bonus associated with certain skills, attacks, and saving throws; the size of the bonus is determined by the character's level, whereas the character's Class and Background determine which checks use the proficiency bonus.

Armor Class (AC), how hard a character is to hit, depends primarily on the type of armor the character wears, further altered by the character's Dexterity modifier. In combat, a monster's AC is essentially the target number needed to hit that creature. *D&D* still uses hit points to determine how much damage a character can take before dying, with various types of attacks and weapons dealing variable amounts of damage depending on how deadly they are.

*D&D* continues to use the nine-alignment system from the first edition of *Advanced Dungeons & Dragons* (*AD&D1e)*, which describes what these alignments mean to players. (See "Alignment" in the glossary.)

Both the *Starter Set* and *Basic Rules* have rules for combat, exploration, various environment-specific rules, equipment and weapons, and spells.

### Setting

The default setting for the latest edition of *D&D* is the Forgotten Realms, an epic fantasy world that has seen many changes over decades of editions, adventures, and stories that have used the setting. (Writers at Wizards of the Coast have assured fans that additional settings are forthcoming.)

The *Starter Set* contains the adventure *The Lost Mine of Phandelver*, an adventure that will help characters progress from levels one through five. Characters begin on the road to the town of Phandelin and take their first steps into the larger setting of the Forgotten Realms as they battle goblins and find clues to the mystery of a forgotten dwarven mine.

### Evaluation

Complexity: 2; the latest iteration of *D&D* presented in this book seems less rules intensive than other recent editions.

Popularity: 4/5; while *D&D* has lost market share to *Pathfinder*, only time will tell if it can once again attain its preeminent place as the number-one best-selling RPG.

Support: 1/5; while there are only a few items available for *D&D* at this time, you can bet that Wizards of the Coast will soon have a host of materials available. Wizards of the Coast writers have also stated that they may soon publish conversion documents for previous editions that will allow players to use their older materials with this new edition.

Completeness: 2; neither the *Starter Set* nor the *Basic Rules* are complete in themselves—you'll have to wait until Wizards of the Coast publishes the three core rulebooks for the complete rules.

Versatility: 3; time has demonstrated that the d20 system, as well as nearly every iteration of the *D&D* system, can be adapted to plenty of other settings and genres beyond fantasy.

Emulation: 5; this score takes into account the fact that, while *D&D* originally emulated other fantasy subgenres of fiction, over four decades it has essentially become its *own* subgenre, with plenty of published recursive fiction to serve as proof.

## Comments

What can we say beyond, "It's *Dungeons & Dragons*—you'll want it in your collection"? Well, one of your friendly authors, who has played *D&D* since 1983, helped to playtest this edition with local teens (don't worry, their parents signed the nondisclosure agreements for them!) and found it to be one of his favorite iterations of the game since . . . well, for many a decade. While we haven't yet seen the final form that the game will take, we can say that this latest edition is a fantastic and fun game worthy of its history and name.

Cost: The *D&D Starter Set* is a $19.99 boxed set; the *D&D Basic Rules* is a free PDF at the Wizards of the Coast website

## Call of Cthulhu, Sixth Edition and Call of Cthulhu, Seventh Edition Quick-Start Rules

Sandy Petersen et al.
Chaosium Inc., 2004 (6th ed.), 2013 (7th ed. Quick-Start Rules)
http://catalog.chaosium.com
Genre Tags: Horror, Investigation
Dice: d4, d6, d8, d20, d%/d100

### Introduction

*Call of Cthulhu* (*CoC*) was the first horror RPG, and it remains one of the preeminent horror RPGs more than two decades later. Although *CoC* uses the *Basic Roleplaying* system as its game engine, its historical importance requires that we give it a separate bibliography entry, and because *CoC* is moving into a seventh edition, we thought we'd see what changes might occur using the seventh edition quick-start rules as a guide.

### System and Characters

*CoC* characters, typically called investigators, have eight attributes called characteristics, including Strength, Constitution, Size, Intelligence, Power (your character's willpower and aptitude for magic), Dexterity, Appearance, and Education. These characteristics range from 3 to 18, with Intelligence and Size ranging from 8 to 18, and Education ranging from 6 to 21. Players generate these characteristics randomly. Players then derive secondary characteristics from their primary characteristics.

One secondary characteristic in particular, Sanity, deserves special attention. As characters encounter the horrors of the Cthulhu mythos, their Sanity decreases, and they may develop psychological illness and aberrant behaviors as a result; thus, Sanity was one of the earliest nonalignment personality mechanics. While there are methods of bolstering a character's Sanity, should it ever reach 0 then the character goes incurably mad.

Players choose a profession depending on the historical era of their game, and spend a number of skill points determined by the profession and the characters' Education and Intelligence scores. Since not every character can be an expert in everything, players might find it best to choose key important skills to raise high rather than try to have a large number of skills at very low levels.

*CoC* is a percentile-based, roll-low system. When making checks, players will attempt to roll under their character's skill value in order to succeed. In the case of an opposed roll, such as in combat, opposing characters make their checks, and the results are compared to one another on a table to determine success. In the case of particularly difficult tests, players will need to roll equal to or under one-half of their skill rank or characteristic percentile. Rolls involving the character's characteristics may require use of a chart, the Resistance Table, to determine a percentage chance for a target number to roll under.

In the course of their investigations, characters may encounter grimoires and tomes of mystical knowledge. Characters may learn spells from these tomes, but beware—the more the characters know of the mind-bending horrors in existence, the more their Sanity drops.

In *CoC*, PCs are notoriously susceptible to violence. Unlike other games, where the designers intend for characters to weather more cinematic action extremes, *CoC* characters are a bit more fragile. Often, *CoC* characters succeed through their perceptiveness, intelligence, and dogged relentlessness, as opposed to their combat prowess—they're called investigators for a reason. That said, it might not be amiss for players to give their characters at least one skill devoted to mayhem—or rather, self-defense—just in case.

## System Changes

For more than three decades, changes to this venerable RPG have been mostly cosmetic. However, the seventh edition has a few major alterations, as demonstrated by the seventh edition quick-start.

Readers might have noticed that while *Basic Roleplaying* and *CoC* are primarily percentile systems, the characteristics are measured in lower increments. These characteristics are a holdover from the *Runequest* game that Chaosium published in 1978, which was meant to be an alternative to *D&D*. Thus, the attributes between the two games are similar, as was how they were generated (usually by rolling a number of d6s). In the *CoC* seventh edition, the players have a set of percentile numbers that they assign to their investigators' characteristics as they choose.

In addition, players may be granted bonus and penalty dice to represent modifiers from the environment. In a percentile system (see the glossary), the player rolls two differently colored ten-sided dice; one is considered the "tens" digit, and the other is considered the "ones" digit; thus a roll of 4 and 7 will be read as a 47. When rolling bonus dice, players roll additional tens dice and select the lowest tens digit for that roll. When rolling penalty dice, players add one or more tens dice to their roll, and have to select the highest, and thus worst, tens digit to calculate their final result.

The sixth edition core rulebook has four introductory adventures for gaming groups, and the seventh edition quick-start has one introductory adventure.

## Setting

*CoC* was one of the earliest RPGs to be fully based on a specific IP. In this case, Chaosium used the stories of pulp writer H. P. Lovecraft as the setting for *CoC*. Collectively referred to as the Cthulhu Mythos, and later added to by other writers (both contemporaries and stylistic successors of Lovecraft), these stories depict a universe where humanity foolishly believes itself to be masters of the planet (and later, space and the cosmos), while ancient horrors that have lain dormant for eons are slowly awakening. Meanwhile, other alien races, both from other planets and Earth's far future, actively study humanity using methods that range from disorienting and maddening to horrifying.

In fact, given what we can learn of the far-future through Lovecraft's stories, humanity as we know it is essentially doomed. This doom, however, ennobles the investigators' struggles, as normal men and women learn of the horrors hidden from the eyes of others and seek to hold them at bay and preserve humanity, if only for one more day.

*CoC* exists as perhaps the best example of converting an existing body of work into an RPG; of using the mechanics and system to fully capture the flavor of a story, setting, or genre; and ensuring that the game plays like the stories read.

## Evaluation

Complexity: 2; *CoC* is an excellent introductory game with easy-to-learn mechanics.

Popularity: 3; while *CoC* isn't everyone's cup of tea, most gamers have at least heard of the game and Lovecraft's stories.

Support: 5; we were tempted to give this a rank of 11, just to make a point—with more than thirty years of published supplements, all of which are compatible with the current edition with only a small amount of tinkering, not to mention a host of fan material on the Internet, a group of *CoC* players never has to go without extra material.

Completeness: 5; while *CoC* has a lot of supplemental material to support it, the game itself is fully complete as is.

Versatility: 3/5; *CoC* can be used to run a variety of horror and/or investigative/mystery games outside of the Cthulhu Mythos as well, and the *Basic Roleplaying* system at the core of *CoC* can be, and has been, used to run just about every gameable genre and subgenre.

Emulation: 5; *CoC* nearly perfectly captures the spirit of Lovecraft's fiction.

## Comments

Run this game for players who enjoy mysteries as well as horror, and refer them to the works of H. P. Lovecraft, the horror stories of Robert E. Howard, August Derleth's later Cthulhu Mythos tales, and Edgar Allan Poe. Fans of the television program *Supernatural* might also enjoy *CoC*.

We would also be remiss if we didn't mention one of the best modern *CoC* settings available, *Delta Green*. In a setting that predates *The X-Files*, *Delta Green* characters are rogue government agents who know the truth about the Cthulhu Mythos and use their status and resources to shut down otherworldly threats. If your characters are interested in a more modern version of *CoC*, then rejoice, for soon *Delta Green* will be released as a stand-alone game!

Cost: Sixth ed.: $39.95 hardcover; $34.95 softcover; $19.22 PDF; Seventh ed. quick-start: $9.95 softcover booklet; free PDF at publisher's website

## A Final Word on Rules, Systems, and Trust

Observant readers will note that, over the course of the book, we tend to point librarians new to RPGs to games that are relatively easy to learn, prepare, and master. Librarians who are already familiar or comfortable with a given system will likely run what they know, but for new GMs, the general level of rules complexity can be a prime factor in choosing a game for your program. We understand that time is precious, and that not every new GM will have the opportunity or desire to read hundreds of pages of rules before starting a program, even if that single book can be used to run years of programming.

While some discussions focus on "rules-heavy" versus "rules-light" games, we tend to discuss how "rules-intensive" an RPG is. More rules-intensive games have a large number of rules for many situations and can have multiple resolution systems for different tasks. A raw measure of the rules intensity is the size of the rulebook(s) needed to play the game; for example, the fourth edition of *D&D* requires three books containing 960 pages of rules. While only 320 pages are necessary for players (even less if a player is primarily concerned with a particular character's abilities), a GM needs to be familiar with an additional 640 pages of this game, little of which includes setting information. Page count alone, however, is not a sufficient measure; the second edition of *Exalted* weighs in at 400 pages and has 48 pages of the book devoted solely to the setting. The number of rules in RPGs is nearly impossible to memorize, and reference to the books is an inevitable part of playing these games.

Less rules-intensive games are generally shorter in length, having fewer rules for character creation and/or conflict resolution. Less rules-intensive systems tend to be easier to learn and remember, tend not to break up the narrative flow of the game, and tend to be more focused on the narrative portrayed in the games. *The Mountain Witch*, by Timothy Kleinert, is an extreme example of this type of RPG, as it is designed to tell only one basic story structure. The challenge for the players and GM lies in how the players create their characters and how they interact to change elements along the overarching narrative framework (Kleinert 2005, 3).

In less rules-intensive games, most of the conflict resolution is left to the GM and players to narrate and agree upon; often players also have the ability to dramatically edit in-game situations by adding elements and even taking narrative control over the scene. Within some of these games there is a blurred line between GM and player as the entire group cooperates to tell a story. Thus, less rules-intensive games can require an even greater level of implicit trust between the GM and the players, a sense of cooperation that was sometimes missing from earlier games. Still, some players do not care for this kind of system, and may think that outcomes should be more defined by the rules and rely less upon the decisions of the GM.

Ultimately, the decision whether to use a more or less rules-intensive game is simply one of taste; players and GMs enjoy what they enjoy, and have different opinions as to which rules, and how many rules, are necessary to run a fun and fair game that effectively models the desired genre, tone, play style, and setting. Either way, RPGs have a high level of GM-player trust built into the social contract, either implicit or explicit, that the players and GM agree to before character creation and the game begins. (For an excellent example of developing both the social contract and setting as a group, see the entry for *Primetime Adventures*.) Chad Underkoffler writes about trust in his game *Truth & Justice*: "The most important part of *T&J* is that it's high trust. Players have to be convinced that the GM isn't going to try and screw them over, and GMs have to believe that the players will have some faith in the game, setting, campaign tone, gaming group, and his or her fairness" (Underkoffler 2005). Librarians must remember that each game group is a unique social system, and the needs of each group will vary, sometimes considerably. The key is for the GM and players to be open and honest in what they expect from the game, and to play in good faith.

## Works Referenced

Kleinert, Timothy. 2005. *The Mountain Witch*. [USA]: Timfire Publishing.
Underkoffler, Chad. 2005. *Truth & Justice*. [USA]: Atomic Sock Monkey Press.

# Appendix A
# Games Listed by Genre Tags

## Action

*Feng Shui: Action Movie Roleplaying*

## African

*Spears of the Dawn*

## Alternate History

*All for One: Regime Diabolique*
*Cold City, v. 1.1*
*Qin: The Warring States*
*Yggdrasill*

## Animals

*Cat: A Little Game about Little Heroes, Revised Edition*
*Mouse Guard Roleplaying Game*

## Asian

*Legend of the Five Rings Roleplaying Game, 4th Edition*
*Qin: The Warring States*

# Cartoons

*Cartoon Action Hour: Season 3*

# Christian

*Dragonraid*

# Comics

*Artesia: Adventures in the Known World*
*Icons: Superpowered Roleplaying*
*Mouse Guard Roleplaying Game*
*Mutants & Masterminds Deluxe Hero's Handbook, Third Edition*

# Conspiracy

*Cold City, v. 1.1*
*Conspiracy X 2.0 (a.k.a. Conspiracy X, Second Edition)*

# Cyberpunk

*Kuro*

# Diceless

*Lords of Olympus*
*Primetime Adventures: A Game of Television Drama, Second Edition*

# Doctor Who

*Doctor Who: Adventures in Time and Space, Eleventh Doctor Edition*

# Fairy Tales

*Faery's Tale Deluxe*
*Seven Leagues: A Fantasy Roleplaying Game of Faerie*

# Fantasy

*All for One: Regime Diabolique*
*Artesia: Adventures in the Known World*
*The Burning Wheel Fantasy Roleplaying System, Gold Edition*
*Cat: A Little Game about Little Heroes, Revised Edition*
*Dragonraid*
*Dungeons & Dragons (fifth ed.): D&D Starter Set and D&D Basic Rules*
*Earthdawn, Third Edition*
*Faery's Tale Deluxe*
*Feng Shui: Action Movie Roleplaying*
*Hero Kids*
*High Valor*
*Legend of the Five Rings Roleplaying Game, 4th Edition*
*Lords of Olympus*
*Mouse Guard Roleplaying Game*
*The One Ring: Adventures Over the Edge of the Wild*
*Pathfinder Roleplaying Game Core Rulebook*
*Prince's Kingdom*
*Qin: The Warring States*
*Reign: A Game of Lords and Leaders*
*Seven Leagues: A Fantasy Roleplaying Game of Faerie*
*Spears of the Dawn*
*Swords & Wizardry Core Rules*
*Yggdrasill*

# Historical

*All for One: Regime Diabolique*
*Cold City, v. 1.1*
*Qin: The Warring States*
*Thou Art but a Warrior, Second Edition*
*Yggdrasill*

## Horror

*Call of Cthulhu, Sixth Edition and Call of Cthulhu, Seventh Edition Quick-Start Rules*
*Cold City, v. 1.1*
*Conspiracy X 2.0 (a.k.a. Conspiracy X, Second Edition)*
*In Nomine*
*Kuro*
*Monsterhearts*
*Night's Black Agents: A Vampire Spy Thriller*
*Weird West*
*Werewolf: The Apocalypse, 20th Anniversary Edition*
*Werewolf: The Forsaken*
*The World of Darkness: Storytelling System Rulebook*

## Investigation

*Call of Cthulhu, Sixth Edition and Call of Cthulhu, Seventh Edition Quick-Start Rules*
*Cold City, v. 1.1*
*Conspiracy X 2.0 (a.k.a. Conspiracy X, Second Edition)*

## Mature Audiences

*Monsterhearts*
*Werewolf: The Apocalypse, 20th Anniversary Edition*
*Werewolf: The Forsaken*

## Multigenre

*Basic Roleplaying: The Chaosium Roleplaying System, Second Edition*
*Cartoon Action Hour: Season 3*
*Fate Core System*
*GenreDiversion 3E Manual*
*GURPS, 4th Edition*
*Primetime Adventures: A Game of Television Drama, Second Edition*
*Prose Descriptive Qualities System (PDQ) Core Rules*
*Risus: The Anything RPG (Version 2.01)*
*Savage Worlds Deluxe Explorer's Edition*

# Mythology

*Lords of Olympus*

# Old School Renaissance

*Mutant Future, Revised Edition*
*Spears of the Dawn*
*Stars without Number (free and core editions)*
*Swords & Wizardry Core Rules*

# Paranormal Romance

*Monsterhearts*

# Post-Apocalypse

*Mutant Future, Revised Edition*
*Numenera*

# Science-Fantasy

*Mutant Future, Revised Edition*
*Numenera*

# Science Fiction

*Black Crusade*
*Deathwatch*
*Doctor Who: Adventures in Time and Space, Eleventh Doctor Edition*
*Feng Shui: Action Movie Roleplaying*
*Firefly Role-Playing Game Core Book*
*Psi\*Run*
*Star Wars: Edge of the Empire Beginner Game and Star Wars: Edge of the
    Empire Roleplaying Game Core Rulebook*
*Stars without Number (free and core editions)*
*Thousand Suns Rulebook*
*Traveller Core Rulebook*

# Space Opera

*Black Crusade*
*Deathwatch*
*Firefly Role-Playing Game Core Book*
*Star Wars: Edge of the Empire Beginner Game and Star Wars: Edge of the Empire Roleplaying Game Core Rulebook*
*Stars without Number (free and core editions)*
*Thousand Suns Rulebook*
*Traveller Core Rulebook*

# Spy

*Cold City, v. 1.1*
*Conspiracy X 2.0 (a.k.a. Conspiracy X, Second Edition)*
*Night's Black Agents: A Vampire Spy Thriller*

# Steampunk

*Lady Blackbird*

# Superhero

*Icons: Superpowered Roleplaying*
*Mutants & Masterminds Deluxe Hero's Handbook, Third Edition*

# Supernatural

*Witch Girls Adventures: The Drama-Diaries Game of Modern Magic and Mischief*
*The World of Darkness: Storytelling System Rulebook*

# Television

*Doctor Who: Adventures in Time and Space, Eleventh Doctor Edition*
*Firefly Role-Playing Game Core Book*
*Primetime Adventures: A Game of Television Drama, Second Edition*

# Thriller

*Night's Black Agents: A Vampire Spy Thriller*

# Time Travel

*Doctor Who: Adventures in Time and Space, Eleventh Doctor Edition*
*Feng Shui: Action Movie Roleplaying*

# Urban Fantasy

*Werewolf: The Apocalypse, 20th Anniversary Edition*
*Werewolf: The Forsaken*
*The World of Darkness: Storytelling System Rulebook*

# Western

*Firefly Role-Playing Game Core Book*
*Weird West*

# Wuxia

*Feng Shui: Action Movie Roleplaying*
*Qin: The Warring States*

# Younger Gamers

*Cartoon Action Hour: Season 3*
*Doctor Who: Adventures in Time and Space, Eleventh Doctor Edition*
*Hero Kids*
*Prince's Kingdom*
*Psi\*Run*

# Appendix B
# Resources

## Where to Buy—RPG-Specific Stores

Bits and Mortar (http://www.bits-and-mortar.com): a cooperative venture
of many RPG publishers that offer free electronic versions of their
RPGs upon proof of purchase of a physical copy from any brick-and-
mortar game or bookstore

DriveThruRPG (http://rpg.drivethrustuff.com): operated by OneBookShelf

Indie Press Revolution (http://www.indiepressrevolution.com/xcart/)

The Indie RPGs Un-store (http://theunstore.com): a consortium of Independent Game Publishers

Lulu (http://www.lulu.com): a self-publishing site where many independent
game creators go to publish their materials

Paizo (http://paizo.com): creators of the *Pathfinder* RPG, with a web store
that sells many other gaming products

RPGNow (https://www.rpgnow.com): also operated by OneBookShelf

Steve Jackson Games (http://www.sjgames.com): publisher of *GURPS*,
with a web store that sells many other gaming products

## Conventions

Comic-Con (http://www.comic-con.org): colossal pop culture celebration
in San Diego, California

ConTessa (http://contessaonline.com): a free, online convention organized
by women, but open to everyone

Dragon Con (http://www.dragoncon.org): Atlanta, Georgia, is the location
of this multimedia and popular culture showcase.

Gary Con (http://www.garycon.com): Named in honor of E. Gary Gygax,
the father of role-playing games (RPGs), and not for the city in

Indiana. Gary Con is an annual gaming convention held in Lake Geneva, Wisconsin.

Gen Con (http://www.gencon.com): Gen Con, the granddaddy of gaming conventions, is held annually in Indianapolis, Indiana. In 2013 approximately 50,000 people attended this four-day gaming extravaganza.

Origins Game Fair (http://originsgamefair.com): Held in Columbus, Ohio, and run by the Game Manufacturers Association (GAMA), the Origins Awards are presented at this convention celebrating gaming.

Pax East (http://east.paxsite.com) and Pax Prime (http://prime.paxsite.com): Penny Arcade's popular costal gaming conventions held in Boston, Massachusetts, and Seattle, Washington

## Websites about Conventions

Game Convention Central: http://gameconventioncentral.com/usa/big-eight-comiccon-dexcon-dragoncon-gencon-origins-paxeast-paxprime-board game-wb/

Wikipedia List of Gaming Conventions: http://en.wikipedia.org/wiki/List_of_gaming_conventions

## Awards

RPGs, like many arts and media, have their own awards. Here is a list of some of those honors.

Diana Jones Award for Excellence in Gaming (http://www.dianajonesaward.org)

ENnie Awards (http://www.ennie-awards.com/blog/): sponsored by EN World

The Indie RPG Awards (http://www.rpg-awards.com): represent some of the best nontraditional RPGs

Origins Awards (http://www.gama.org/OriginsAwards/tabid/2720/Default.aspx): GAMA presents the Origins Awards and includes the categories of "Best Roleplaying Game" and "Best Roleplaying Supplement."

## Advice for Players and Game Masters

Laws, Robin D. 2002. *Robin's Laws of Good Game Mastering*. [S.l]: Steve Jackson Games.

Laws, Robin D. 2010. *Hamlet's Hit Points: What Three Classic Narratives Tell Us about Roleplaying Games*. Roseville, Minn: Gameplaywright Press.

Rosenberg, Aaron. 2003. *Gamemastering Secrets*. 2nd ed. Randolph, Mass: Grey Ghost Press. PDF e-book.

Stolze, Greg. *How to Play Roleplaying Games*. 2006. http://www.gregstolze .com/downloads.html

Vecchione, Phil. 2012. *Never Unprepared: The Complete Game Master's Guide to Session Prep*. Murray, Utah: Engine Publishing.

Vecchione, Phil, and Walt Ciechanowski. 2013. Odyssey: *The Compete Game Master's Guide to Campaign Management*. Murray, Utah: Engine Publishing.

## Informative Blogs, Podcasts, and Websites

Dragonsfoot (http://www.dragonsfoot.org): a website dedicated to the first edition of *Advanced Dungeons and Dragons*

*The Escapist* (http://www.theescapist.com/index.htm): with the exception of Stackpole, few people have done more than William J. Walton to advocate gaming and dispel the panic and negative stereotypes of gaming. The Escapist also creates a base on the Internet that promotes a healthy view and celebration of RPGs.

*Game Geeks RPG* (http://gamegeeksrpg.com): Kurt Wiegel posts reviews as short video clips.

*Gnome Stew* (http://www.gnomestew.com): a blog about game mastering

*Grognardia* (http://grognardia.blogspot.com): longtime game writer James Maliszewski's blog

ICv2 (http://www.icv2.com/): top website for gaming industry news

*Ken and Robin Talk about Stuff* (http://www.kenandrobintalkaboutstuff. com): entertaining discussion of multifarious game-related topics by authors and game designers Kenneth Hite and Robin D. Laws

*Roleplaying Tips* (http://www.roleplayingtips.com): a blog by Johnn Four with fantastic tips for game masters (GMs) and players

RPG Geek (http://rpggeek.com)

RPG.net (http://www.rpg.net): longtime forum for RPG discussions

The RPG Site (http://www.therpgsite.com): a no-holds barred forum for RPG discussions

Story Games (http://www.story-games.com): a leading forum for discussing indie RPGs

*Studies about Fantasy Role-Playing Games* (http://www.rpgstudies.net):
includes a link to Michael A. Stackpole's Pulling Report: http://www.rpg
studies.net/stackpole/pulling_report.html.

*Wil Wheaton's Tabletop* (https://wilwheaton.net/category/tabletop/): occasionally reviews RPGs

*Wired*'s *GeekDad* column (http://www.wired.com/geekdad/): occasionally
has RPG reviews

## Websites and Apps to Enhance Your Gaming Experience

Chris Pound's Generators (http://generators.christopherpound.com/)

Dice Apps: There are many good dice apps; pick one that you like.

Fake Name Generator (http://www.fakenamegenerator.com/): will even
make a QR code for the "person"

Prismatic Art Collection (http://www.prismaticart.com): free collection of
images celebrating the multicultural diversity of heroes

Obsidian Portal (https://www.obsidianportal.com): an online "GM Note-
book" to track your games, characters, and adventures

QR Code Generator (https://www.unitaglive.com/qrcode): may be used to
promote your collection or game

Random Generator (http://random-generator.com/index.php?title=Main
_Page)

Random Name Generator (http://random-name-generator.info/)

Roll20 (http://roll20.net): an online space for gaming, in case your patrons
are spread over too large a geographic area for regular in-person
sessions.

## Miscellaneous Cool Tools

Chessex (http://www.chessex.com/): maker extraordinaire of dice, game
mats, etc.

Klutzke, Carl. 2007. *StoryCards Roleplaing Game*. Dogtown Games.
http://storycardsrpg.com

Obsidian Serpent Games LLC. 2012. *RPG Inspiration Cards*. Obsidian
Serpent Games LLC. https://www.thegamecrafter.com/games/rpg-in
spiration-cards

Paizo Publishing. 2011. *Gamemastery Plot Twist Cards Flashbacks*. Paizo
Pub LLC. http://paizo.com

Stephens, Lisa. 2010. *Gamemastery Plot Twist Cards*. Paizo Pub LLC. http://paizo.com

## RPG Holidays

Free RPG Day (http://www.freerpgday.com): Visit your friendly local game stores for one-shot games and a chance to pick up some free quick-start rules, adventure modules, and other swag.

International Game Day @ Your Library (http://igd.ala.org): a perfect time to promote your gaming group and RPG collection

International GMs Day (http://gmsday.com): March 4

International Tabletop Day (http://www.tabletopday.com): Watch for special promotions on this day—another great day for a gaming program.

Read an RPG Book in Public Week (http://www.theescapist.com/read rpgsinpublic/): actually three weeks, intended to gain visibility for the hobby

## For Your Amusement

Assorted Intricacies. 2011. "Roll a d6." Song. http://youtube/54VJWHL2K3I

*Dork Tower.* Comics. (http://www.dorktower.com)

*Knights of the Dinner Table.* Comics. http://www.kodtweb.com

*Order of the Stick.* Comics. http://www.giantitp.com/Comics.html

Tucker, S. J. 2011. *Playing D&D.* Song. http://music.sjtucker.com/track/digital-only-bonus-track-d-d

Vancil, Matt, Jeff Madsen, Tish Lopez, Don Early, Nathan Rice, Carol Roscoe, Brian Lewis, Scott C. Brown, Christian Doyle, and Jen Page. 2008. *The Gamers Dorkness Rising.* [United States]: Anthem Pictures. Movie sequel to *The Gamers*, filled with gaming, romance, gaming, friendship, gaming, forgiveness, and gaming.

Vancil, Matt, Mike Shimkus, Phil M. Price, and Nathan Rice. 2003. *The Gamers.* Tacoma, Wash.: Dead Gentlemen Productions. Low-budget movie that celebrates gaming with friends.

# Index

# About the Authors

STEVEN A. TORRES-ROMAN, MLIS, is teen librarian at DeKalb Public Library, DeKalb, IL. He has worked extensively with teens and literacy for the last ten years, and is the author of Libraries Unlimited's Read On . . . Science Fiction: Reading Lists for Every Taste. Torres-Roman holds a master of arts degree in English in addition to his master's degree in library and information sciences.

CASON E. SNOW, MLIS, is metadata librarian/cataloger at University of Maine—Orono. He is the author of several articles on role playing in libraries including "Playing with History: A Look at Video Games, World History, and Libraries"; "Tabletop Fantasy RPGs: Tips for Introducing Role-Playing Games in Your Library"; and "Dragons in the Stacks: An Introduction to Role-Playing Games and Their Value to Libraries." He received a master's degree in library and information science from the University of Wisconsin—Milwaukee and a master of arts degree in history from Northern Illinois University.